BEACON LIGHTS OF HISTORY.

GALILEO AT PISA

After the painting by F. ROYBET

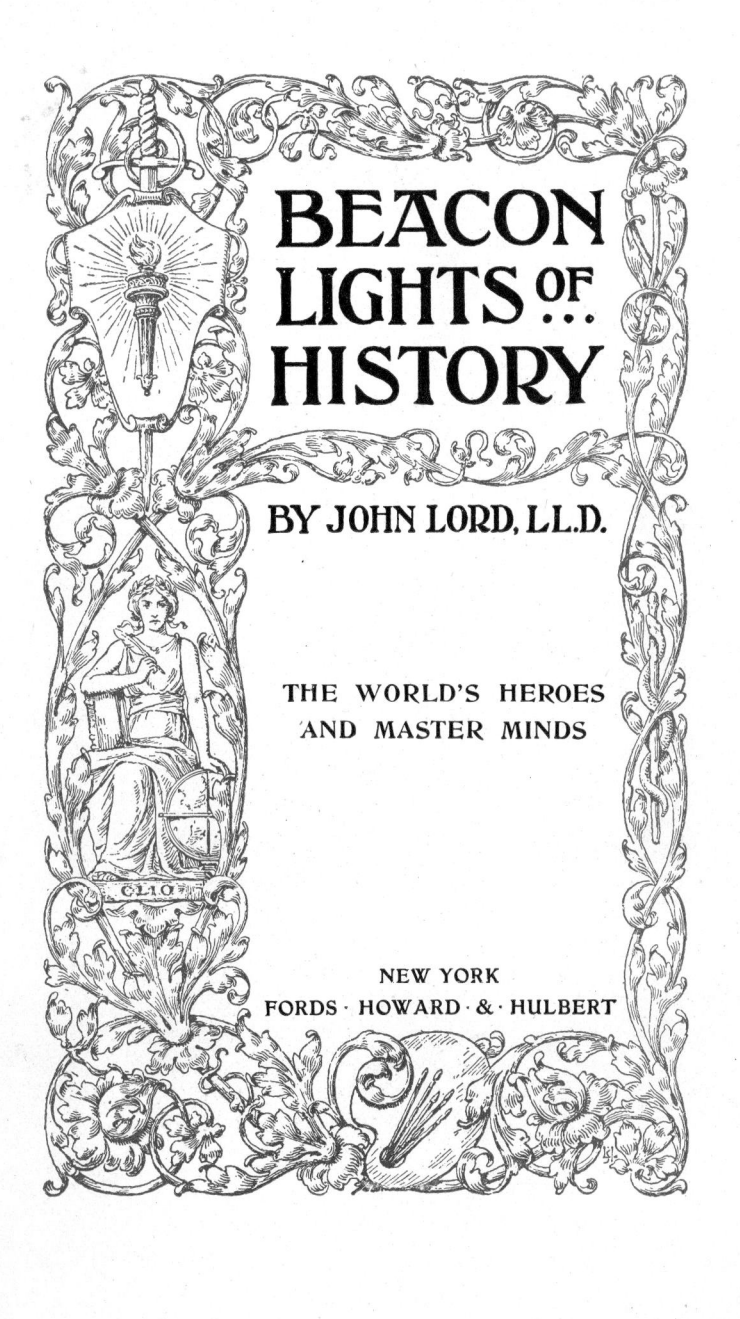

BEACON LIGHTS OF HISTORY

BY JOHN LORD, LL.D.

THE WORLD'S HEROES
AND MASTER MINDS

NEW YORK
FORDS · HOWARD · & · HULBERT

BEACON LIGHTS

OF HISTORY.

By JOHN LORD, LL.D.,

AUTHOR OF "THE OLD ROMAN WORLD," "MODERN EUROPE,"
ETC., ETC.

VOLUME VI.

RENAISSANCE AND REFORMATION.

NEW YORK:
FORDS, HOWARD & HULBERT
BOSTON: JOHN QUINCY ADAMS AND COMPANY
LONDON: THE WAVERLY BOOK COMPANY, LTD.
1913

Copyright, 1885,
By JOHN LORD.

Entered at Stationers' Hall

THE UNIVERSITY PRESS, CAMBRIDGE, MASS., U. S. A.

VOL. VI.

RENAISSANCE AND REFORMATION.

CONTENTS.

DANTE.

Rise of Modern Poetry.

	PAGE
The antiquity of Poetry	23
The greatness of Poets	24
Their influence on Civilization	25
The true poet one of the rarest of men	25
The pre-eminence of Homer, Dante, Shakspeare, and Goethe	26
Characteristics of Dante	27
His precocity	28
His moral wisdom and great attainments	29
His terrible scorn and his isolation	30
State of society when Dante was born	31
His banishment	32
Guelphs and Ghibellines	33
Dante stimulated to his great task by an absorbing sentiment	34
Beatrice	35
Dante's passion for Beatrice analyzed	36
The worship of ideal qualities the foundation of lofty love	37
The mystery of love	38–40
Its exalted realism	41
Dedication of Dante's life-labors to the departed Beatrice	42

CONTENTS.

	PAGE
The Divine Comedy; a study	43
The Inferno; its graphic pictures	44
Its connection with the ideas of the Middle Ages	44
The physical hell of Dante in its connection with the Mediæval doctrine of Retribution	45
The Purgatorio; its moral wisdom	46
Origin of the doctrine of Purgatory	47
Its consolation amid the speculations of despair	48
The Paradiso	49
Its discussion of grand themes	50
The Divina Commedia makes an epoch in civilization	51
Dante's life an epic	52
His exalted character	53
His posthumous influence	54, 55

GEOFFREY CHAUCER.

ENGLISH LIFE IN THE FOURTEENTH CENTURY.

The characteristics of the fourteenth century	59
Its great events and characters	60
State of society in England when Chaucer arose	61
His early life	63
His intimacy with John of Gaunt, the great Duke of Lancaster	64
His prosperity	65
His poetry	66
The Canterbury Tales	68
Their fidelity to Nature and to English life	70
Connection of his poetry with the formation of the English Language	74
The Pilgrims of the Canterbury Tales	75–79

CONTENTS.

	PAGE
Chaucer's views of women and of love	81
His description of popular sports and amusements	82
The preponderance of country life in the fourteenth century	84
Chaucer's description of popular superstitions	85
Of ecclesiastical abuses	86
His emancipation from the ideas of the Middle Ages	87
Peculiarities of his poetry	88
Chaucer's private life	89
The respect in which he was held	90
Influence of his poetry	91

CHRISTOPHER COLUMBUS.

MARITIME DISCOVERIES.

Marco Polo	95
His travels	96
The geographical problems of the fourteenth century	97
Sought to be solved by Christopher Columbus	98
The difficulties he had to encounter	99
Regarded as a visionary man	100
His persistence	101
Influence of women in great enterprises	102
Columbus introduced to Queen Isabella	103
Excuses for his opponents	104
The Queen favors his projects	105
The first voyage of Columbus	106
Its dangers	107
Discovery of the Bahama Islands	108
Discovery of Cuba and Hispaniola	109
Columbus returns to Spain	109
The excitement and enthusiasm produced by his discoveries	110

	PAGE
His second voyage	110
Extravagant expectations of Columbus	111
Disasters of the colonists	112
Decline of the popularity of Columbus	112
His third voyage	113
His arrest and disgrace	114
His fourth voyage	115
His death	115
Greatness of his services	116
Results of his discoveries	117, 118
Colonization	119
The mines of Peru and Mexico	119
The effects on Europe of the rapid increase of the precious metals	120
True sources of national wealth	121–125
The destinies of America	126–129
Its true mission	130–138

SAVONAROLA.

Unsuccessful Reforms.

The age of Savonarola	141
Revival of Classic Literature	142
Ecclesiastical corruptions	142
Religious apathy; awakened intelligence; infidel spirit	143
Youth of Savonarola	144
His piety	145
Begins to preach	146
His success at Florence	146
Peculiarities of his eloquence	147
Death of Lorenzo de' Medici	147
Savonarola as a political leader	148

	PAGE
Denunciation of tyranny	149
His influence in giving a constitution to the Florentines	150
Difficulties of Constitution-making	151
His method of teaching political science	152
Peculiarities of the new Rule	153
Its great wisdom	154
Savonarola as reformer	155
As moralist	156
Terrible denunciation of sin in high places	157
A prophet of woe	159
Contrast between Savonarola and Luther	160–163
The sermons of Savonarola	164
His marvellous eloquence	165
Its peculiarities	167
The enemies of Savonarola	168
Savonarola persecuted	169
His appeal to Europe	170
The people desert him	171
Months of torment	172, 173
His martyrdom	174
His character	175, 176
His posthumous influence	177–179

MICHAEL ANGELO.

THE REVIVAL OF ART.

Michael Angelo as representative of reviving Art	183
Ennobling effects of Art when inspired by lofty sentiments	184
Brilliancy of Art in the sixteenth century	185–188
Early life of Michael Angelo	189
His aptitude for Art	189
Patronized by Lorenzo de' Medici	190

CONTENTS.

	PAGE
Sculpture later in its development than Architecture	191
The chief works of Michael Angelo as sculptor	192
The peculiarity of his sculptures	193
Michael Angelo as painter	193
History of painting in the Middle Ages	194
Da Vinci	195
The frescos of the Sistine Chapel	196
The Last Judgment	197
The cartoon of the battle of Pisa	198
The variety as well as moral grandeur of Michael Angelo's paintings	199
Ennobling influence of his works	200
His works as architect	201
St. Peter's Church	202–205
Revival of Roman and Grecian Architecture	206
Contrasted with Gothic Architecture	207
Michael Angelo rescues the beauties of Paganism	209
Not responsible for absurdities of the Renaissance	210
Greatness of Michael Angelo as a man	211
His industry, temperance, dignity of character, love of Art for Art's sake	212
His indifference to rewards and praises	213
His transcendent fame	214

MARTIN LUTHER.

THE PROTESTANT REFORMATION.

Luther's predecessors	217
Corruptions of the Church	218
Luther the man for the work of reform	219
His peculiarities	220
His early piety	221

CONTENTS.

	PAGE
Enters a Monastery	222
His religious experience	223
Made Professor of Divinity at Wittenberg	224
The Pope in great need of money to complete St. Peter's	225
Indulgences; principles on which they were based	226
Luther, indignant, preaches Justification by Faith	227
His immense popularity	227
Grace the cardinal principle of the Reformation	228
The Reformation began as a religious movement	229
How the defence of Luther's doctrine led to the recognition of the supreme authority of the Scriptures	230–232
Public disputation at Leipsic between Luther and Eck	234
Connection between the advocacy of the Bible as a supreme authority and the right of private judgment	235
Religious liberty a sequence of private judgment	236–240
Connection between religious and civil liberty	241–242
Contrast between Leo I. and Luther	243-245
Luther as reformer	246
His boldness and popularity	247
He alarms Rome	248
His translation of the Bible, his hymns, and other works	249
Summoned by imperial authority to the Diet of Worms	250
His memorable defence	250
His immortal legacies	251
His death and character	252

THOMAS CRANMER.

THE ENGLISH REFORMATION.

Importance of the English Reformation	255
Cranmer its best exponent	256

CONTENTS.

	PAGE
What was effected during the reign of Henry VIII.	256
Thomas Cromwell	257
Suppression of Monasteries	258
Their opposition to the revival of Learning	259
Their exceeding corruption	260
Their great wealth and its confiscation	262
Ecclesiastical courts	264
Sir Thomas More; his execution	265
Main feature of Henry VIII.'s anti-clerical measures	266
Fall of Cromwell	267
Rise of Cranmer	268
His characteristics	269
His wise moderation	270
His fortunate suggestions to Henry VIII.	271
Made Archbishop of Canterbury	271
Difficulties of his position	272
Reforms made by the government, not by the people	273
Accession of Edward VI.	273
Cranmer's Church reforms: open communion; abolition of the Mass; new English liturgy	274
Marriage among the clergy; the Forty-two Articles	275
Accession of Mary	276
Persecution of the Reformers	277
Reactionary measures	278
Arrest, weakness, and recantation of Cranmer	279, 280
His noble death; his character	281
Death of Mary	282
Accession of Elizabeth, and return of exiles to England	282
The Elizabethan Age	283
Conservative reforms and conciliatory measures	284, 285
The Thirty-nine Articles	286
Nonconformists	287
Their doctrines and discipline	288
The great Puritan controversy	289

	PAGE
The Puritans represent the popular side of the Reformation	290
Their theology	291, 292
Their moral discipline	293
Their connection with civil liberty	294
Summary of the English Reformation	294, 295

IGNATIUS LOYOLA.

RISE AND INFLUENCE OF THE JESUITS.

The counter-reformation effected by the Jesuits	299
Picture of the times; theological doctrines	300
The Monastic Orders no longer available	301
Ignatius Loyola	302
His early life	303
Founds a new order of Monks	303
Wonderful spread of the Society of Jesus	304
Their efficient organization	305
Causes of success in general	306
Virtues and abilities of the early Jesuits	307, 308
Their devotion and bravery	309
Jesuit Missions	310
Veneration for Loyola; his "Spiritual Exercises"	310
Lainez	311
Singular obedience exacted of the members of the Society	312
Absolute power of the General of the Order	313
Voluntary submission of Jesuits to complete despotism	314
The Jesuits adapt themselves to the circumstances of society	315
Causes of the decline of their influence	317
Corruption of most human institutions	318
The Jesuits become rich and then corrupt	319, 320
Ésprit de corps of the Jesuits	321

Their doctrine of expediency	322, 323
Their political intrigues	324
Persecution of the Protestants	325
The enemies they made	326
Madame de Pompadour	327
Suppression of the Order	328
Their return to power	330
Reasons why Protestants fear and dislike them	331

JOHN CALVIN.

Protestant Theology.

John Calvin's position	335
His early life and precocity	336
Becomes a leader of Protestants	337
Removes to Geneva	337
His habits and character	338
Temporary exile	339
Convention at Frankfort	340
Melancthon, Luther, Calvin, and Catholic doctrines	341
Return to Geneva, and marriage	342
Calvin compared with Luther	343, 344
Calvin as a legislator	345
His reform	346
His views of the Eucharist	347
Excommunication, etc.	349
His dislike of ceremonies and festivals	350
The simplicity of the worship of God	350
His ideas of church government	351
Absence of toleration	352
Church and State	353, 354

CONTENTS.

	PAGE
Exaltation of preaching	355
Calvin as a theologian; his Institutes	356, 357
His doctrine of Predestination	358
His general doctrines in harmony with Mediæval theology	358
His views of sin and forgiveness; Calvinism	359–362
He exacts the same authority to logical deduction from admitted truths as to direct declarations of Scripture	363
Puritans led away by Calvin's intellectuality	364
His whole theology radiates from the doctrine of the majesty of God and the littleness of man	365
To him a personal God is everything	366, 367
Defects of his system	368, 369
Calvin an aristocrat	371
His intellectual qualities	372
His prodigious labors	373
His severe characteristics	374–376
His vast influence	377
His immortal fame	378–380

LORD BACON.

THE NEW PHILOSOPHY.

	PAGE
Lord Bacon as portrayed by Macaulay	383
His great defects of character	384
Contrast made between the man and the philosopher	385
Bacon's youth and accomplishments	387
Enters Parliament	388
Seeks office	389
At the height of fortune and fame	390
His misfortunes	391
Consideration of charges against him	392–396
His counterbalancing merits	397, 398

CONTENTS.

	PAGE
The exaltation by Macaulay of material life	399–402
Bacon made its exponent	403
But the aims of Bacon were higher	404
The true spirit of his philosophy	405
Deductive philosophies	407–409
His new method	410
Bacon's Works	411–415
Relations of his philosophy	416, 417
Material science and knowledge	418
Comparison of knowledge with wisdom	420–424

GALILEO.

ASTRONOMICAL DISCOVERIES.

A brilliant portent	427
The greatness of the sixteenth century	428
Artists, scholars, reformers, religious defenders	429
Maritime discoveries	430
Literary, ecclesiastical, political achievements	431
Youth of Galileo	432
His early discoveries	433
Genius for mathematics	434
Professor at Pisa	435
Ridicules the old philosophers; invents the thermometer	436
Compared with Kepler	437
Galileo teaches the doctrines of Copernicus	438
Gives offence by his railleries and mockeries	439
Theology and science	440
Astronomical knowledge of the Ancients	441
Utilization of science	442
Construction of the first telescope	443
Galileo's reward	444
His successive discoveries	445

CONTENTS.

	PAGE
His enemies	446
High scientific rank in Europe	447
Hostility of the Church	448
Galileo summoned before the Inquisition; his condemnation and admonition	449
His new offences	450
Summoned before a council of Cardinals	451
His humiliation	452
His recantations	453
Consideration of his position	454
Greatness of mind rather than character	455
His confinement at Arceti	456
Opposition to science	457
His melancholy old age and blindness	458
Visited by John Milton; comparison of the two, when blind	459
Consequence of Galileo's discoveries	460
Later results	461
Vastness of the universe	462
Grandeur of astronomical science	463

LIST OF ILLUSTRATIONS
VOLUME VI.

	PAGE
Galileo at Pisa . . . . *Frontispiece*	
After the painting by F. Roybet.	
Dante in Florence	37
After the painting by Rafaeli Sorbi.	
The Canterbury Pilgrimage	71
From the frieze by R. W. W. Sewell.	
Columbus at the Court of Spain	105
After the painting by Vaczlav Brozik, Metropolitan Museum, New York.	
Savonarola	145
From the statue by E. Pazzi, Uffizi Gallery, Florence.	
Michael Angelo in His Studio Visited by Pope Julius II.	193
After the painting by Haman.	
Luther Preaching at Wartburg	243
After the painting by Hugo Vogel.	
Henry VIII. of England	273
After the painting by Hans Holbein, Windsor Castle, England.	
Cranmer at the Traitor's Gate	281
After the painting by Frederick Goodall.	
Madame de Pompadour	327
After the painting by Fr. Boucher.	
John Calvin	361
From a contemporaneous painting.	
Lord Francis Bacon	401
After the painting by T. Van Somer.	
Galileo Galilei	431
After the painting by J. Sustermans, Uffizi Gallery, Florence.	

DANTE.

A. D. 1265–1321.

RISE OF MODERN POETRY.

BEACON LIGHTS OF HISTORY.

DANTE.

RISE OF MODERN POETRY.

THE first great genius who aroused his country from the torpor of the Middle Ages was a poet. Poetry, then, was the first influence which elevated the human mind amid the miseries of a gloomy period, if we may except the schools of philosophy which flourished in the rising universities. But poetry probably preceded all other forms of culture in Europe, even as it preceded philosophy and art in Greece. The gay Provençal singers were harbingers of Dante, even as unknown poets prepared the way for Homer. And as Homer was the creator of Grecian literature, so Dante, by his immortal comedy, gave the first great impulse to Italian thought. Hence poets are great benefactors, and we will not let them die in our memories or hearts. We crown them, when alive, with laurels and praises; and when they die, we erect monuments to their honor. They are dear to us, since their writings give perpetual pleasure, and appeal to our loftiest sentiments. They appeal not merely to consecrated ideas and feelings, but they strive to conform to the principles of immortal art. Every great poet is as much an artist as the sculptor or the painter; and art survives learning itself. Varro, the most learned of the Romans, is forgotten, when Virgil is familiar to every school-boy. Cicero himself would not have been immortal, if his essays and orations had not conformed to the principles of art. Even an historian who would live must be an artist, like Voltaire or Macaulay. A cumbrous, or heavy, or pedantic historian will never be read, even if his learning be praised by all the critics of Germany.

Poets are the great artists of language. They even create languages, like Homer and Shakspeare. They are the ornaments of literature. But they are more than ornaments. They are the sages whose sayings are treasured up and valued and quoted from age to age, because of the inspiration which is given to them,— an insight into the mysteries of the soul and the secrets of life. A good song is never lost; a good poem is never buried, like a system of philosophy, but has an inherent vitality, like the melodies of the son of Jesse. Real poetry is something, too, beyond elaborate versification, which is one of the literary fashions, and passes away like other fashions unless redeemed by something that arouses the soul, and elevates it, and appeals to the consciousness of universal humanity. It is the poets who make revelations, like prophets and sages of old; it is they who invest history with interest, like Shakspeare and Racine, and preserve what is most vital and valuable in it. They even adorn philosophy, like Lucretius, when he speculated on the systems of the Ionian philosophers. They certainly impress powerfully on the mind the truths of theology, as Watts and Cowper and Wesley did in their noble lyrics. So that the most rapt and imaginative of men, if artists, utilize the whole realm of knowledge, and diffuse it, and perpetuate it in artistic forms. But real poets are rare, even if there are many who glory in the jingle of language and the structure of rhyme. Poetry, to live, must have a soul, and it must combine rare things, — art, music, genius, original thought, wisdom made still richer by learning, and, above all, a power of appealing to inner sentiments, which all feel, yet are reluctant to express. So choice are the gifts, so grand are the qualities, so varied the attainments of truly great poets, that very few are born in a whole generation and in nations that number twenty or forty millions of people. They are the rarest of gifted men. Every nation can boast of its illustrious lawyers, statesmen, physicians, and orators; but they can point only to a few of their poets with pride. We can count on the fingers of one of our hands all those worthy of poetic fame who now live in this great country of intellectual and civilized men, — one for every ten millions. How great the pre-eminence even of ordinary poets! How very great the pre-eminence of those few whom all ages and nations admire!

The critics assign to Dante a pre-eminence over most of those we call immortal. Only two or three other poets in the whole realm of literature, ancient or modern, dispute his throne. We compare him with Homer and Shakspeare, and perhaps Goethe, alone. Civilization glories in Virgil, Milton, Tasso, Racine, Pope, and Byron, — all immortal artists; but it points to only four men concerning whose transcendent creative power there is unanimity of judgment, — prodigies of genius, to whose influence and fame we can assign no limits; stars of such surpassing brilliancy that we can only gaze and wonder, — growing brighter and brighter, too, with the progress of ages; so remarkable that no barbarism will ever obscure their brightness, so original that all imitation of them becomes impossible and absurd. So great is original genius, directed by art and consecrated to lofty sentiments.

I have assumed the difficult task of presenting one of these great lights. But I do not presume to analyze his great poem, or to point out critically its excellencies. This would be beyond my powers, even if I were an Italian. It takes a poet to reveal a poet. Nor is criticism interesting to ordinary minds, even in the hands of masters. I should make critics laugh if I were to attempt to dissect the Divine Comedy. Although, in an English dress, it is known to most people who pretend to be cultivated, yet it is not more read than the "Paradise Lost" or the "Faerie Queene," being too deep and learned for some, and understood by nobody without a tolerable acquaintance with the Middle Ages, which it interprets, — the superstitions, the loves, the hatreds, the ideas of ages which can never more return. All I can do — all that is safe for me to attempt — is to show the circumstances and conditions in which it was written, the sentiments which prompted it, its historical results, its general scope and end, and whatever makes its author stand out to us as a living man, bearing the sorrows and revelling in the joys of that high life which gave to him extraordinary moral wisdom, and made him a prophet and teacher to all generations. He was a man of sorrows, of resentments, fierce and implacable, but whose "love was as transcendent as his scorn," — a man of vast experiences and intense convictions and superhuman earnestness, despising the world which he sought to elevate, living isolated in the midst of society, a wanderer and a sage, meditating constantly on the grandest themes, lost in ecstatic reveries, familiar with abstruse theories, versed in all the wisdom of his day and in the history of the past, a believer in God and immortality, in rewards and punishments, and perpetually soaring to comprehend the mysteries of existence, and those ennobling truths which constitute the joy and the hope of renovated and emancipated and glorified spirits in the realms of eternal bliss. All this is history, and it is history alone which I seek to teach, — the outward life of a great man, with glimpses, if I can, of those visions of beauty and truth in which his soul lived, and which visions and experiences constitute his peculiar greatness. Dante was not so close an observer of human nature as Shakspeare, nor so great a painter of human actions as Homer, nor so learned a scholar as Milton; but his soul was more serious than either, — he was deeper, more intense than they; while in pathos, in earnestness, and in fiery emphasis he has been surpassed only by Hebrew poets and prophets.

It would seem from his numerous biographies that he was remarkable from a boy; that he was a youthful prodigy; that he was precocious, like Cicero and Pascal; that he early made great attainments, giving utterance to living thoughts and feelings, like Bacon, among boyish companions; lisping in numbers, like Pope, before he could write prose; different from all other boys, since no time can be fixed when he did not think and feel like a person of maturer years. Born in Florence, of the noble family of the Alighieri, in the year 1265, his early education devolved upon his mother, his father having died while the boy was very young. His mother's friend, Brunetto Latini, famous as statesman and scholarly poet, was of great assistance in directing his tastes and studies. As a mere youth he wrote sonnets, such as Sordello the Troubadour would not disdain to own. He delights, as a boy, in those inquiries which gave fame to Bonaventura. He has an intuitive contempt for all quacks and pretenders. At Paris he maintains fourteen different theses, propounded by learned men, on different subjects, and gains universal admiration. He is early selected by his native city for important offices, which he fills with honor. In wit he encounters no superiors. He scorches courts by sarcasms which he can not restrain. He offends the great by a superiority which he does not attempt to veil. He affects no humility, for his nature is doubtless proud; he is even offensively conscious and arrogant. When Florence is deliberating about the choice of an ambassador to Rome, he playfully, yet still arrogantly, exclaims: "If I remain behind, who goes? and if I go, who remains behind?" His countenance, so austere and thoughtful, impresses all beholders with a sort of inborn greatness; his lip, in Giotto's portrait, is curled disdainfully, as if he lived among fools or knaves. He is given to no youthful excesses; he lives simply and frugally. He rarely speaks unless spoken to; he is absorbed apparently in thought. Without a commanding physical person, he is a marked man to everybody, even when he deems himself a stranger. Women gaze at him with wonder and admiration, though he disdains their praises and avoids their flatteries. Men make way for him as he passes them, unconsciously. "Behold," said a group of ladies, as he walked slowly by them, "there is a man who has visited hell!" To the close of his life he was a great devourer of books, and digested their contents. His studies were as various as they were profound. He was familiar with the ancient poets and historians and philosophers; he was still better acquainted with the abstruse speculations of the schoolmen. He delighted in universities and scholastic retreats; from the cares and duties of public life he would retire to solitary labors, and dignify his retirement by improving studies. He did not live in a cell, like Jerome, or a cave, like Mohammed; but no man was ever more indebted to solitude and meditation than he for that insight and inspiration which communion with God and great ideas alone can give.

And yet, though a recluse and student, he had great experiences with life. He was born among the higher ranks of society. He inherited an ample patrimony. He did not shrink from public affairs. He was intensely patriotic, like Michael Angelo ; he gave himself up to the good of his country, like Savonarola. Florence was small, but it was important; it was already a capital, and a centre of industry. He represented its interests in various courts. He lived with princes and nobles. He took an active part in all public matters and disputations ; he was even familiar with the intrigues of parties ; he was a politician as well as scholar. He entered into the contests between Popes and Emperors respecting the independence of Italy. He was not conversant with art, for the great sculptors and painters had not then arisen. The age was still dark ; the mariner's compass had not been invented, chimneys had not been introduced, the comforts of life were few. Dames of highest rank still spent their days over the distaff or in combing flax. There were no grand structures but cathedral churches. Life was laborious, dismal, and turbulent. Law and order did not reign in cities or villages. The poor were oppressed by nobles. Commerce was small and manufactures scarce. Men lived in dreary houses, without luxuries, on coarse bread and fruit and vegetables. The crusades had not come to an end. It was the age of bad popes and quarrelsome nobles, and lazy monks and haughty bishops, and ignorant people, steeped in gloomy superstitions, two hundred years before America was discovered, and two hundred and fifty years before Michael Angelo erected the dome of St. Peter's.

But there was faith in the world, and rough virtues, sincerity, and earnestness of character, though life was dismal. Men believed in immortality and in expiation for sin. The rising universities had gifted scholars whose abstruse speculations have never been rivalled for acuteness and severity of logic. There were bards and minstrels, and chivalric knights and tournaments and tilts, and village *fêtes* and hospitable convents and gentle ladies, — gentle and lovely even in all states of civilization, winning by their graces and inspiring men to deeds of heroism and gallantry.

In one of those domestic revolutions which were so common in Italy Dante was banished, and his property was confiscated; and he at the age of thirty-five, about the year 1300, when Giotto was painting portraits, was sent forth a wanderer and an exile, now poor and unimportant, to eat the bread of strangers and climb other people's stairs; and so obnoxious was he to the dominant party in his native city for his bitter spirit, that he was destined never to return to his home and friends. His ancestors, boasting of Roman descent, belonged to the patriotic party, — the Guelphs, who had the ascendency in his early years, — that party which defended the claims of the Popes against the Emperors of Germany. But this party had its divisions and rival families, — those that sided with the old feudal nobles who had once ruled the city, and the new mercantile families that surpassed them in wealth and popular favor. So, expelled by a fraction of his own party that had gained power, Dante went over to the Ghibellines, and became an adherent of imperial authority until he died.

It was in his wanderings from court to court and castle to castle and convent to convent and university to university, that he acquired that profound experience with men and the world which fitted him for his great task. "Not as victorious knight on the field of Campaldino, not as leader of the Guelph aristocracy at Florence, not as prior, not as ambassador," but as a wanderer did he acquire his moral wisdom. He was a striking example of the severe experiences to which nearly all great benefactors have been subjected, — Abraham the exile, in the wilderness, in Egypt, among Philistines, among robbers and barbaric chieftains; the Prince Siddârtha, who founded Buddhism, in his wanderings among the various Indian nations who bowed down to Brahma; and, still greater, the Apostle Paul, in his protracted martyrdom among Pagan idolaters and boastful philosophers, in Asia and in Europe. These and others may be cited, who led a life of self-denial and reproach in order to spread the truths which save mankind. We naturally call their lot hard, even though they chose it; but it is the school of greatness. It was sad to see the wisest and best man of his day, — a man of family, of culture, of wealth, of learning, loving leisure, attached to his home and country, accustomed to honor and independence, — doomed to exile, poverty, neglect, and hatred, without those compensations which men of genius in our time secure. But I would not attempt to excite pity for an outward condition which developed the higher virtues, — for a thorny path which led to the regions of eternal light. Dante may have walked in bitter tears to Paradise, but after the fashion of saints and martyrs in all ages of our world. He need but cast his eyes on that emblem which was erected on every pinnacle of Mediæval churches to symbolize passing suffering with salvation infinite, — the great and august creed of the age in which he lived, though now buried amid the triumphs of an imposing material civilization whose end is the adoration of the majesty of man rather than the majesty of God, the wonders of creation rather than the greatness of the Creator.

But something more was required in order to write an immortal poem than even native genius, great learning, and profound experience. The soul must be stimulated to the work by an absorbing and ennobling passion. This passion Dante had; and it is as memorable as the mortal loves of Abélard and Héloïse, and infinitely more exalting, since it was spiritual and immortal, — even the adoration of his lamented and departed Beatrice.

I wish to dwell for a moment, perhaps longer than to some may seem dignified, on this ideal or sentimental love. It may seem trivial and unimportant to the eye of youth, or a man of the world, or a woman of sensual nature, or to unthinking fools and butterflies; but it is invested with dignity to one who meditates on the mysteries of the soul, the wonders of our higher nature, — one of the things which arrest the attention of philosophers.

It is recorded and attested, even by Dante himself, that at the early age of nine he fell in love with Beatrice, — a little girl of one of his neighbors, — and that he wrote to her sonnets as the mistress of his devotion. How could he have written sonnets without an inspiration, unless he felt sentiments higher than we associate with either boys or girls? The boy was father of the man. "She appeared to me," says the poet, " at a festival, dressed in that most noble and honorable color, scarlet, — girded and ornamented in a manner suitable to her age; and from that moment love ruled my soul. And after many days had passed, it happened that, passing through the street, she turned her eyes to the spot where I stood, and with ineffable courtesy she greeted me; and this had such an effect on me that it seemed I had reached the furthest limit of blessedness. I took refuge in the solitude of my chamber; and, thinking over what had happened to me, I proposed to write a sonnet, since I had already acquired the art of putting words into rhyme." This, from his " Vita Nuova," his first work, relating to the "new life" which this love awoke in his young soul.

Thus, according to Dante's own statement, was the seed of a never-ending passion planted in his soul, — the small beginning, so insignificant to cynical eyes, that it would almost seem preposterous to allude to it; as if this fancy for a little girl in scarlet, and in a boy but nine years of age, could ripen into anything worthy to be soberly mentioned by a grave and earnest poet, in the full maturity of his genius, — worthy to give direction to his lofty intellect, worthy to be the occasion of the greatest poem the world has seen from Homer to modern times. Absurd! ridiculous! Great rivers cannot rise from such a spring; tall trees cannot grow from such a little acorn. Thus reasons the man who does not take cognizance of the mighty mysteries of human life. If anything tempted the boy to write sonnets to a little girl, it must have been the chivalric element in society at that period, when even boys were required to choose objects of devotion, and to whom they were to be loyal, and whose honor they were bound to defend. But the grave poet, in the decline of his life, makes this simple confession, as the begin-

DANTE IN FLORENCE

After the painting by Rafaelli Sorbi

ning of that sentiment which never afterwards departed from him, and which inspired him to his grandest efforts.

But this youthful attachment was unfortunate. Beatrice did not return his passion, and had no conception of its force, and perhaps was not even worthy to call it forth. She may have been beautiful; she may have been gifted; she may have been commonplace. It matters little whether she was intellectual or not, beautiful or not. It was not the flesh and blood he saw, but the image of beauty and loveliness which his own mind created. He idealized the girl; she was to him all that he fancied. But she never encouraged him; she denied his greetings, and even avoided his society. At last she died, when he was twenty-seven, and left him — to use his own expression — " to ruminate on death, and envy whomsoever dies." To console himself, he read Boëthius, and religious philosophy was ever afterwards his favorite study. Nor did serenity come, so deep were his sentiments, so powerful was his imagination, until he had formed an exalted purpose to write a poem in her honor, and worthy of his love. " If it please Him through whom all things come," said Dante, " that my life be spared, I hope to tell such things of her as never before have been seen by any one."

Now what inspired so strange a purpose? Was it a Platonic sentiment, like the love of Petrarch for Laura, or something that we cannot explain, and yet real, — a mystery of the soul in its deepest cravings and aspirations? And is love, among mortals generally, based on such a foundation? Is it flesh and blood we love; is it the intellect; is it the character; is it the soul; is it what is inherently interesting in woman, and which everybody can see, — the real virtues of the heart and charms of physical beauty? Or is it what we fancy in the object of our adoration, what exists already in our own minds, — the archetypes of eternal ideas of beauty and grace? And do all men worship these forms of beauty which the imagination creates? Can any woman, or any man, seen exactly as they are, incite a love which is kindred to worship? And is any love worthy to be called love, if it does not inspire emotions which prompt to self-sacrifice, labor, and lofty ends? Can a woman's smiles incite to Herculean energies, and drive the willing worshipper to Aönian heights, unless under these smiles are seen the light of life and the blessedness of supernatural fervor? Is there, and can there be, a perpetuity in mortal charms without the recognition or the supposition of a moral beauty connected with them, which alone is pure and imperishable, and which alone creates the sacred ecstasy that revels in the enjoyment of what is divine, or what is supposed to be divine, not in man, but in the conceptions of man, — the ever-blazing glories of goodness or of truth which the excited soul doth see in the eyes and expression of the adored image? It is these archetypes of divinity, real or fancied, which give to love all that is enduring. Destroy these, take away the real or fancied glories of the soul and mind, and the holy flame soon burns out. No mortal love can last, no mortal love is beautiful, unless the visions which the mind creates are not more or less realized in the object of it, or when a person, either man or woman, is not capable of seeing ideal perfections. The loves of savages are the loves of brutes. The more exalted the character and the soul, the greater is the capacity of love, and the deeper its fervor. It is not the object of love which creates this fervor, but the mind which is capable of investing it with glories. There could not have been such intensity in Dante's love had he not been gifted with the power of creating so lofty and beautiful an ideal; and it was this he worshipped, — not the real Beatrice, but the angelic beauty he thought he saw in her. Why could he not see the perfections he adored shining in other women, who perhaps had a higher claim to them? Ah, that is the mystery! And you cannot solve it any easier than you can tell why a flower blooms or a seed germinates. And why was it that Dante, with his great experience, could in later life see the qualities he adored in no other woman than in the cold and unappreciative girl who avoided him? Suppose she had become his wife, might he not have been disenchanted, and his veneration been succeeded by a bitter disappointment? Yet, while the delusion lasted, no other woman could have filled her place; in no other woman could he have seen such charms; no other love could have inspired his soul to make such labors.

I would not be understood as declaring that married love must be necessarily a disenchantment. I would not thus libel humanity, and insult plain reason and experience. Many loves *are* happy, and burn brighter and brighter to the end; but it is because there are many who are worthy of them, both men and women, — because the ideal, which the mind created, *is* realized to a greater or less degree, although the loftier the archetype, the less seldom is it found. Nor is it necessary that perfection should be found. A person may have faults which alienate and disenchant, but with these there may be virtues so radiant that the worship, though imperfect, remains, — a respect, on the whole, so great that the soul is lifted to admiration. Who can love this perishable form, unless one sees in it some traits which belong to superior and immortal natures? And hence the sentiment, when pure, creates a sort of companionship of beings robed in celestial light, and exorcises those degrading passions which belong to earth. But Dante saw no imperfections in

Beatrice: perhaps he had no opportunity to see them. His own soul was so filled with love, his mind soared to such exalted regions of adoration, that when she passed away he saw her only in the beatified state, in company with saints and angels; and he was wrapped in ecstasies which knew no end, — the unbroken adoration of beauty, grace, and truth, even of those eternal ideas on which Plato based all that is certain, and all that is worth living for; that sublime realism without which life is a failure, and this world is "a mockery, a delusion, and a snare."

This is the history and exposition of that love for Beatrice with which the whole spiritual life of Dante is identified, and without which the "Divine Comedy" might not have been written. I may have given to it disproportionate attention; and it is true I might have allegorized it, and for love of a woman I might have substituted love for an art, — even the art of poetry, in which his soul doubtless lived, even as Michael Angelo, his greatest fellow-countryman, lived in the adoration of beauty, grace, and majesty. Oh, happy and favored is the person who lives in the enjoyment of an art! It may be humble; it may be grand. It may be music; it may be painting, or sculpture, or architecture, or poetry, or oratory, or landscape gardening, yea, even farming, or needle-work, or house decoration, — anything which employs the higher faculties of the mind, and brings order out of confusion, and takes one from himself, from the drudgery of mechanical labors, even if it be no higher than carving a mantelpiece or making a savory dish; for all these things imply creation, alike the test and the reward of genius itself, which almost every human being possesses, in some form or other, to a greater or less degree, — one of the kindest gifts of Deity to man.

The great artist, kindled by his visions of imperishable loveliness in the person of his departed Beatrice, now resolves to dedicate to her honor his great life-labor, — even his immortal poem, which should be a transcript of his thoughts, a mirror of his life, a record of his sorrows, a painting of his experiences, a description of what he saw, a digest of his great meditations, a thesaurus of the treasures of the Mediæval age, an exposition of its great and leading ideas in philosophy and in religion. Every great man wishes to leave behind some monument of his labors, to bless or instruct mankind. Any man without some form of this noble ambition lives in vain, even if his monument be no more than a cultivated farm rescued from wildness and sterility.

Now Dante's monument is "the marvellous, mystic, unfathomable song," in which he sang his sorrows and his joys, revealed his visions, and recorded the passions and sentiments of his age. It never can be popular, because it is so difficult to be understood, and because its leading ideas are not in harmony with those which are now received. I doubt if anybody can delight in that poem, unless he sympathizes with the ideas of the Middle Ages; or, at least, unless he is familiar with them, and with the historical characters who lived in those turbulent and gloomy times. There is more talk and pretension about that book than any one that I know of. Like the "Faerie Queene" or the "Paradise Lost," it is a study rather than a recreation; one of those productions which an educated person ought to read in the course of his life, and which if he can read in the original, and has read, is apt to boast of, — like climbing a lofty mountain, enjoyable to some with youth and vigor and enthusiasm and love of nature, but a very toilsome thing to most people, especially if old and short-winded and gouty.

In the year 1309 the first part of the "Divine Comedy," the *Inferno*, was finished by Dante, at the age of forty-four, in the tenth year of his pilgrimage, under the roof of the Marquis of Lunigiana; and it was intrusted to the care of Fra Ilario, a monk living on the beautiful Ligurian shores. As everybody knows, it is a vivid, graphic picture of what was supposed to be the infernal regions, where great sinners are punished with various torments forever and ever. It is interesting for the excellence of the poetry, the brilliant analyses of characters, the allusion to historical events, the bitter invectives, the intense sarcasms, and the serious, earnest spirit which underlies the descriptions. But there is very little of gentleness or compassion, in view of the protracted torments of the sufferers. We stand aghast in view of the miseries and monsters, furies and gorgons, snakes and fires, demons, filth, lakes of pitch, pools of blood, plains of scorching sands, circles, and chimeras dire, — a physical hell of utter and unspeakable dreariness and despair, awfully and powerfully described, but still repulsive. In each of the dismal abodes, far down in the bowels of the earth, which Dante is supposed to have visited with Virgil as a guide, in which some infernal deity presides, all sorts of physical tortures are accumulated, inflicted on traitors, murderers, robbers, — men who have committed great crimes, unpunished in their lifetime; such men as Cain, Judas, Ugolino, — men consigned to an infamous immortality. On the great culprits of history, and of Italy especially, Dante virtually sits in judgment; and he consigns them equally to various torments which we shudder to think of.

And here let me say, as a general criticism, that in the *Inferno* are brought out in tremendous language the opinions of the Middle Ages in reference to retribution. Dante does not rise above them, with all his genius; he is not emancipated from them. It is the rarest thing in this world for any man, however profound his intellect and bold his spirit, to be emancipated from the great and leading ideas of his age. Abraham was, and Moses, and the founder of Buddhism, and Socrates, and Mohammed, and Luther; but they were reformers, more or less divinely commissioned, with supernatural aid in many instances to give them wisdom. But Homer was not, nor Euripides, nor the great scholastics of the Middle Ages, nor even popes. The venerated doctors and philosophers, prelates, scholars, nobles, kings, to say nothing of the people, thought as Dante did in reference to future punishment, — that it was physical, awful, accumulative, infinite, endless; the wrath of avenging deity displayed in pains and agonies inflicted on the body, like the tortures of inquisitors, thus appealing to the fears of men, on which chiefly the power of the clergy was based. Nor in these views of endless physical sufferings, as if the body itself were eternal and indestructible, is there the refinement of Milton, who placed misery in the upbraidings of conscience, in mental torture rather than bodily, in the everlasting pride and rebellion of the followers of Satan and his fallen angels. It was these awful views of protracted and eternal physical torments, — not the hell of the Bible, but the hell of priests, of human invention, — which gives to the Middle Ages a sorrowful and repulsive light, thus nursing superstition and working on the fears of mankind, rather than on the conscience and the sense of moral accountability. But how could Dante have represented the ideas of the Middle Ages, if he had not painted his *Inferno* in the darkest colors that the imagination could conceive, unless he had soared beyond what is revealed into the unfathomable and mysterious and unrevealed regions of the second death?

After various wanderings in France and Italy, and after an interval of three years, Dante produced the second part of the poem, — the *Purgatorio*, — in which he assumes another style, and sings another song. In this we are introduced to an illustrious company, — many beloved friends, poets, musicians, philosophers, generals, even prelates and popes, whose deeds and thoughts were on the whole beneficent. These illustrions men temporarily expiate the sins of anger, of envy, avarice, gluttony, pride, ambition, — the great defects which were blended with virtues, and which are to be purged out of them by suffering. Their torments are milder, and amid them they discourse on the principles of moral wisdom. They utter noble sentiments; they discuss great themes; they show how vain is wealth and power and fame; they preach sermons. In these discourses, Dante shows his familiarity with history and philosophy; he unfolds that moral wisdom for which he is most distinguished. His scorn is now tempered with tenderness. He shows a true humanity; he is more forgiving, more generous, more sympathetic. He is more lofty, if he is not more intense. He sees the end of expiations: the sufferers will be restored to peace and joy.

But even in his purgatory, as in his hell, he paints the ideas of his age. He makes no new or extraordinary revelations. He arrives at no new philosophy. He is the Christian poet, after the pattern of his age.

It is plain that the Middle Ages must have accepted or invented some relief from punishment, or every Christian country would have been overwhelmed with the blackness of despair. Men could not live, if they felt they could not expiate their sins. Who could smile or joke or eat or sleep or have any pleasure, if he thought seriously there would be no cessation or release from endless pains? Who could discharge his ordinary duties or perform his daily occupations, if his father or his mother or his sister or his brother or his wife or his son or his daughter might not be finally forgiven for the frailties of an imperfect nature which he had inherited? The Catholic Church, in its benignity,— at what time I do not know,— opened the future of hope amid the speculations of despair. She saved the Middle Ages from universal gloom. If speculation or logic or tradition or scripture pointed to a hell of reprobation, there must be also a purgatory as the field of expiation,—

for expiation there must be for sin, somewhere, somehow, according to immutable laws, unless a mantle of universal forgiveness were spread over sinners who in this life had given no sufficient proofs of repentance and faith. Expiation was the great element of Mediæval theology. It may have been borrowed from India, but it was engrafted on the Christian system. Sometimes it was made to take place in this life; when the sinner, having pleased God, entered at once upon heavenly beatitudes. Hence fastings, scourgings, self-laceration, ascetic rigors in dress and food, pilgrimages, — all to purchase forgiveness; which idea of forgiveness was scattered to the winds by Luther, and replaced by grace, — faith in Christ attested by a righteous life. I allude to this notion of purgatory, which early entered into the creeds of theologians, and which was adopted by the Catholic Church, to show how powerful it was when human consciousness sought a relief from the pains of endless physical torments.

After Dante had written his *Purgatorio*, he retired to the picturesque mountains which separate Tuscany from Modena and Bologna; and in the hospitium of an ancient monastery, "on the woody summit of a rock from which he might gaze on his ungrateful country, he renewed his studies in philosophy and theology." There, too, in that calm retreat, he commenced his

Paradiso, the subject of profound meditations on what was held in highest value in the Middle Ages. The themes are theological and metaphysical. They are such as interested Thomas Aquinas and Bonaventura, Anselm and Bernard. They are such as do not interest this age, — even the most gifted minds, — for our times are comparatively indifferent to metaphysical subtleties and speculations. Beatrice and Peter and Benedict alike discourse on the recondite subjects of the Bible in the style of Mediæval doctors. The themes are great, — the incarnation, the immortality of the soul, the resurrection of the body, salvation by faith, the triumph of Christ, the glory of Paradise, the mysteries of the divine and human natures; and with these disquisitions are reproofs of bad popes, and even of some of the bad customs of the Church, like indulgences, and the corruptions of the monastic system. The *Paradiso* is a thesaurus of Mediæval theology, — obscure, but lofty, mixed up with all the learning of the age, even of the lives of saints and heroes and kings and prophets. Saint Peter examines Dante upon faith, James upon hope, and John upon charity. Virgil here has ceased to be his guide; but Beatrice, robed in celestial loveliness, conducts him from circle to circle, and explains the sublimest doctrines and resolves his mortal doubts, — the object still of his adoration, and inferior only to the mother of our Lord, *regina angelorum, mater caris-*

sima, whom the Church even then devoutly worshipped, and to whom the greatest sages prayed.

> "Thou virgin mother, daughter of thy Son,
> Humble and high beyond all other creatures,
> The limit fixed of the eternal counsel, —
> Thou art the one who such nobility
> To human nature gave, that its Creator
> Did not disdain to make himself its creature.
> Not only thy benignity gives succor
> To him who asketh it, but oftentimes
> Forerunneth of its own accord the asking.
> In thee compassion is; in thee is pity;
> In thee magnificence; in thee unites
> Whate'er of goodness is in any creature."

In the glorious meditation of those grand subjects which had such a charm for Benedict and Bernard, and which almost offset the barbarism and misery of the Middle Ages, — to many still regarded as "ages of faith," — Dante seemingly forgets his wrongs; and in the company of her whom he adores he seems to revel in the solemn ecstasy of a soul transported to the realms of eternal light. He lives now with the angels and the mysteries, —

> "Like to the fire
> That in a cloud imprisoned doth break out expansive.
> . . . .
> Thus, in that heavenly banqueting his soul
> Outgrew himself, and, in the transport lost,
> Holds no remembrance now of what she was."

The Paradise of Dante is not gloomy, although it be obscure and indefinite. It is the unexplored world of thought and knowledge, the explanation of dogmas which his age accepted. It is a revelation of glories such as only a lofty soul could conceive, but could not paint, — a supernal happiness given only to favored mortals, to saints and martyrs who have triumphed over the seductions of sense and the temptations of life, — a beatified state of blended ecstasy and love.

"Had I a tongue in eloquence as rich as is the coloring in fancy's loom,
'Twere all too poor to utter the least part of that enchantment."

Such is this great poem; in all its parts and exposition of the ideas of the age, — sometimes fierce and sometimes tender, profound and infantine, lofty and degraded, like the Church itself, which conserved these sentiments. It is an intensely religious poem, and yet more theological than Christian, and full of classical allusions to pagan heroes and sages, — a most remarkable production considering the age, and, when we remember that it is without a prototype in any language, a glorious monument of reviving literature, both original and powerful.

Its appearance was of course an epoch, calling out the admiration of Italians, and of all who could understand it, — of all who appreciated its moral wisdom in every other country of Europe. And its fame has been steadily increasing, although I fear much of the popular enthusiasm is exaggerated and unfelt. One who can read Italian well may see its "fiery emphasis and depth," its condensed thought and language, its supernal scorn and supernal love, its bitterness and its forgiveness; but very few sympathize with its theology or its philosophy, or care at all for the men whose crimes he punishes, and whose virtues he rewards.

But there is great interest in the man, as well as in the poem which he made the mirror of his life, and the register of his sorrows and of those speculations in which he sought to banish the remembrance of his misfortunes. His life, like his poem, is an epic. We sympathize with his resentments, "which exile and poverty made perpetually fresh." "The sincerity of his early passion for Beatrice," says Hallam, "pierces through the veil of allegory which surrounds her, while the memory of his injuries pursues him into the immensity of eternal light; and even in the company of saints and angels his unforgiving spirit darkens at the name of Florence. . . . He combines the profoundest feelings of religion with those patriotic recollections which were suggested by the reappearance of the illustrious dead."

Next to Michael Angelo he was the best of all famous Italians, stained by no marked defects but bitterness, pride, and scorn; while his piety, his patriotism, and elevation of soul stand out in marked contrast with the selfishness and venality and hypocrisy and cruelty of the leading men in the history of his times. "He wrote with his heart's blood;" he wrote in poverty, exile, grief, and neglect; he wrote like an inspired prophet of old. He seems to have been specially raised up to exalt virtue, and vindicate the ways of God to man, and prepare the way for a new civilization. He breathes angry defiance to all tyrants; he consigns even popes to the torments he created. He ridicules fools; he exposes knaves. He detests oppression; he is a prophet of liberty. He sees into all shams and all hypocrisies, and denounces lies. He is temperate in eating and drinking; he has no vices. He believes in friendship, in love, in truth. He labors for the good of his countrymen. He is affectionate to those who comprehend him. He accepts hospitalities, but will not stoop to meanness or injustice. He will not return to his native city, which he loves so well, even when permitted, if obliged to submit to humiliating ceremonies. He even refuses a laurel crown from any city but from the one in which he was born. No honors could tempt him to be untrue unto himself; no tasks are too humble to perform, if he can make himself useful. At Ravenna he gives lectures to the people in their own language, regarding the restoration of the Latin impossible, and wishing to bring into estimation the richness of the vernacular tongue. And when his work is done he dies, before he becomes old (1321), having fulfilled his vow. His last retreat was at Ravenna, and his last days were soothed with gentle attentions from Guido da Polenta, that kind duke who revived his fainting hopes. It was in his service, as ambassador to Venice, that Dante sickened and died. A funeral sermon was pronounced upon him by his friend the duke, and beautiful monuments were erected to his memory. Too late the Florentines begged for his remains, and did justice to the man and the poet; as well they might, since his is the proudest name connected with their annals. He is indeed one of the great benefactors of the world itself, for the richness of his immortal legacy.

Could the proscribed and exiled poet, as he wandered, isolated and alone, over the vine-clad hills of Italy, and as he stopped here and there at some friendly monastery, wearied and hungry, have cast his prophetic eye down the vistas of the ages; could he have seen what honors would be bestowed upon his name, and how his poem, written in sorrow, would be scattered in joy among all nations, giving a new direction to human thought, shining as a fixed star in the realms of genius, and kindling into shining brightness what is only a reflection of its rays; yea, how it would be committed to memory in the rising universities, and be commented on by the most learned expositors in all the schools of

Europe, lauded to the skies by his countrymen, received by the whole world as a unique, original, unapproachable production, suggesting grand thoughts to Milton, reappearing even in the creations of Michael Angelo, coloring art itself whenever art seeks the sublime and beautiful, inspiring all subsequent literature, dignifying the life of letters, and gilding philosophy as well as poetry with new glories, — could he have seen all this, how his exultant soul would have rejoiced, even as did Abraham, when, amid the ashes of the funeral pyre he had prepared for Isaac, he saw the future glories of his descendants; or as Bacon, when, amid calumnies, he foresaw that his name and memory would be held in honor by posterity, and that his method would be received by all future philosophers as one of the priceless boons of genius to mankind!

AUTHORITIES.

Vita Nuova; Divina Commedia, — Translations by Carey and Longfellow; Boccaccio's Life of Dante; Wright's St. Patrick's Purgatory; Dante et la Philosophie Catholique du Treizième Siècle, par Ozinan; Labitte, La Divine Comédie avant Dante; Balbo's Life and Times of Dante; Hallam's Middle Ages; Napier's Florentine History; Villani; Leigh Hunt's Stories from the Italian Poets; Botta's Life of Dante; J. R. Lowell's article on Dante in American Cyclopædia; Milman's Latin Christianity; Carlyle's Heroes and Hero-worship; Macaulay's Essays; The Divina Commedia from the German of Schelling; Voltaire's Dictionnaire Philosophique; La Divine Comédie, by Lamennais; Dante, by Labitte.

GEOFFREY CHAUCER.

A. D. 1340–1400.

ENGLISH LIFE IN THE FOURTEENTH CENTURY.

GEOFFREY CHAUCER.

ENGLISH LIFE IN THE FOURTEENTH CENTURY.

THE age which produced Chaucer was a transition period from the Middle Ages to modern times, midway between Dante and Michael Angelo. Chaucer was the contemporary of Wyclif, with whom the Middle Ages may appropriately be said to close, or modern history to begin.

The fourteenth century is interesting for the awakening, especially in Italy, of literature and art; for the wars between the French and English, and the English and the Scots; for the rivalry between the Italian republics; for the efforts of Rienzi to establish popular freedom at Rome; for the insurrection of the Flemish weavers, under the Van Arteveldes, against their feudal oppressors; for the terrible "**Jacquerie**" in Paris; for the insurrection of Wat Tyler in England; for the Swiss confederation; for a schism in the Church when the popes retired to Avignon; for the aggrandizement of the Visconti at Milan and the Medici at Florence;

for incipient religious reforms under Wyclif in England and John Huss in Bohemia; for the foundation of new colleges at Oxford and Cambridge; for the establishment of guilds in London; for the exploration of distant countries; for the dreadful pestilence which swept over Europe, known in England as the Black Death; for the development of modern languages by the poets; and for the rise of the English House of Commons as a great constitutional power.

In most of these movements we see especially a simultaneous rising among the people, in the more civilized countries of Europe, to obtain charters of freedom and municipal and political privileges, extorted from monarchs in their necessities. The fourteenth century was marked by protests and warfare equally against feudal institutions and royal tyranny. The way was prepared by the wars of kings, which crippled their resources, as the Crusades had done a century before. The supreme miseries of the people led them to political revolts and insurrections, — blind but fierce movements, not inspired by ideas of liberty, but by a sense of oppression and degradation. Accompanying these popular insurrections were religious protests against the corrupt institutions of the Church.

In the midst of these popular agitations, aggressive and needless wars, public miseries and calamities, baronial aggrandizement, religious inquiries, parliamentary encroachment, and reviving taste for literature and art, Chaucer arose.

His remarkable career extended over the last half of the fourteenth century, when public events were of considerable historical importance. It was then that parliamentary history became interesting. Until then the barons, clergy, knights of the shire, and burgesses of the town, summoned to assist the royal councils, deliberated in separate chambers or halls; but in the reign of Edward III. the representatives of the knights of the shires and the burgesses united their interests and formed a body strong enough to check royal encroachments, and became known henceforth as the House of Commons. In thirty years this body had wrested from the Crown the power of arbitrary taxation, had forced upon it new ministers, and had established the principle that the redress of grievances preceded grants of supply. Edward III. was compelled to grant twenty parliamentary confirmations of Magna Charta. At the close of his reign, it was conceded that taxes could be raised only by consent of the Commons; and they had sufficient power, also, to prevent the collection of the tax which the Pope had levied on the country since the time of John, called Peter's Pence. The latter part of the fourteenth century must not be regarded as an era of the triumph of popular rights, but as the period when these rights began to be asserted. Long and dreary was the march of the people to complete political enfranchisement from the rebellion under Wat Tyler to the passage of the Reform Bill in our times. But the Commons made a memorable stand against Edward III. when he was the most powerful sovereign of western Europe, one which would have been impossible had not this able and ambitious sovereign been embroiled in desperate war both with the Scotch and French.

With the assertion of political rights we notice the beginning of commercial enterprise and manufacturing industry. A colony of Flemish weavers was established in England by the enlightened king, although wool continued to be exported. It was not until the time of Elizabeth that the raw material was consumed at home.

Still, the condition of the common people was dreary enough at this time, when compared with what it is in our age. They perhaps were better fed on the necessities of life than they are now. All meats were comparatively cheaper; but they had no luxuries, not even wheaten bread. Their houses were small and dingy, and a single chamber sufficed for a whole family, both male and female. Neither glass windows nor chimneys were then in use, nor knives nor forks, nor tea nor coffee; not even potatoes, still less tropical fruits. The people had neither bed-clothes, nor carpets, nor glass nor crockery ware, nor cotton dresses, nor books, nor schools. They were robbed by feudal masters, and cheated and imposed upon by friars and pedlers; but a grim cheerfulness shone above their discomforts and miseries, and crime was uncommon and severely punished. They amused themselves with rough sports, and cherished religious sentiments. They were brave and patriotic.

It was to describe the habits and customs of these people, as well as those of the classes above them, to give dignity to consecrated sentiments and to shape the English language, that Chaucer was raised up.

He was born, it is generally supposed, in the year 1340; but nothing is definitely known of him till 1357, when Edward III. had been reigning about thirty years. It is surmised that his father was a respectable citizen of London; that he was educated at Cambridge and Oxford; that he went to Paris to complete his education in the most famous university in the world; that he then extensively travelled in France, Holland, and Flanders, after which he became a student of law in the Inner Temple. Even then he was known as a poet, and his learning and accomplishments attracted the attention of Edward III., who was a patron of genius, and who gave him a house in Woodstock, near the royal palace. At this time Chaucer was a handsome, witty, modest, dignified man of letters, in easy circumstances, moving in the higher ranks of society, and already known for his "Troilus and Cresseide," which was then doubtless the best poem in the language.

It was then that the intimacy began between him and John of Gaunt, a youth of eighteen, then Earl of Richmond, fourth son of Edward III., afterwards known as the great Duke of Lancaster, — the most powerful nobleman that ever lived in England, also the richest, possessing large estates in eighteen counties, as well as six earldoms. This friendship between the poet and the first prince of the blood, after the Prince of Wales, seems to have arisen from the admiration of John of Gaunt for the genius and accomplishments of Chaucer, who was about ten years the elder. It was not until the prince became the Duke of Lancaster that he was the friend and protector of Wyclif, — and from different reasons, seeing that the Oxford scholar and theologian could be of use to him in his warfare against the clergy, who were hostile to his ambitious designs. Chaucer he loved as a bright and witty companion; Wyclif he honored as the most learned churchman of the age.

The next authentic event in Chaucer's life occurred in 1359, when he accompanied the king to France in that fruitless expedition which was soon followed by the peace of Brétigny. In this unfortunate campaign Chaucer was taken prisoner, but was ransomed by his sovereign for £16, — about equal to £300 in these times. He had probably before this been installed at court as a gentleman of the bedchamber, on a stipend which would now be equal to £250 a year. He seems to have been a favorite with the court, after he had written his first great poem. It is singular that in a rude and ignorant age poets should have received much greater honor than in our enlightened times. Gower was patronized by the Duke of Gloucester, as Chaucer was by the Duke of Lancaster, and Petrarch and Boccaccio were in Italy by princes and nobles. Even learning was held in more reverence in the fourteenth century than it is in the nineteenth. The scholastic doctor was one of the great dignitaries of the age, as well as of the schools, and ranked with bishops and abbots. Wyclif at one time was the most influential man in the English Church, sitting in Parliament, and sent by the king on important diplomatic missions. So Chaucer, with less claim, received valuable offices and land-grants, which made him a wealthy man; and he was also sent on important missions in the company of nobles. He lived at the court. His son Thomas married one of the richest heiresses in the kingdom, and became speaker of the House of Commons; while his daughter Alice married the Duke of Suffolk, whose grandson was declared by Richard III. to be his heir, and came near becoming King of England. Chaucer's wife's sister married the Duke of Lancaster himself; so he was allied with the royal family, if not by blood, at least by ambitious marriage connections.

I know of no poet in the history of England who occupied so high a social position as did Chaucer, or who received so many honors. The poet of the people was the companion of kings and princes. At one time he had a reverse of fortune, when his friend and patron, the Duke of Lancaster, was in disgrace and in voluntary banishment during the minority of Richard II., against whom he had intrigued, and who afterwards was dethroned by Henry IV., a son of the Duke of Lancaster. While the Duke of Gloucester was in power, Chaucer was deprived of his offices and revenues for two or three years, and was even imprisoned in the Tower; but when Lancaster returned from the Continent, his offices and revenues were restored. His latter days were luxurious and honored. At fifty-one he gave up his public duties as a collector of customs, chiefly on wool, and retired to Woodstock and spent the remainder of his fortunate life in dignified leisure and literary labors. In addition to his revenues, the Duke of Lancaster, who was virtually the ruler of the land during the reign of Richard II., gave him the castle of Donnington, with its park and gardens; so that he became a man of territorial influence. At the age of fifty-eight he removed to London, and took a house in the precincts of Westminster Abbey, where the chapel of Henry VII. now stands. He died the following year, and was buried in the Abbey church, — that sepulchre of princes and bishops and abbots. His body was deposited in the place now known as the Poets' Corner, and a fitting monument to his genius was erected over his remains, as the first great poet that had appeared in England, probably only surpassed in genius by Shakspeare, until the language assumed its present form. He was regarded as a moral phenomenon, whom kings and princes delighted to honor. As Leonardo da Vinci died in the arms of Francis I., so Chaucer rested in his grave near the bodies of those sovereigns and princes with whom he lived in intimacy and friendship. It was the rarity of his gifts, his great attainments, elegant manners, and refined tastes which made him the companion of the great, since at that time only princes and nobles and ecclesiastical dignitaries could appreciate his genius or enjoy his writings.

Although Chaucer had written several poems which were admired in his day, and made translations from the French, among which was the "Roman de la Rose," the most popular poem of the Middle Ages, — a poem which represented the difficulties attendant on the passion of love, under the emblem of a rose which had to be plucked amid thorns, — yet his best works were written in the leisure of declining years.

The occupation of the poet during the last twelve years of his life was in writing his "Canterbury Tales," on which his fame chiefly rests; written not for money, but because he was impelled to write it, as all true poets write and all great artists paint, — *ex animo,* — because they cannot help writing and painting, as the solace and enjoyment of life. For his day these tales were a great work of art, evidently written with great care. They are also stamped with the inspiration of genius, although the stories themselves were copied in the main from the French and Italian, even as the French and Italians copied from Oriental writers, whose works were translated into the languages of Europe; so that the romances of the Middle Ages were originally produced in India, Persia, and Arabia. Absolute creation is very rare. Even Shakspeare, the most original of poets, was indebted to French and Italian writers for the plots of many of his best dramas. Who can tell the remote sources of human invention; who knows the then popular songs which Homer probably incorporated in his epics; who can trace the fountains of those streams which have fertilized the literary world? — and hence, how shallow the criticism which would detract from literary genius because it is indebted, more or less, to the men who have lived ages ago. It is the way of putting things which constitutes the merit of men of genius. What has Voltaire or Hume or Froude told the world, essentially, that it did not know before? Read, for instance, half-a-dozen historians on Joan of Arc: they all relate substantially the same facts. Genius and originality are seen in the reflections and deductions and grand sentiments prompted by the narrative. Let half-a-dozen distinguished and learned theologians write sermons on Abraham or Moses or David: they will all be different, yet the main facts will be common to all.

The "Canterbury Tales" are great creations, from the humor, the wit, the naturalness, the vividness of description, and the beauty of the sentiments displayed in them, although sullied by occasional vulgarities and impurities, which, however, in all their coarseness do not corrupt the mind. Byron complained of their coarseness, but Byron's poetry is far more demoralizing. The age was coarse, not the mind of the author. And after five hundred years, with all the obscurity of language and obsolete modes of spelling, they still give pleasure to the true lovers of poetry when they have once mastered the language, which is not, after all, very difficult. It is true that most people prefer to read the great masters of poetry in later times; but the "Canterbury Tales" are interesting and instructive to those who study the history of language and literature. They are links in the civilization of England. They paint the age more vividly and accurately than any known history. The men and women of the fourteenth century, of all ranks, stand out to us in fresh and living colors. We see them in their dress, their feasts, their dwellings, their language, their habits, and their manners. Amid all the changes in human thought and in social institutions the characters appeal to our common humanity, essentially the same under all human conditions. The men and women of the fourteenth century love and hate, eat and drink, laugh and talk, as they do in the nineteenth. They delight, as we do, in the varieties of dress, of parade, and luxurious feasts. Although the form of these has changed, they are alive to the same sentiments which move us. They like fun and jokes and amusement as much as we. They abhor the same class of defects which disgust us, — hypocrisies, shams, lies. The inner circle of their friendship is the same as ours to-day, based on sincerity and admiration. There is the same infinite variety in character, and yet the same uniformity. The human heart beats to the same sentiments that it does under all civilizations and conditions of life. No people can live without friendship and sympathy and love; and these are ultimate sentiments of the soul, which are as eternal as the ideas of Plato. Why do the Psalms of David, written for an Oriental people four thousand

THE CANTERBURY PILGRIMAGE
(Section of Frieze by R. W. Sewell in the house of Mr. George Gould at Lakewood, N. J.)

Copyright, 1898, by C. Klackner

years ago, excite the same emotions in the minds of the people of England or France or America that they did among the Jews? It is because they appeal to our common humanity, which never changes, — the same to-day as it was in the beginning, and will be to the end. It is only form and fashion which change; men remain the same. The men and women of the Bible talked nearly the same as we do, and seem to have had as great light on the primal principles of wisdom and truth and virtue. Who can improve on the sagacity and worldly wisdom of the Proverbs of Solomon? They have a perennial freshness, and appeal to universal experience. It is this fidelity to nature which is one of the great charms of Shakspeare. We quote his brief sayings as expressive of what we feel and know of the certitudes of our moral and intellectual life. They will last forever, under every variety of government, of social institutions, of races, and of languages. And they will last because these every-day sentiments are put in such pithy, compressed, unique, and novel form, like the Proverbs of Solomon or the sayings of Epictetus. All nations and ages alike recognize the moral wisdom in the sayings of those immortal sages whose writings have delighted and enlightened the world, because they appeal to consciousness or experience.

Now it must be confessed that the poetry of Chaucer

does not abound in the moral wisdom and spiritual insight and profound reflections on the great mysteries of human life which stand out so conspicuously in the writings of Dante, Shakspeare, Milton, Goethe, and other first-class poets. He does not describe the inner life, but the outward habits and condition of the people of his times. He is not serious enough, nor learned enough, to enter upon the discussion of those high themes which agitated the schools and universities, as Dante did one hundred years before. He tells us how monks and friars lived, not how they dreamed and speculated. Nor are his sarcasms scorching and bitter, but rather humorous and laughable. He shows himself to be a genial and loving companion, not an austere teacher of disagreeable truths. He is not solemn and intense, like Dante; he does not give wings to his fancy, like Spenser; he has not the divine insight of Shakspeare; he is not learned, like Milton; he is not sarcastic, like Pope; he does not rouse the passions, like Byron; he is not meditative, like Wordsworth, — but he paints nature with great accuracy and delicacy, as also the men and women of his age, as they appeared in their outward life. He describes the passion of love with great tenderness and simplicity. In all his poems, love is his greatest theme, — which he bases, not on physical charms, but the moral beauty of the soul. In his earlier life he does not seem to have done full justice to women, whom he ridicules, but does not despise; in whom he indeed sees the graces of chivalry, but not the intellectual attraction of cultivated life. But later in life, when his experiences are broader and more profound, he makes amends for his former mistakes. In his "Legend of Good Women," which he wrote at the command of Anne of Bohemia, wife of Richard II., he eulogizes the sex and paints the most exalted sentiments of the heart. He not only had great vividness in the description of his characters, but doubtless great dramatic talent, which his age did not call out. His descriptions of nature are very fresh and beautiful, indicating a great love of nature, — flowers, trees, birds, lawns, gardens, waterfalls, falcons, dogs, horses, with whom he almost talked. He had a great sense of the ridiculous; hence his humor and fun and droll descriptions, which will ever interest because they are so fresh and vivid. And as a poet he continually improved as he advanced in life. His last works are his best, showing the care and labor he bestowed, as well as his fidelity to nature. I am amazed, considering his time, that he was so great an artist without having a knowledge of the principles of art as taught by the great masters of composition.

But, as has been already said, his distinguishing excellence is vivid and natural description of the life and habits, not the opinions, of the people of the fourteenth century, described without exaggeration or effort for effect. He paints his age as Molière paints the times of Louis XIV., and Homer the heroic periods of Grecian history. This fidelity to nature and inexhaustible humor and living freshness and perpetual variety are the eternal charms of the "Canterbury Tales." They bring before the eye the varied professions and trades and habits and customs of the fourteenth century. We see how our ancestors dressed and talked and ate; what pleasures delighted them, what animosities moved them, what sentiments elevated them, and what follies made them ridiculous. The same naturalness and humor which marked "Don Quixote" and the "Decameron" also are seen in the "Canterbury Tales." Chaucer freed himself from all the affectations and extravagances and artificiality which characterized the poetry of the Middle Ages. With him began a new style in writing. He and Wyclif are the creators of English literature. They did not create a language, but they formed and polished it.

The various persons who figure in the "Canterbury Tales" are too well known for me to enlarge upon. Who can add anything to the Prologue in which Chaucer himself describes the varied characters and habits and appearance of the pilgrims to the shrine of Thomas à Becket at Canterbury? There are thirty of these pilgrims, including the poet himself, embracing nearly all the professions and trades then known, except the higher dignitaries of Church and State, who are not supposed to mix freely in ordinary intercourse, and whom it would be unwise to paint in their marked peculiarities. The most prominent person, as to social standing, is probably the knight. He is not a nobleman, but he has fought in many battles, and has travelled extensively. His cassock is soiled, and his horse is strong but not gay, — a very respectable man, courteous and gallant, a soldier corresponding to a modern colonel or captain. His son, the esquire, is a youth of twenty, with curled locks and embroidered dress, shining in various colors like the flowers of May, gay as a bird, active as a deer, and gentle as a maiden. The yeoman who attends them both is clad in green like a forester, with arrows and feathers, bearing the heavy sword and buckler of his master. The prioress is another respectable person, coy and simple, with dainty fingers, small mouth, and clean attire, — a refined sort of a woman for that age, ornamented with corals and brooch, so stately as to be held in reverence, yet so sentimental as to weep for a mouse caught in a trap: all characteristic of a respectable, kind-hearted lady who has lived in seclusion. A monk, of course, in the fourteenth century was everywhere to be seen; and a monk we have among the pilgrims, riding a "dainty" horse, accompanied with greyhounds, loving fur trimmings on his Benedictine habit and a fat swan to roast. The friar, too, we see, — a mendicant, yet merry and full of dalliances, beloved by the common women, to whom he gave easy absolution; a jolly vagabond, who knew all the taverns, and who carried on his portly person pins and songs and relics to sell or to give away. And there was the merchant, with forked beard and Flemish beaver hat and neatly clasped boots, bragging of his gains and selling French crowns, but on the whole a worthy man. The Oxford clerk or scholar is one of the company, silent and sententious, as lean as the horse on which he rode, with threadbare coat, and books of Aristotle and his philosophy which he valued more than gold, of which indeed he could boast but little, — a man anxious to learn, and still more to teach. The sergeant of the law is another prominent figure, wary and wise, discreet and dignified, bustling and busy, yet not so busy as he seemed to be, wearing a coat of divers colors, and riding very badly. A franklin, or country gentleman, mixes with the company, with a white beard and red complexion; one of Epicurus's own sons, who held that ale and wheaten bread and fish and dainty flesh, partridge fat, were pure felicity; evidently a man given to hospitality, —

> "His table dormant in his hall alway
> Stood ready covered all the longe day."

He was a sheriff, also, to enforce the law, and to be present at all the county sessions. The doctor, of course, could not be left out of the company, — a man who knew the cause of every malady, versed in magic as well as physic, and grounded also in astronomy; who held that gold is the best of cordials, and knew how to keep what he gained; not luxurious in his diet, but careful what he ate and drank. The village miller is not forgotten in this motley crowd, — rough, brutal, drunken, big and brawn, with a red beard and a wart on his nose, and a mouth as wide as a furnace, a reveller and a jangler, accustomed to take toll thrice, and given to all the sins that then abounded. He is the most repulsive figure in the crowd, both vulgar and wicked. In contrast with him is the *reve*, or steward, of a lordly house, — a slender, choleric man, feared by servants and gamekeepers, yet in favor with his lord, since he always had money to lend, although it belonged to his master; an adroit agent and manager, who so complicated his accounts that no auditor could unravel them or any person bring him in arrears. He rode a fine dappled-gray stallion, wore a long blue overcoat, and carried a rusty sword, — evidently a proud and prosperous man. With a monk and friar, the picture would be incomplete without a pardoner, or seller of indulgences, with yellow hair and smooth face, loaded with a pillow-case of relics and pieces of the true cross, of which there were probably cartloads in every country in Europe, and of which the popes had an inexhaustible supply. This sleek and gentle pedler of indulgences rode side by side with a repulsive officer of the Church, with a fiery red face, of whom children were afraid, fond of garlic and onions and strong wine, and speaking only Latin law-terms when he was drunk, but withal a good fellow, abating his lewdness and drunkenness. In contrast with the pardoner and "sompnour" we see the poor parson, full of goodness, charity, and love, — a true shepherd and no mercenary, who waited upon no pomp and sought no worldly gains, happy only in the virtues which he both taught and lived. Some think that Chaucer had in view the learned Wyclif when he described the most interesting character of the whole group. With him was a ploughman, his brother, as good and pious as he, living in peace with all the world, paying tithes cheerfully, laborious and conscientious, the forerunner of the Puritan yeoman.

Of this motley company of pilgrims, I have already spoken of the prioress, — a woman of high position. In contrast with her is the wife of Bath, who has travelled extensively, even to Jerusalem and Rome; charitable, kind-hearted, jolly, and talkative, but bold and masculine and coarse, with a red face and red stockings, and a hat as big as a shield, and sharp spurs on her feet, indicating that she sat on her ambler like a man.

There are other characters which I cannot stop to mention, — the sailor, browned by the seas and sun, and full of stolen Bordeaux wine; the haberdasher; the carpenter; the weaver; the dyer; the tapestry-worker; the cook, to boil the chickens and the marrow-bones, and bake the pies and tarts, — mostly people from the middle and lower ranks of society, whose clothes are gaudy, manners rough, and language coarse. But all classes and trades and professions seem to be represented, except nobles, bishops, and abbots, — dignitaries whom, perhaps, Chaucer is reluctant to describe and caricature.

To beguile the time on the journey to Canterbury, all these various pilgrims are required to tell some story peculiar to their separate walks of life; and it is these stories which afford the best description we have of the manners and customs of the fourteenth century, as well as of its leading sentiments and ideas.

The knight was required to tell his story first, and it naturally was one of love and adventure. Although the scene of it was laid in ancient Greece, it delineates the institution of chivalry and the manners and sentiments it produced. No writer of that age, except perhaps Froissart, paints the connection of chivalry with the graces of the soul and the moral beauty which poetry associates with the female sex as Chaucer does. The aristocratic woman of chivalry, while delighting in martial sports, and hence masculine and haughty, is also condescending, tender, and gracious. The heroic and dignified self-respect with which chivalry invested woman exalted the passion of love. Allied with reverence for woman was loyalty to the prince. The rough warrior again becomes a gentleman, and has access to the best society. Whatever may have been the degrees of rank, the haughtiest nobleman associated with the penniless knight, if only he were a gentleman and well born, on terms of social equality, since chivalry, while it created distinctions, also levelled those which wealth and power naturally created among the higher class. Yet chivalry did not exalt woman outside of noble ranks. The plebeian woman neither has the graces of the high-born lady, nor does she excite that reverence for the sex which marked her condition in the feudal castle. "Tournaments and courts of love were not framed for village churls, but for high-born dames and mighty earls."

Chaucer in his description of women in ordinary life does not seem to have a very high regard for them. They are weak or coarse or sensual, though attentive to their domestic duties, and generally virtuous. An exception is made of Virginia, in the doctor's tale, who is represented as beautiful and modest, radiant in simplicity, discreet and true. But the wife of Bath is disgusting from her coarse talk and coarser manners. Her tale is to show what a woman likes best, which, according to her, is to bear rule over her husband and household. The prioress is conventional and weak, aping courtly manners. The wife of the host of the Tabard inn is a vixen and shrew, who calls her husband a milksop, and is so formidable with both her tongue and her hands that he is glad to make his escape from her whenever he can. The pretty wife of the carpenter, gentle and slender, with her white apron and open dress, is anything but intellectual, — a mere sensual beauty. Most of these women are innocent of toothbrushes, and give and receive thrashings, and sing songs without a fastidious taste, and beat their servants and nag their husbands. But they are good cooks, and understand the arts of brewing and baking and roasting and preserving and pickling, as well as of spinning and knitting and embroidering. They are supreme in their households; they keep the keys and lock up the wine. They are gossiping, and love to receive their female visitors. They do not do much shopping, for shops were very primitive, with but few things to sell. Their knowledge is very limited, and confined to domestic matters. They are on the whole modest, but are the victims of friars and pedlers. They have more liberty than we should naturally suppose, but have not yet learned to discriminate between duties and rights. There are few disputed questions between them and their husbands, but the duty of obedience seems to have been recognized. But if oppressed, they always are free with their tongues; they give good advice, and do not spare reproaches in language which in our times we should not call particularly choice. They are all fond of dress, and wear gay colors, without much regard to artistic effect.

In regard to the sports and amusements of the people, we learn much from Chaucer. In one sense the England of his day was merry; that is, the people were noisy and rough in their enjoyments. There was frequent ringing of the bells; there were the horn of the huntsman and the excitements of the chase; there was boisterous mirth in the village ale-house; there were frequent holidays, and dances around May-poles covered with ribbons and flowers and flags; there were wandering minstrels and jesters and jugglers, and cock-fightings and foot-ball and games at archery; there were wrestling matches and morris-dancing and bear-baiting. But the exhilaration of the people was abnormal, like the merriment of negroes on a Southern plantation,—a sort of rebound from misery and burdens, which found a vent in noise and practical jokes when the ordinary restraint was removed. The uproarious joy was a sort of defiance of the semi-slavery to which workmen were doomed; for when they could be impressed by the king's architect and paid whatever he chose to give them, there could not have been much real contentment, which is generally placid and calm. There is one thing in which all classes delighted in the fourteenth century, and that was a garden, in which flowers bloomed, — things of beauty which were as highly valued as the useful. Moreover, there was a zest in rural sports now seldom seen, especially among the upper classes who could afford to hunt and fish. There was no excitement more delightful to gentlemen and ladies than that of hawking, and it infinitely surpassed in interest any rural sport whatever in our day, under any circumstances. Hawks trained to do the work of fowling-pieces were therefore greater pets than any dogs that now are the company of sportsmen. A lady without a falcon on her wrist, when mounted on her richly caparisoned steed for a morning's sport, was very rare indeed.

An instructive feature of the " Canterbury Tales " is the view which Chaucer gives us of the food and houses and dresses of the people. "In the Nonne's Prestes' Tale we see the cottage and manner of life of a poor widow." She has three daughters, three pigs, three oxen, and a sheep. Her house had only two rooms, — an eating-room, which also served for a kitchen and sitting-room, and a bower or bedchamber, — both without a chimney, with holes pierced to let in the light. The table was a board put upon trestles, to be removed when the meal of black bread and milk, and perchance an egg with bacon, was over. The three slept without sheets or blankets on a rude bed, covered only with their ordinary day-clothes. Their kitchen utensils were a brass pot or two for boiling, a few wooden platters, an iron candlestick, and a knife or two; while the furniture was composed of two or three chairs and stools, with a frame in the wall, with shelves, for clothes and utensils. The manciple and the cook of the company seem to indicate that living among the well-to-do classes was a very generous and a very serious part of life, on which a high estimate was placed, since food in any variety, though plentiful at times, was not always to be had, and therefore precarious. "Guests at table were paired, and ate, every pair, out of the same plate or off the same trencher." But the bill of fare at a franklin's feast would be deemed anything but poor, even in our times, — "bacon and pea-soup, oysters, fish, stewed beef, chickens, capons, roast goose, pig, veal, lamb, kid, pigeon, with custard, apples and pears, cheese and spiced cakes." All these with abundance of wine and ale.

The "Canterbury Tales" remind us of the vast preponderance of the country over town and city life. Chaucer, like Shakspeare, revels in the simple glories of nature, which he describes like a man feeling it to be a joy to be near to "Mother Earth," with her rich bounties. The birds that usher in the day, the flowers which beautify the lawn, the green hills and vales, with ever-changing hues like the clouds and the skies, yet fruitful in wheat and grass; the domestic animals, so mute and patient, the bracing air of approaching winter, the genial breezes of the spring, — of all these does the poet sing with charming simplicity and grace, yea, in melodious numbers; for nothing is more marvellous than the music and rhythm of his lines, although they are not enriched with learned allusions or much moral wisdom, and do not march in the stately and majestic measure of Shakspeare or of Milton.

But the most interesting and instructive of the "Canterbury Tales" are those which relate to the religious life, the morals, the superstitions, and ecclesiastical abuses of the times. In these we see the need of the reformation of which Wyclif was the morning light. In these we see the hypocrisies and sensualities of both monks and friars, relieved somewhat by the virtues of the simple parish priest or poor parson, in contrast with the wealth and luxury of the regular clergy, as monks were called, in their princely monasteries, where the lordly abbot vied with both baron and bishop in the magnificence of his ordinary life. We see before us the Mediæval clergy in all their privileges, and yet in all their ignorance and superstition, shielded from the punishment of crime and the operation of all ordinary laws (a sturdy defiance of the temporal powers), the agents and ministers of a foreign power, armed with the terrors of hell and the grave. Besides the prioress and the nuns' priest, we see in living light the habits and pretensions of the lazy monk, the venal friar and pardoner, and the noisy summoner for ecclesiastical offences: hunters and gluttons are they, with greyhounds and furs, greasy and fat, and full of dalliances; at home in taverns, unprincipled but agreeable vagabonds, who cheat and rob the people, and make a mockery of what is most sacred on the earth. These privileged mendicants, with their relics and indulgences, their arts and their lies, and the scandals they create, are treated by Chaucer with blended humor and severity, showing a mind as enlightened as that of the great scholar at Oxford, who heads the movement against Rome and the abuses at which she connived if she did not encourage. And there is something intensely English in his disgust and scorn,—brave for his day, yet shielded by the great duke who was at once his protector and friend, as he was of Wyclif himself,—in his severer denunciation, and advocacy of doctrines which neither Chaucer nor the Duke of Lancaster understood, and which, if they had, they would not have sympathized with nor encouraged. In these attacks on ecclesiastics and ecclesiastical abuses,

Chaucer should be studied with Wyclif and the early reformers, although he would not have gone so far as they, and led, unlike them, a worldly life. Thus by these poems he has rendered a service to his country, outside his literary legacy, which has always been held in value. The father of English poetry belonged to the school of progress and of inquiry, like his great contemporaries on the Continent. But while he paints the manners, customs, and characters of the fourteenth century, he does not throw light on the great ideas which agitated or enslaved the age. He is too real and practical for that. He describes the outward, not the inner life. He was not serious enough — I doubt if he was learned enough — to enter into the disquisitions of schoolmen, or the mazes of the scholastic philosophy, or the meditations of almost inspired sages. It is not the joys of heaven or the terrors of hell on which he discourses, but of men and women as they lived around him, in their daily habits and occupations. We must go to Wyclif if we would know the theological or philosophical doctrines which interested the learned. Chaucer only tells how monks and friars lived, not how they speculated or preached. We see enough, however, to feel that he was emancipated from the ideas of the Middle Ages, and had cast off their gloom, their superstition, and their despair. The only things he liked of those dreary times were their courts of love and their chivalric glories.

I do not propose to analyze the poetry of Chaucer, or enter upon a critical inquiry as to his relative merits in comparison with the other great poets. It is sufficient for me to know that critics place him very high as an original poet, although it is admitted that he drew much of his material from French and Italian authors. He was, for his day, a great linguist. He had travelled extensively, and could speak Latin, French, and Italian with fluency. He knew Petrarch and other eminent Italians. One is amazed that in such an age he could have written so well, for he had no great models to help him in his own language. If occasionally indecent, he is not corrupting. He never deliberately disseminates moral poison; and when he speaks of love, he treats almost solely of the simple and genuine emotions of the heart.

The best criticism that I have read of Chaucer's poetry is that of Adolphus William Ward; although as a biography it is not so full or so interesting as that of Godwin or even Morley. In no life that I have read are the mental characteristics of our poet so ably drawn,—"his practical good sense," his love of books, his still deeper love of nature, his naïveté, the readiness of his description, the brightness of his imagery, the easy flow of his diction, the vividness with which he describes character; his inventiveness, his readiness of illustration, his musical rhythm, his gaiety and cheerfulness, his vivacity and joyousness, his pathos and tenderness, his keen sense of the ridiculous and power of satire, without being bitter, so that his wit and fun are harmless, and perpetually pleasing.

He doubtless had great dramatic talent, but he did not live in a dramatic age. His especial excellence, never surpassed, was his power of observing and drawing character, united with boundless humor and cheerful fun. And his descriptions of nature are as true and unstinted as his descriptions of men and women, so that he is as fresh as the month of May. In his poetry is life; and hence his immortal fame. He is not so great as Spenser or Shakspeare or Milton; but he has the same vitality as they, and is as wonderful as they considering his age and opportunities, — a poet who constantly improved as he advanced in life, and whose greatest work was written in his old age.

Unfortunately, we know but little of Chaucer's habits and experiences, his trials and disappointments, his friendships or his hatreds. What we do know of him raises our esteem. Though convivial, he was temperate; though genial, he was a silent observer, quiet in his manners, modest in his intercourse with the world, walking with downcast eye, but letting nothing escape his notice. He believed in friendship, and kept his friends to the end, and was stained neither by envy nor by pride, — as frank as he was affectionate, as gentle as he was witty. Living with princes and nobles, he never descended to gross adulation, and never wrote a line of approval of the usurpation of Henry IV., although his bread depended on Henry's favor, and he was also the son of the king's earliest and best friend. He was not a religious man, nor was he an immoral man, judged by the standard of his age. He probably was worldly, as he lived in courts. We do not see in him the stern virtues of Dante or Milton; nothing of that moral earnestness which marked the only other great man with whom he was contemporary, — he who is called the "morning star" of the Reformation. But then we know nothing about him which calls out severe reprobation. He was patriotic, and had the confidence of his sovereign, else he would not have been employed on important missions. And the sweetness of his character may be inferred from his long and tender friendship with Gower, whom some in that age considered the greater poet. He was probably luxurious in his habits, but intemperate use of wine he detested and avoided. He was portly in his person, but refinement marked his features. He was a gentleman, according to the severest code of chivalric excellence; always a favorite with ladies, and equally admired by the knights and barons of a brilliant court. No poet was ever more honored in his life or lamented in his death, as his beautiful monument in Westminster Abbey would seem to attest. That monument is the earliest that was erected to the memory of a poet in that Pantheon of English men of rank and genius; and it will probably be as long preserved as any of those sculptured urns and animated busts which seek to keep alive the memory of the illustrious dead,—of those who, though dead, yet speak to all future generations.

AUTHORITIES.

Chaucer's own works, especially the Canterbury Tales; publications of the Chaucer Society; Pauli's History of England; ordinary Histories of England which relate to the reigns of Edward III. and Richard II., especially Green's History of the English People; Life of Chaucer, by William Godwin (4 volumes, London, 1804); Tyrwhitt's edition of Canterbury Tales; Speglet's edition of Chaucer; Warton's History of English Poetry; St. Palaye's History of Chivalry; Chaucer's England, by Matthew Browne (London, 1869); Sir Harris Nicholas's Life of Chaucer; The Riches of Chaucer, by Charles Cowden Clarke; Morley's Life of Chaucer. The latest work is a Life and Criticism of Chaucer, by Adolphus William Ward. There is also a Guide to Chaucer, by H. G. Fleary. See also Skeat's collected edition of Chaucer's Works, brought out under the auspices of the Early English Text Society.

CHRISTOPHER COLUMBUS.

A. D. 1446-1506.

MARITIME DISCOVERIES.

CHRISTOPHER COLUMBUS.

MARITIME DISCOVERIES.

ABOUT thirteen hundred years ago, when Attila the Hun, called "the scourge of God," was overrunning the falling empire of the Romans, some of the noblest citizens of the small cities of the Adriatic fled, with their families and effects, to the inaccessible marshes and islands at the extremity of that sea, and formed a permanent settlement. They became fishermen and small traders. In process of time they united their islands together by bridges, and laid the foundation of a mercantile state. Thither resorted the merchants of Mediæval Europe to make exchanges. Thus Venice became rich and powerful, and in the twelfth century it was one of the prosperous states of Europe, ruled by an oligarchy of the leading merchants.

Contemporaneous with Dante, one of the most distinguished citizens of this mercantile mart, Marco Polo, impelled by the curiosity which reviving commerce excited and the restless adventure of a crusading age, visited the court of the Great Khan of Tartary, whose empire was the largest in the world. After a residence of seventeen years, during which he was loaded with honors, he returned to his native country, not by the ordinary route, but by coasting the eastern shores of Asia, through the Indian Ocean, up the Persian Gulf, and thence through Bagdad and Constantinople, bringing with him immense wealth in precious stones and other Eastern commodities. The report of his wonderful adventures interested all Europe, for he was supposed to have found the Tarshish of the Scriptures, that land of gold and spices which had enriched the Tyrian merchants in the time of Solomon, — men supposed by some to have sailed around the Cape of Good Hope in their three years' voyages. Among the wonderful things which Polo had seen was a city on an island off the coast of China, which was represented to contain six hundred thousand families, so rich that the palaces of its nobles were covered with plates of gold, so inviting that odoriferous plants and flowers diffused the most grateful perfumes, so strong that even the Tartar conquerors of China could not subdue it. This island, known now as Japan, was called Cipango, and was supposed to be inexhaustible in riches, especially when the reports of Polo were confirmed by Sir John Mandeville, an English traveller in the time of Edward III., — and with even greater exaggerations, since he represented the royal palace to be more than six miles in circumference, occupied by three hundred thousand men.

In an awakening age of enterprise, when chivalry had not passed away, nor the credulity of the Middle Ages, the reports of this Cipango inflamed the imagination of Europe, and to reach it became at once the desire and the problem of adventurers and merchants. But how could this El Dorado be reached? Not by sailing round Africa; for to sail South, in popular estimation, was to encounter torrid suns with ever increasing heat, and suffocating vapors, and unknown dangers. The scientific world had lost the knowledge of what even the ancients knew. Nobody surmised that there was a Cape of Good Hope which could be doubled, and would open the way to the Indian Ocean and its islands of spices and gold. Nor could this Cipango be reached by crossing the Eastern Continent, for the journey was full of perils, dangers, and insurmountable obstacles.

Among those who meditated on this geographical mystery was a young sea captain of Genoa, who had studied in the University of Pavia, but spent his early life upon the waves,—intelligent, enterprising, visionary, yet practical, with boundless ambition, not to conquer kingdoms, but to discover new realms. Born probably in 1446, in the year 1470 he married the daughter of an Italian navigator living in Lisbon; and, inheriting with her some valuable Portuguese charts and maritime journals, he settled in Lisbon and took up chart-making as a means of livelihood. Being thus trained in both the art and the science of navigation, his active mind seized upon the most interesting theme of the day. His studies and experience convinced him that the Cipango of Marco Polo could be reached by sailing directly west. He knew that the earth was round, and he inferred from the plants and carved wood and even human bodies that had occasionally floated from the West, that there must be unknown islands on the western coasts of the Atlantic, and that this ocean, never yet crossed, was the common boundary of both Europe and Asia; in short, that the Cipango could be reached by sailing west. And he believed the thing to be practicable, for the magnetic needle had been discovered, or brought from the East by Polo, which always pointed to the North Star, so that mariners could sail in the darkest nights; and also another instrument had been made, essentially the modern quadrant, by which latitude could be measured. He supposed that after sailing west, about eight hundred leagues, by the aid of compass and quadrant, and such charts as he had collected and collated, he should find the land of gold and spices by which he would become rich and famous.

This was not an absurd speculation to a man of the intellect and knowledge of Columbus. To his mind there were but few physical difficulties if he only had the ships, and the men bold enough to embark with him, and the patronage which was necessary for so novel and daring an enterprise. The difficulties to be surmounted were not so much physical as moral. It was the surmounting of moral difficulties which gives to Columbus his true greatness as a man of genius and resources. These moral obstacles were so vast as to be all but insurmountable, since he had to contend with all the established ideas of his age, — the superstitions of sailors, the prejudices of learned men, and general geographical ignorance. He himself had neither money, nor ships, nor powerful friends. Nobody believed in him; all ridiculed him; some insulted him. Who would furnish money to a man who was supposed to be half crazy, — certainly visionary and wild; a rash adventurer who would not only absorb money but imperil life? Learned men would not listen to him, and powerful people derided him, and princes were too absorbed in wars and pleasure to give him a helping hand. Aid could come only from some great state or wealthy prince; but both states and princes were deaf and dumb to him. It was a most extraordinary inspiration of genius in the fifteenth century which created, not an opinion, but a conviction that Asia could be reached by sailing west;

and how were common minds to comprehend such a novel idea? If a century later, with all the blaze of reviving art and science and learning, the most learned people ridiculed the idea that the earth revolved around the sun, even when it was proved by all the certitudes of mathematical demonstration and unerring observations, how could the prejudiced and narrow-minded priests of the time of Columbus, who controlled the most important affairs of state, be made to comprehend that an unknown ocean, full of terrors, could be crossed by frail ships, and that even a successful voyage would open marts of inexhaustible wealth? All was clear enough to this scientific and enterprising mariner; and the inward assurance that he was right in his calculation gave to his character a blended boldness, arrogance, and dignity which was offensive to men of exalted station, and ill became a stranger and adventurer with a thread-bare coat, and everything which indicated poverty, neglect, and hardship, and without any visible means of living but by the making and selling of charts.

Hence we cannot wonder at the seventeen years of poverty, neglect, ridicule, disappointment, and deferred hopes, such as make the heart sick, which elapsed after Columbus was persuaded of the truth of his theory, before he could find anybody enlightened enough to believe in him, or powerful enough to assist him.

Wrapped up in those glorious visions which come only to a man of superlative genius, and which make him insensible to heat and cold and scanty fare, even to reproach and scorn, this intrepid soul, inspired by a great and original idea, wandered from city to city, and country to country, and court to court, to present the certain greatness and wealth of any state that would embark in his enterprise. But all were alike cynical, cold, unbelieving, and even insulting. He opposes overwhelming, universal, and overpowering ideas. To have surmounted these amid such protracted opposition and discouragement constitutes his greatness; and finally to prove his position by absolute experiment and hazardous enterprise makes him one of the greatest of human benefactors, whose fame will last through all the generations of men. And as I survey that lonely, abstracted, disappointed, and derided man, — poor and unimportant, so harassed by debt that his creditors seized even his maps and charts, obliged to fly from one country to another to escape imprisonment, without even listeners and still less friends, and yet with ever-increasing faith in his cause, utterly unconquerable, alone in opposition to all the world, — I think I see the most persistent man of enterprise that I have read of in history. Critics ambitious to say something new may rake out slanders from the archives of enemies, and discover faults which derogate from the character we have been taught to admire and venerate; they may even point out spots, which we cannot disprove, in that sun of glorious brightness, which shed its beneficent rays over a century of darkness,—but this we know, that, whatever may be the force of detraction, his fame has been steadily increasing, even on the admission of his slanderers, for three centuries, and that he now shines as a fixed star in the constellation of the great lights of modern times, not alone because he succeeded in crossing the ocean, when once embarked on it, but for surmounting the moral difficulties which lay in his way before he could embark upon it, and for being finally instrumental in conferring the greatest boon that our world has received from any mortal man, since Noah entered into the ark.

I think it is Lamartine who has said that truly immortal benefactors have seldom been able to accomplish their mission without the encouragement of either saints or women. This is emphatically true in the case of Columbus. The door to success was at last opened to him by a friendly and sympathetic friar of a Franciscan convent near the little port of Palos, in Andalusia. The sun-burned and disappointed adventurer (for that is what he was), wearied and hungry, and nearly discouraged, stopped at the convent-door to get a morsel of bread for his famished son, who attended him in his pilgrimage. The prior of that obscure convent was the first who comprehended the man of genius, not so much because he was an enlightened scholar, but because his pious soul was full of kindly sympathy, showing that the instincts of love are kindred to the inspirations of genius. It was the voice of Ali and Cadijeh that strengthened Mohammed. It was Catherine von Bora who sustained Luther in his gigantic task. The worthy friar, struck by the noble bearing of a man so poor and wearied, became delighted with the conversation of his guest, who opened to him both his heart and his schemes. He forwarded his plans by a letter to a powerful ecclesiastic, who introduced him to the Spanish Court, then one of the most powerful, and certainly the proudest and most punctilious, in Europe. Ferdinand of Aragon was polite, yet wary and incredulous; but Isabella of Castile listened more kindly to the stranger, whom the greatness of his mission inspired with eloquence. Like the saint of the convent, she, and she alone of her splendid court, divined that there was something to be heeded in the words of Columbus, and gave her womanly and royal encouragement, although too much engrossed with the conquest of Grenada and the cares of her kingdom to pay that immediate attention which Columbus entreated.

I may not dwell on the vexatious delays and the protracted discouragements of Columbus after the Queen had given her ear to his enthusiastic prophecies of the future glories of the kingdom. To the court and to the universities and to the great ecclesiastics he was still a visionary and a needy adventurer; and they quoted, in refutation of his theory, those Scripture texts which were hurled in greater wrath against Galileo when he announced his brilliant discoveries. There are, from some unfathomed reason, always texts found in the sacred writings which seem to conflict with both science and a profound theology; and the pedants, as well as the hypocrites and usurpers, have always shielded themselves behind these in their opposition to new opinions. I will not be hard upon them, for often they are good men, simply unable to throw off the shackles of ages of ignorance and tyranny. People should not be subjected to lasting reproach because they cannot emancipate themselves from prevailing ideas. If those prejudiced courtiers and scholastics who ridiculed Columbus could only have seen with his clearer insight, they might have loaded him with favors. But they were blinded and selfish and envious. Nor was it until Columbus convinced his sovereigns that the risk was small for so great a promised gain, that he was finally commissioned to undertake his voyage. The promised boon was the riches of Oriental countries, boundless and magnificent, — countries not to be discovered, but already known, only hard and perhaps impossible to reach. And

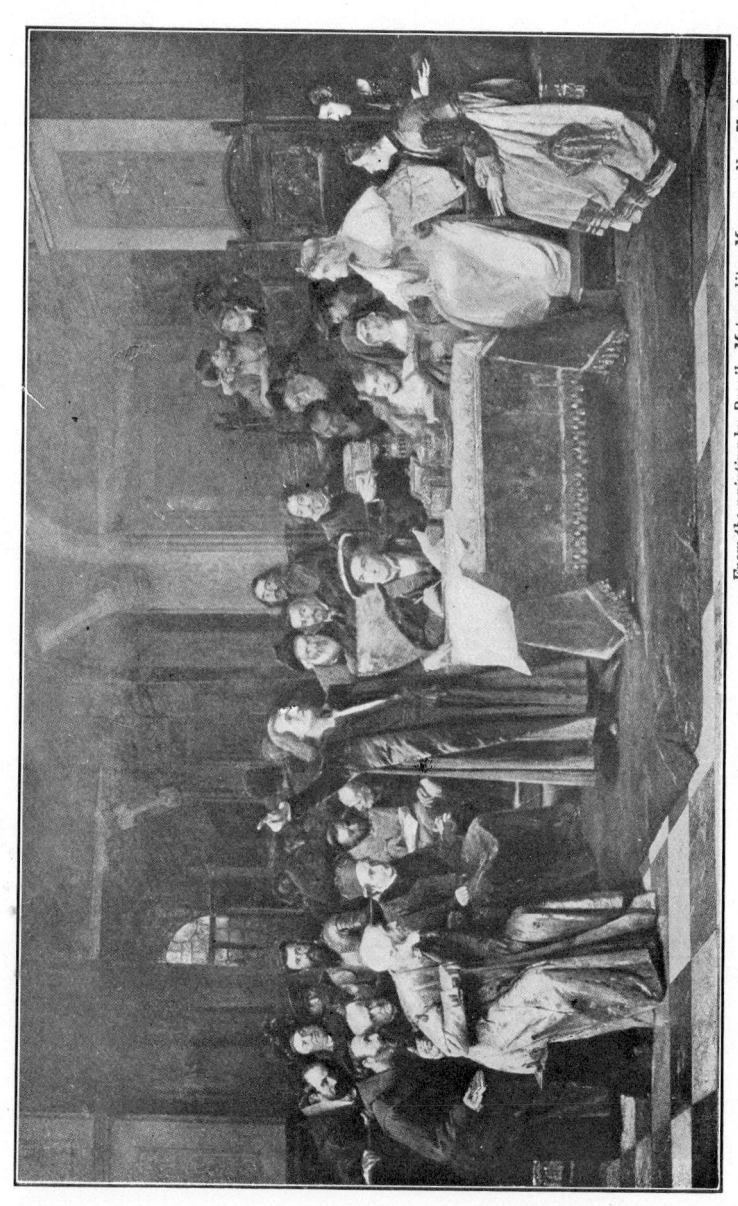

From the painting by Brozik, Metropolitan Museum, New York

COLUMBUS AT THE COURT OF SPAIN

Columbus himself was so firmly persuaded of the existence of these riches, and of his ability to secure them, and they were so exaggerated by his imagination, that his own demands were extravagant and preposterous, as must have seemed to an incredulous court,—that he, a stranger, an adventurer, almost a beggar even, should in case of success be made viceroy and admiral over the unexplored realm, and with a tenth of all the riches he should collect or seize; and that these high offices — almost regal — should also be continued not only through his own life, but through the lives of his heirs from generation to generation, thus raising him to a possible rank higher than that of any of the dukes and grandees of Spain.

Ferdinand and Isabella, however, readily promised all that the persistent and enthusiastic adventurer demanded, doubtless with the feeling that there was not more than one chance in a hundred that he would ever be heard from again, but that this one chance was well worth all and more than they expended,— a possibility of indefinite aggrandizement. To the eyes of Ferdinand there was a prospect — remote, indeed — of adding to the power of the Spanish monarchy; and it is probable that the pious Isabella contemplated also the conversion of the heathen to Christianity. It is possible that some motives may have also influenced Columbus kindred to this,—a renewed crusade against Saracen infidels, which he might undertake from the wealth he was so confident of securing. But the probabilities are that Columbus was urged on to his career by ambitious and worldly motives chiefly, or else he would not have been so greedy to secure honors and wealth, nor would have been so jealous of his dignity when he had attained power. To me Columbus was no more a saint than Sir Francis Drake was when he so unscrupulously robbed every ship he could lay his hands upon, although both of them observed the outward forms of religious worship peculiar to their respective creeds and education. There were no unbelievers in that age. Both Catholics and Protestants, like the ancient Pharisees, were scrupulous in what were supposed to be religious duties, — though these too often were divorced from morality. It is Columbus only as an intrepid, enthusiastic, enlightened navigator, in pursuit of a new world of boundless wealth, that I can see him; and it was for his ultimate success in discovering this world, amid so many difficulties, that he is to be regarded as a great benefactor, of the glory of which no ingenuity or malice can rob him.

At last he sets sail, August 3, 1492, and, singularly enough, from Palos, within sight of the little convent where he had received his first encouragement. He embarked in three small vessels, the largest of which was less than one hundred tons, and two without decks, but having high poops and sterns inclosed. What an insignificant flotilla for such a voyage! But it would seem that the Admiral, with great sagacity, deemed small vessels best adapted to his purpose, in order to enter safely shallow harbors and sail near the coast.

He sails in the most propitious season of the year, and is aided by steady trade-winds which waft his ships gently through the unknown ocean. He meets with no obstacles of any account. The skies are serene, the sea is as smooth as the waters of an inland lake; and he is comforted, as he advances to the west, by the appearance of strange birds and weeds and plants that indicate nearness to the land. He has only two objects of solicitude,— the variations of the magnetic needle, and the superstitious fears of his men; the last he succeeds in allaying by inventing plausible theories, and by concealing the real distance he has traversed. He encourages them by inflaming their cupidity. He is nearly baffled by their mutinous spirit. He is in danger, not from coral reefs and whirlpools and sunken rocks and tempests, as at first was feared, but from his men themselves, who clamor to return. It is his faith and moral courage and fertility of resources which we most admire. Days pass in alternate hope and disappointment, amid angry clamors, in great anxiety, for no land appears after he has sailed far beyond the points where he expected to find it. The world is larger than even he has supposed. He promises great rewards to the one who shall first see the unknown shores. It is said that he himself was the first to discover land by observing a flickering light, which is exceedingly improbable, as he was several leagues from shore; but certain it is, that the very night the land was seen from the Admiral's vessel, it was also discovered by one of the seamen on board another ship. The problem of the age was at last solved. A new continent was given to Ferdinand and Isabella.

On the 12th of October Columbus lands — not, however, on the continent, as he supposed, but on an island — in great pomp, as admiral of the seas and viceroy of the king, in a purple doublet, and with a drawn sword in one hand and the standard of Spain in the other, followed by officers in appropriate costume, and a friar bearing the emblem of our redemption, which is solemnly planted on the shore, and the land called San Salvador. This little island, one of the Bahamas, is not, however, gilded with the anticipated splendors of Oriental countries. He finds neither gold, nor jewels, nor silks, nor spices, nor any signs of civilization; only naked men and women, without any indication of wealth or culture or power. But he finds a soft and genial climate, and a soil of unparalleled fertility, and trees and shrubs as green as Andalusia in spring, and birds with every variety of plumage, and insects glistening with every color of the rainbow; while the natives are gentle and unsuspecting and full of worship. Columbus is disappointed, but not discouraged. He sets sail to find the real Cipango of which he is in search. He cruises among the Bahama islands, discovers Cuba and Hispaniola (now called Hayti), explores their coasts, holds peaceful intercourse with the natives, and is transported with enthusiasm in view of the beauty of the country and its great capacities; but he sees no gold, only a few ornaments to show that there is gold somewhere near, if it only could be found. Nor has he reached the Cipango of his dreams, but new countries, of which there was no record or suspicion of existence, yet of vast extent, and fertile beyond knowledge. He is puzzled, but filled with intoxicating joy. He has performed a great feat. He has doubtless added indefinitely to the dominion of Spain.

Columbus leaves a small colony on the island of Hispaniola, and with the trophies of his discoveries returns to Spain, without serious obstacles, except a short detention in Portugal, whither he was driven by a storm. His stories fill the whole civilized world with wonder. He is welcomed with the most cordial and enthusiastic reception; the people gaze at him with admiration. His sovereigns rise at his approach, and seat him beside themselves on their gilded and canopied throne; he has made them a present worthy of a god. What honors could be too great for such a man! Even envy pales before the universal exhilaration. He enters into the most august circles as an equal; his dignities and honors are confirmed; he is loaded with presents and favors; he is the most marked personage in Europe; he is almost stifled with the incense of royal and popular idolatry. Never was a subject more honored and caressed. The imagination of a chivalrous and lively people is inflamed with the wildest expectations, for although he returned with but little of the expected wealth, he has pointed out a land rich in unfathomed mines.

A second and larger expedition is soon projected. Everybody wishes to join it. All press to join the fortunate admiral who has added a continent to civilization. The proudest nobles, with the armor and horses of chivalry, embark with artisans and miners for another voyage, now without solicitude or fear, but with unbounded hopes of wealth, — especially hardy adventurers and broken-down families of rank anxious to retrieve their fortunes. The pendulum of a nation's thought swings from the extreme of doubt and cynicism to the opposite extreme of faith and exhilaration. Spain was ripe for the harvest. Eight hundred years' desperate contest with the Moors had made the nation bold, heroic, adventurous. There were no such warriors in all Europe. Nowhere were there such chivalric virtues. No people were then animated with such martial enthusiasm, such unfettered imagination, such heroic daring, as were the subjects of Ferdinand and Isabella. They were a people to conquer a world; not merely heroic and enterprising, but fresh with religious enthusiasm. They had expelled the infidels from Spain; they would fight for the honor of the Cross in any clime or land.

The hopes held out by Columbus were extravagant; and these extravagant expectations were the occasion of his fall and subsequent sorrows and humiliation. Doubtless he was sincere, but he was infatuated. He could only see the gold of Cipango. He was as confident of enriching his followers as he had been of discovering new realms. He was as enthusiastic as Sir Walter Raleigh a century later, and made promises as rash as he, and created the same exalted hopes, to be followed by bitter disappointments; and consequently he incurred the same hostilities and met the same downfall.

This second expedition was undertaken in seventeen vessels, carrying fifteen hundred people, all full of animation and hope, and some of them with intentions to settle in the newly discovered country until they had made their fortunes. They arrived at Hispaniola in March, of the year 1493, only to discover that the men left behind on the first voyage to secure their settlement were all despoiled or murdered; that the natives had proved treacherous, or that the Spaniards had abused their confidence and forfeited their friendship. They were exposed to new hostilities: they found the climate unhealthy; their numbers rapidly dwindled away from disease or poor food; starvation stared them in the face, in spite of the fertility of the soil; dissensions and jealousies arose; they were governed with great difficulty, for the haughty hidalgoes were unused to menial labor, and labor of the most irksome kind was necessary; law and order were relaxed. The blame of disaster was laid upon the Admiral, who was accused of deceiving them; evil reports were sent to Spain, accusing him of incapacity, cruelty, and oppression; gold was found only in small quantities; some of the leading men mutinied; general discontent arose; the greater part of the colonists were disabled from sickness and debility; no gold of any amount was sent back to Spain, only five hundred Indian slaves to be sold instead, which led to renewed hostilities with the natives, and the necessity for their subjugation. All of these evils created bitter disappointment in Spain and discontent with the measures and government of Columbus himself, so that a commission of inquiry was sent to Hispaniola, headed by Aguado, who assumed arrogant authority, and made it necessary for Columbus to return to Spain without adding essentially to his discoveries. He sailed around

Cuba and Jamaica and other islands, but as yet had not seen the mainland or found mines of gold or silver.

He landed in Spain, in 1496, to find that his popularity had declined and the old enthusiasm had grown cold. With him landed a feeble train of emaciated men, who had nothing to relate but sickness, hardship, and disappointment. The sovereigns, however, received him kindly; but he was depressed and sad, and clothed himself with the habit of a Franciscan friar, to denote his humility and dejection. He displayed a few golden collars and bracelets as trophies, with some Indians; but these no longer dazzled the crowd.

It was not until 1498 that Columbus was enabled to make his third voyage, having experienced great delay from the general disappointment. Instead of seventeen vessels, he could collect but six. In this voyage he reached the mainland, — that part called Paria, near the mouth of the Orinoco, in South America, but he supposed it to be an island. It was fruitful and populous, and the air was sweetened with the perfumes of flowers. Yet he did not explore the coast to any extent, but made his way to Hispaniola, where he had left the discontented colony, himself broken in health, a victim of gout, haggard from anxiety, and emaciated by pain. His splendid constitution was now undermined from his various hardships and cares.

He found the colony in a worse state than when he

left it under the care of his brother Bartholomew. The Indians had proved hostile; the colonists were lazy and turbulent; mutiny had broken out; factions prevailed, as well as general misery and discontent. The horrors of famine had succeeded wars with the natives. There was a general desire to leave the settlement. Columbus tried to restore order and confidence; but the difficulty of governing such a disorderly set of adventurers was too great even for him. He was obliged to resort to severities that made him more and more unpopular. The complaints of his enemies reached Spain. He was most cruelly misrepresented and slandered; and in the general disappointment, and the constant drain upon the mother country to support the colony, his enemies gained the ear of his sovereigns, and strong doubts arose in their minds about his capacity for government. So a royal commission was sent out,—an officer named Bovadilla, with absolute power to examine into the state of the colony, and supplant, if necessary, the authority of Columbus. The result was the arrest of Columbus and his brothers, who were sent to Spain in chains. What a change of fortune! I will not detail the accusations against him, just or unjust. It is mournful enough to see the old man brought home in irons from the world he had discovered and given to Spain. The injustice and cruelty which he received produced a reaction, and he was once more kindly received at court, with the promise that his grievances should be redressed and his property and dignities restored.

Columbus was allowed to make one more voyage of discovery, but nothing came of it except renewed troubles, hardships, dangers, and difficulties; wars with the natives, perils of the sea, discontents, disappointments; and when at last he returned to Spain, in 1504, — broken with age and infirmities, after twelve years of harassing cares, labors, and dangers (a checkered career of glory and suffering), — nothing remained but to prepare for his final rest. He had not made a fortune; he had not enriched his patrons, — but he had discovered a continent. His last days were spent in disquieting and fruitless negotiations to perpetuate his honors among his descendants. He was ever jealous and tenacious of his dignities. Ferdinand was polite, but selfish and cold; nor can this calculating prince ever be vindicated from the stain of gross ingratitude. Columbus died in the year 1506, at the age of sixty, a disappointed man. But honors were ultimately bestowed upon his heirs, who became grandees and dukes, and intermarried with the proudest families of Spain; and it is also said that Ferdinand himself, after the death of the great navigator, caused a monument to be erected to his memory with this inscription: "To Castile and Leon Columbus gave a new world." But no man of that century needed less than Columbus a monument to perpetuate his immortal fame.

I think that historians belittle Columbus when they would excite our pity for his misfortunes. They insult the dignity of all struggling souls, and make utilitarians of all benefactors, and give false views of success. Few benefactors, on the whole, were ever more richly rewarded than he. He died Admiral of the Seas, a grandee of Spain,—having bishops for his eulogists and princes for his mourners, — the founder of an illustrious house, whose name and memory gave glory even to the Spanish throne. And even if he had not been rewarded with material gains, it was enough to feel that he had conferred a benefit on the world which could scarcely be appreciated in his lifetime, — a benefit so transcendent that its results could be seen only by future generations. Who could adequately pay him for his services; who could estimate the value of his gift? What though they load him to-day with honors, or cast him tomorrow into chains?—that is the fate of all immortal benefactors since our world began. His great soul should have soared beyond vulgar rewards. In the loftiness of his self-consciousness he should have accepted, without a murmur, whatever fortune awaited him. Had he merely given to civilization a new style of buttons, or an improved envelope, or a punch for a railway conductor, or a spring for a carriage, or a mining tool, or a screw, or revolver, or reaper, the inventors of which have "seen millions in them," and been cheated out of his gains, he might have whimpered over his wrongs. How few benefactors have received even as much as he; for he won dignities, admiration, and undying fame. We scarcely know the names of many who have made grand bequests. Who invented the mariner's compass? Who gave the lyre to primeval ages, or the blacksmith's forge, or the letters of the alphabet, or the arch in architecture, or glass for windows? Who solved the first problem of geometry? Who first sang the odes which Homer incorporated with the Iliad? Who first turned up the earth with a plough? Who first used the weaver's shuttle? Who devised the cathedrals of the Middle Ages? Who gave the keel to ships? Who was the first that raised bread by yeast? Who invented chimneys? But all ages will know that Columbus discovered America; and his monuments are in every land, and his greatness is painted by the ablest historians.

But I will not enlarge on the rewards Columbus received, or the ingratitude which succeeded them, by force of envy or from the disappointment of worldly men in not realizing all the gold that he promised. Let me allude to the results of his discovery.

The first we notice was the marvellous stimulus to maritime adventures. Europe was inflamed with a desire to extend geographical knowledge, or add new countries to the realms of European sovereigns.

Within four years of the discovery of the West India Islands by Columbus, Cabot had sailed past Newfoundland, and Vasco da Gama had doubled the Cape of Good Hope, and laid the foundation of the Portuguese empire in the East Indies. In 1499 Ojeda, one of the companions of Columbus, and Amerigo Vespucci discovered Brazil. In 1500 Cortereal, a Portuguese, explored the Gulf of St. Lawrence. In 1505 Francesco de Almeira established factories along the coast of Malabar. In 1510 the Spaniards formed settlements on the mainland at Panama. In 1511 the Portuguese established themselves at Malacca. In 1513 Balboa crossed the Isthmus of Darien and reached the Pacific Ocean. The year after that, Ponce de Leon had visited Florida. In 1515 the Rio de la Plata was navigated; and in 1517 the Portuguese had begun to trade with China and Bengal. As early as 1520 Cortes had taken Mexico, and completed the conquest of that rich country the following year. In 1522 Cano circumnavigated the globe. In 1524 Pizarro discovered Peru, which in less than twelve years was completely subjugated,— the year when California was discovered by Cortes. In 1542 the Portuguese were admitted to trade with Japan. In 1576 Frobisher sought a North-western passage to India; and the following year Sir Francis

Drake commenced his more famous voyages under the auspices of Elizabeth. In 1578 Sir Humphrey Gilbert colonized Virginia, followed rapidly by other English settlements, until before the century closed the whole continent was colonized either by Spaniards, or Portuguese, or English, or French, or Dutch. All countries came in to share the prizes held out by the discovery of the New World.

Colonization followed the voyages of discovery. It was animated by the hope of finding gold and precious stones. It was carried on under great discouragements and hardships and unforeseen difficulties. As a general thing, the colonists were not accustomed to manual labor; they were adventurers and broken-down dependents on great families, who found restraint irksome and the drudgeries of their new life almost unendurable. Nor did they intend, at the outset, permanent settlements; they expected to accumulate gold and silver, and then return to their country. They had sought to improve their condition, and their condition became forlorn. They were exposed to sickness from malaria, poor food, and hardship; they were molested by the natives whom they constantly provoked; they were subject to cruel treatment on the part of royal governors. They melted away wherever they settled, by famine, disease, and war, whether in South or North America. They were discontented and disappointed, and not easily governed; the chieftains quarrelled with each other, and were disgraced by rapacity and cruelty. They did not find what they expected. They were lonely and desolate, and longed to return to the homes they had left, but were frequently without means to return, — doomed to remain where they were, and die. Colonization had no dignity until men went to the New World for religious liberty, or to work upon the soil. The conquest of Mexico and Peru, however, opened up the mining of gold and silver, which were finally found in great abundance. And when the richness of these countries in the precious metals was finally established, then a regular stream of emigrants flocked to the American shores. Gold was at last found, but not until thousands had miserably perished.

The mines of Mexico and Peru undoubtedly enriched Spain, and filled Europe with envy and emulation. A stream of gold flowed to the mother country, and the caravels which transported the treasures of the new world became objects of plunder to all nations hostile to Spain. The seas were full of pirates. Sir Francis Drake was an undoubted pirate, and returned, after his long voyage around the world, with immense treasure, which he had stolen. Then followed, with the eager search after gold and silver, a rapid demoralization in all maritime countries.

It would be interesting to show how the sudden

accumulation of wealth by Spain led to luxury, arrogance, and idleness, followed by degeneracy and decay, since those virtues on which the strength of man is based are weakened by sudden wealth. Industry declined in proportion as Spain became enriched by the precious metals. But this inquiry is foreign to my object.

A still more interesting inquiry arises, how far the nations of Europe were really enriched by the rapid accumulation of gold and silver. The search for the precious metals may have stimulated commercial enterprise, but it is not so clear that it added to the substantial wealth of Europe, except so far as it promoted industry. Gold is not wealth; it is simply the exponent of wealth. Real wealth is in farms and shops and ships, — in the various channels of industry, in the results of human labor. So far as the precious metals enter into useful manufactures, or into articles of beauty and taste, they are indeed inherently valuable. Mirrors, plate, jewelry, watches, gilded furniture, the adornments of the person, in an important sense, constitute wealth, since all nations value them, and will pay for them as they do for corn or oil. So far as they are connected with art, they are valuable in the same sense as statues and pictures, on which labor has been expended. There is something useful, and even necessary, besides food and raiment and houses. The gold which ornamented Solomon's temple, or the Minerva of Phidias, or the garments of Leo X., had a value. The ring which is a present to brides is a part of a marriage ceremony. The golden watch, which never tarnishes, is more valuable inherently than a pewter one, because it remains beautiful. Thus when gold enters into ornaments deemed indispensable, or into manufactures which are needed, it has an inherent value, — it is wealth.

But when gold is a mere medium of exchange, — its chief use, — then it has only a conventional value; I mean, it does not make a nation rich or poor, since the rarer it is the more it will purchase of the necessaries of life. A pound's weight of gold, in ancient Greece, or in Mediæval Europe, would purchase as much wheat as twenty pounds' weight will purchase to-day. If the mines of Mexico or Peru or California had never been worked, the gold in the civilized world three hundred years ago would have been as valuable for banking purposes, or as an exchange for agricultural products, as twenty times its present quantity, since it would have bought as much as twenty times the quantity will buy to-day. Make diamonds as plenty as crystals, they would be worth no more than crystals, if they were not harder and more beautiful. Make gold as plenty as silver, it would be worth no more than silver, except for manufacturing purposes; it would be worth no more to bankers and merchants. The vast increase in the production of the precious metals simply increased the value of the commodities for which they were exchanged. A laborer can purchase no more bread with a dollar to-day than he could with five cents three hundred years ago. Five cents were really as much wealth three hundred years ago as a dollar is to-day. Wherein, then, has the increase in the precious metals added to the wealth of the world, if a twentieth part of the gold and silver now in circulation would buy as much land, or furniture, or wheat, or oil three hundred years ago as the whole amount now used as money will buy to-day? Had no gold or silver mines been discovered in America, the gold and silver would have appreciated in value in proportion to the wear of them. In other words, the scarcer the gold and silver the more the same will purchase of the fruits of human industry. So industry is the wealth, not the gold. It is the cultivated farms and the manufactures and the buildings and the internal improvements of a country which constitute its real wealth, since these represent its industry, — the labor of men. Mines, indeed, employ the labor of men, but they do not furnish food for the body, or raiment to wear, or houses to live in, or fuel for cooking, or any purpose whatever of human comfort or necessity, — only a material for ornament; which I grant is wealth, so far as ornament is for the welfare of man. The marbles of ancient Greece were very valuable for the labor expended on them, either for architecture or for ornament.

Gold and silver were early selected as useful and convenient articles for exchange, like bank-notes, and so far have inherent value as they supply that necessity; but if a fourth part of the gold and silver in existence would supply that necessity, the remaining three-fourths are as inherently valueless as the paper on which bank-notes are printed. Their value consists in what they represent of the labors and industries of men.

Now Spain ultimately became poor, in spite of the influx of gold and silver from the American mines, because industries of all kinds declined. People were diverted from useful callings by the mighty delusion which gold discoveries created. These discoveries had the same effect on industry, which is the wealth of nations, as the support of standing armies has in our day. They diverted men from legitimate callings. The miners had to be supported like soldiers; and, worse, the sudden influx of gold and silver intoxicated men and stimulated speculation. An army of speculators do not enrich a nation, since they rob each other. They cause money to change hands; they do not stimulate industry. They do not create wealth; they simply make it flow from one person to another.

But speculations sometimes create activity in enterprise; they inflame desires for wealth, and cause people to make greater exertions. In that sense the discovery of American mines gave a stimulus to commerce and travel and energy. People rushed to America for gold: these people had to be fed and clothed. Then farmers and manufacturers followed the gold-hunters; they tilled the soil to feed the miners. The new farms which dotted the region of the gold-diggers added to the wealth of the country in which the mines were located. Colonization followed gold-digging. But it was America that became enriched, not the old countries from which the miners came, except so far as the old countries furnished tools and ships and fabrics, for doubtless commerce and manufacturing were stimulated. So far, the wealth of the world increased; but the men who returned to riot in luxury and idleness did not stimulate enterprise. They made others idle also. The necessity of labor was lost sight of.

And yet if one country became idle, another country may have become industrious. There can be but little question that the discovery of the American mines gave commerce and manufactures and agriculture, on the whole, a stimulus. This was particularly seen in England. England grew rich from industry and enterprise, as Spain became poor from idleness and luxury. The silver and gold, diffused throughout Europe, ultimately found their way into the pockets of Englishmen, who made a market for their manufactures. It was not alone the precious metals which enriched England, but the will and power to produce those articles of industry for which the rest of the world parted with their gold and silver. What has made France rich since the Revolution? Those innumerable articles of taste and elegance — fabrics and wines — for which all Europe parted with their specie; not war, not conquest, not mines. Why till recently was Germany so poor? Because it had so little to sell to other nations; because industry was cramped by standing armies and despotic governments.

One thing is certain, that the discovery of America opened a new field for industry and enterprise to all the discontented and impoverished and oppressed Europeans who emigrated. At first they emigrated to dig silver and gold. The opening of mines required labor, and miners were obliged to part with their gold for the necessaries of life. Thus California in our day has become peopled with farmers and merchants and manufacturers, as well as miners. Many came to America expecting to find gold, and were disappointed, and were obliged to turn agriculturists, as in Virginia. Many came to New England from political and religious motives. But all came to better their fortunes. Gradually the United States and Canada became populated from east to west and from north to south. The surplus population of Europe poured itself into the wilds of America. Generally the emigrants were farmers. With the growth of agricultural industry were developed commerce and manufactures. Thus, materially, the world was immensely benefited. A new continent was opened for industry. No matter what the form of government may be, — I might almost say no matter what the morals and religion of the people may be, — so long as there is land to occupy, and to be sold cheap, the continent will fill up, and will be as densely populated as Europe or Asia, because the natural advantages are good. The rivers and the lakes will be navigated; the products of the country will be exchanged for European and Asiatic products; wealth will certainly increase, and increase indefinitely. There is no calculating the future resources and wealth of the New World, especially in the United States. There are no conceivable bounds to their future commerce, manufactures, and agricultural products. We can predict with certainty the rise of new cities, villas, palaces, material splendor, limited only to the increasing resources and population of the country. Who can tell the number of miles of new railroads yet to be made; the new inventions to abridge human labor; what great empires are destined to rise; what unknown forms of luxury will be found out; what new and magnificent trophies of art and science will gradually be seen; what mechanism, what material glories, are sure to come? This is not speculation. Nothing can retard the growth of America in material wealth and glory. The splendid external will call forth more panegyrics than the old Roman world which fancied itself eternal. The tower of the new Babel will rise to the clouds, and be seen in all its glory throughout the earth and sea. No Fourth of July orator ever exaggerated the future destinies of America in a material point of view. No "spread-eagle" politician even conceived what will be sure to come.

And what then? Grant the most indefinite expansion, — the growth of empires whose splendor and wealth and power shall utterly eclipse the glories of the Old World. All this is probable. But when we have dwelt on the future material expansion; when we have given wings to imagination, and feel that even imagination cannot reach the probable realities in a material aspect, — then our predictions and calculations stop. Beyond material glories we cannot count with certainty. The world has witnessed many powerful empires which have passed away, and left "not a rack behind." What remains of the antediluvian world? — not even a spike of Noah's ark, larger and stronger than any modern ship. What remains of Nineveh, of Babylon, of Thebes, of Tyre, of Carthage,

— those great centres of wealth and power? What remains of Roman greatness even, except in laws and literature and renovated statues? Remember there is an undeviating uniformity in the past history of nations. What is the simple story of all the ages?— industry, wealth, corruption, decay, and ruin. What conservative power has been strong enough to arrest the ruin of the nations of antiquity? Have not material forces and glories been developed and exhibited, whatever the religion and morals of the fallen nations? Cannot a country grow materially to a certain point, under the most adverse influences, in a religious and moral point of view? Yet for lack of religion and morals the nations perished, and their Babel-towers were buried in the dust. They perished for lack of true conservative forces; at least that is the judgment of historians. Nobody doubts the splendor of the material glories of the ancient nations. The ruins of Baalbec, of Palmyra, of Athens, prove this, to say nothing of history. The material glories of the ancient nations may be surpassed by our modern wonders; but yet all the material glories of the ancient nations passed away.

Now if this is to be the destiny of America, — an unbounded material growth, followed by corruption and ruin, — then Columbus has simply extended the realm for men to try material experiments. Make New York a second Carthage, and Boston a second Athens, and Philadelphia a second Antioch, and Washington a second Rome, and we simply repeat the old experiments. Did not the Romans have nearly all we have, materially, except our modern scientific inventions?

But has America no higher destiny than to repeat the old experiments, and improve upon them, and become rich and powerful? Has she no higher and nobler mission? Can she lay hold of forces that the Old World never had, such as will prevent the uniform doom of nations? I maintain that there is no reason that can be urged, based on history and experience, why she should escape the fate of the nations of antiquity, unless new forces arise on this continent different from what the world has known, and which have a conservative influence. If America has a great mission to declare and to fulfil, she must put forth altogether new forces, and these not material. And these alone will save her and save the world. It is mournful to contemplate even the future magnificent material glories of America if these are not to be preserved, if these are to share the fate of ancient wonders. It is obvious that the real glory of America is to be something entirely different from that of which the ancients boasted. And this is to be moral and spiritual, — that which the ancients lacked.

This leads me to speak of the moral consequences

of the discovery of America, — infinitely grander than any material wonders, of which the world has been full, of which every form of paganism has boasted, which nearly everywhere has perished, and which must necessarily perish everywhere, without new forces to preserve them.

In a moral point of view scarcely anything good immediately resulted, at least to Europe, by the discovery of America. It excited the wildest spirit of adventure, the most unscrupulous cupidity, the most demoralizing speculation. It created jealousies and wars. The cruelties and injustices inflicted on the Indians were revolting. Nothing in the annals of the world exceeds the wickedness of the Spaniards in the conquest of Peru and Mexico. That conquest is the most dismal and least glorious in human history. We see in it no poetry, or heroism, or necessity; we read of nothing but its crimes. The Jesuits, in their missionary zeal, partly redeemed the cruelties; but they soon imposed a despotic yoke, and made their religion pay. Monopolies scandalously increased, and the New World was regarded only as spoil. The tone of moral feeling was lowered everywhere, for the nations were crazed with the hope of sudden accumulations. Spain became enervated and demoralized.

On America itself the demoralization was even more marked. There never was such a state of moral degradation in any Christian country as in South America. Three centuries have passed, and the low state of morals continues. Contrast Mexico and Peru with the United States, morally and intellectually. What seeds of vice did not the Spaniards plant! How the old natives melted away!

And then, to add to the moral evils attending colonization, was the introduction of African slaves, especially in the West Indies and the Southern States of North America. Christendom seems to have lost the sense of morality. Slavery more than counterbalances all other advantages together. It was the stain of the seventeenth and eighteenth centuries. Not merely slaves, but the slave-trade, increase the horrors of the frightful picture. America became associated, in the minds of Europeans, with gold-hunting, slavery, and cruelty to Indians. Better that the country had remained undiscovered than that such vices and miseries should be introduced into the most fertile parts of the New World.

I cannot see that civilization gained anything, morally, by the discovery of America, until the new settlers were animated by other motives than a desire for sudden wealth. When the country became colonized by men who sought liberty to worship God, — men of lofty purposes, willing to undergo sufferings and danger in order to plant the seeds of a higher civilization, — then there arose new forms of social and political life. Such men were those who colonized New England. And, say what you will, in spite of all the disagreeable sides of the Puritan character, it was the Puritans who gave a new impulse to civilization in its higher sense. They founded schools and colleges and churches. They introduced a new form of political life by their town-meetings, in which liberty was nurtured, and all local improvements were regulated. It was the autonomy of towns on which the political structure of New England rested. In them was born that true representative government which has gradually spread towards the West. The colonies were embryo States,—States afterwards to be bound together by a stronger tie than that of a league. The New England States, after the war of Independence, were the defenders and advocates of a federal and central power. An entirely new political organization was gradually formed, resting equally on such pillars as independent townships and independent States, and these represented by delegates in a national centre.

So we believe America was discovered, not so much to furnish a field for indefinite material expansion, with European arts and fashions,—which would simply assimilate America to the Old World, with all its dangers and vices and follies,—but to introduce new forms of government, new social institutions, new customs and manners, new experiments in liberty, new religious organizations, new modes to ameliorate the necessary evils of life. It was discovered that men might labor and enjoy the fruits of industry in a new mode, unfettered by the restraints which the institutions of Europe imposed. America is a new field in which to try experiments in government and social life, which cannot be tried in the older nations without sweeping and dangerous revolutions; and new institutions have arisen which are our pride and boast, and which are the wonder and admiration of Europe. America is the only country under the sun in which there is self-government, — a government which purely represents the wishes of the people, where universal suffrage is not a mockery. And if America has a destiny to fulfil for other nations, she must give them something more valuable than reaping machines, palace cars, and horse railroads. She must give, not only machinery to abridge labor, but institutions and ideas to expand the mind and elevate the soul, — something by which the poor can rise and assert their rights. Unless something is developed here which cannot be developed in other countries, in the way of new spiritual and intellectual forces, which have a conservative influence, then I cannot see how America can long continue to be the home and refuge of the poor and miserable of other lands. A new and better spirit must vivify schools and colleges and philanthropic enterprises than that which has prevailed in older nations.

Unless something new is born here which has a peculiar power to save, wherein will America ultimately differ from other parts of Christendom? We must have schools in which the heart as well as the brain is educated, and newspapers which aspire to something higher than to fan prejudices and appeal to perverted tastes. Our hope is not in books which teach infidelity under the name of science, nor in pulpits which cannot be sustained without sensational oratory, nor in journals which trade on the religious sentiments of the people, nor in Sabbath-school books which are an insult to the human understanding, nor in colleges which fit youth merely for making money, nor in schools of technology to give an impulse to material interests, nor in legislatures controlled by monopolists, nor in judges elected by demagogues, nor in philanthropic societies to ventilate unpractical theories. These will neither renovate nor conserve what is most precious in life. Unless a nation grows morally as well as materially, there is something wrong at the core of society. As I have said, no material expansion will avail, if society becomes rotten at the core. America is a glorious boon to civilization, but only as she fulfils a new mission in history, — not to become more potent in material forces, but in those spiritual agencies which prevent corruption and decay. An infidel professor, calling himself a savant, may tell you that there is nothing certain or great but in the direction of science to utilities, even as he may glory in a philosophy which ignores a creator and takes cognizance only of a creation.

As I survey the growing and enormous moral evils which degrade society, here as everywhere, in spite of Bunker Hills and Plymouth Rocks, and all the windy declamations of politicians and philanthropists, and all the advance in useful mechanisms, I am sometimes tempted to propound inquiries which suggest the old, mournful story of the decline and ruin of States and Empires. I ask myself, Why should America be an exception to the uniform fate of nations, as history has demonstrated? Why should not good institutions be perverted here, as in all other countries and ages of the world? Where has civilization shown any striking triumphs, except in inventions to abridge the labors of mankind and make men comfortable and rich? Is there nothing before us, then, but the triumphs of material life, to end as mournfully as the materialism of antiquity? If so, then Christianity is a most dismal failure, is a defeated power, like all other forms of religion which failed to save. But is it a failure? Are we really swinging back to Paganism? Is the time to be hailed when all religions will be considered by the philosopher as equally false and equally useful? Is there nothing more cheerful for us to contemplate than what the old Pagan philosophy holds out,— man destined to live like brutes or butterflies, and pass away into the infinity of time and space, like inert matter, decomposed, absorbed, and entering into new and everlasting combinations? Is America to become like Europe and Asia in all essential elements of life? Has she no other mission than to add to perishable glories? Is she to teach the world nothing new in education and philanthropy and government? Are all her struggles in behalf of liberty in vain?

We all know that Christianity is the only hope of the world. The question is, whether America is or is not more favorable for its healthy developments and applications than the other countries of Christendom are. We believe that it is. If it is not, then America is only a new field for the spread and triumph of material forces. If it is, we may look forward to such improvements in education, in political institutions, in social life, in religious organizations, in philanthropical enterprise, that the country will be sought by the poor and enslaved classes of Europe more for its moral and intellectual advantages than for its mines or farms; the objects of the Puritan settlers will be gained, and the grandeur of the discovery of a New World will be established.

> " What sought they thus afar?
> Bright jewels of the mine?
> The wealth of seas, — the spoils of war?
> They sought for Faith's pure shrine.

Ay, call it holy ground,
   The soil where first they trod;
They've left unstained what there they found,—
   Freedom to worship God."

AUTHORITIES.

Prescott's Ferdinand and Isabella; Washington Irving; Cabot's Voyages, and other early navigators; Columbus, by De Costa; Life of Columbus, by Bossi and Spatono; Relations de Quatre Voyage par Christopher Colomb; Drake's World Encompassed; Murray's Historical Account of Discoveries; Hernando, Historia del Amirante; History of Commerce; Lives of Pizarro and Cortes; Frobisher's Voyages; Histories of Herrera, Las Casas, Gomera, and Peter Martyr; Navarrete's Collections; Memoir of Cabot, by Richard Biddle; Hakluyt's Voyages; Dr. Lardner's Cyclopædia, — History of Maritime and Inland Discovery; Anderson's History of Commerce; Oviedo's General History of the West Indies; History of the New World, by Geronimo Benzoni; Goodrich's Life of Christopher Columbus.

SAVONAROLA.

A. D. 1452–1498.

UNSUCCESSFUL REFORMS.

SAVONAROLA.

UNSUCCESSFUL REFORMS.

THIS Lecture is intended to set forth a memorable movement in the Roman Catholic Church,—a reformation of morals, preceding the greater movement of Luther to produce a reformation of both morals and doctrines. As the representative of this movement I take Savonarola, concerning whom much has of late been written; more, I think, because he was a Florentine in a remarkable age,—the age of artists and of reviving literature,—than because he was a martyr, battling with evils which no one man was capable of removing. His life was more a protest than a victory. He was an unsuccessful reformer, and yet he prepared the way for that religious revival which afterward took place in the Catholic Church itself. His spirit was not revolutionary, like that of the Saxon monk, and yet it was progressive. His soul was in active sympathy with every emancipating idea of his age. He was the incarnation of a fervid, living, active piety amid forms and formulas, a fearless exposer of all shams, an uncompromising enemy to the blended atheism and idolatry of his ungodly age. He was the contemporary of political, worldly, warlike, unscrupulous popes, disgraced by nepotism and personal vices, — men who aimed to extend not a spiritual but temporal dominion, and who scandalized the highest position in the Christian world, as attested by all reliable historians, whether Catholic or Protestant. However infallible the Catholic Church claims to be, it has never been denied that some of her highest dignitaries have been subject to grave reproaches, both in their character and their influence. Such men were Sixtus IV., Julius II., and Alexander VI., — able, probably, for it is very seldom that the popes have not been distinguished for something, but men, nevertheless, who were a disgrace to the superb position they had succeeded in reaching.

The great feature of that age was the revival of classical learning and artistic triumphs in sculpture, painting, and architecture, blended with infidel levity and social corruptions, so that it is both interesting and hideous. It is interesting for its triumphs of genius, its dispersion of the shadows of the Middle Ages, the commencement of great enterprises and of a marked refinement of manners and tastes; it is hideous for its venalities, its murders, its debaucheries, its unblushing wickedness, and its disgraceful levities, when God and duty and self-restraint were alike ignored. Cruel tyrants reigned in cities, and rapacious priests fattened on the credulity of the people. Think of monks itinerating Europe to sell indulgences for sin; of monasteries and convents filled, not with sublime enthusiasts as in earlier times, but with gluttons and sensualists, living in concubinage and greedy of the very things which primitive monasticism denounced and abhorred! Think of boys elevated to episcopal thrones, and the sons of popes made cardinals and princes! Think of churches desecrated by spectacles which were demoralizing, and a worship of saints and images which had become idolatrous, — a degrading superstition among the people, an infidel apathy among the higher classes: not infidel speculations, for these were reserved for more enlightened times, but an indifference to what is ennobling, to all vital religion, worthy of the Sophists in the time of Socrates!

It was in this age of religious apathy and scandalous vices, yet of awakening intelligence and artistic glories, when the greatest enthusiasm was manifested for the revived literature and sculptured marbles of classic Greece and Rome, that Savonarola appeared in Florence as a reformer and preacher and statesman, near the close of the fifteenth century, when Columbus was seeking a western passage to India; when Michael Angelo was moulding the "Battle of Hercules with the

Centaurs;" when Ficino was teaching the philosophy of Plato; when Alexander VI. was making princes of his natural children; when Bramante was making plans for a new St. Peter's; when Cardinal Bembo was writing Latin essays; when Lorenzo de' Medici was the flattered patron of both scholars and artists, and the city over which he ruled with so much magnificence was the most attractive place in Europe, next to that other city on the banks of the Tiber, whose wonders and glories have never been exhausted, and will probably survive the revolutions of unknown empires.

But Savonarola was not a native of Florence. He was born in the year 1452 at Ferrara, belonged to a good family, and received an expensive education, being destined to the profession of medicine. He was a sad, solitary, pensive, but precocious young man, whose youth was marked by an unfortunate attachment to a haughty Florentine girl. He did not cherish her memory and dedicate to her a life-labor, like Dante, but became very dejected and very pious. His piety assumed, of course, the ascetic type, for there was scarcely any other in that age, and he entered a Dominican convent, as Luther, a few years later, entered an Augustinian. But he was not an original genius, or a bold and independent thinker like Luther, so he was not emancipated from the ideas of his age. How

From the statue by E. Pazzi, Uffizi Galleries, Florence

SAVONAROLA

few men can go counter to prevailing ideas! It takes a prodigious genius, and a fearless, inquiring mind, to break away from their bondage. Abraham could renounce the idolatries which surrounded him, when called by a supernatural voice; Paul could give up the Phariseeism which reigned in the Jewish schools and synagogues, when stricken blind by the hand of God; Luther could break away from monastic rules and papal denunciation, when taught by the Bible the true ground of justification,—but Savonarola could not. He pursued the path to heaven in the beaten track, after the fashion of Jerome and Bernard and Thomas Aquinas, after the style of the Middle Ages, and was sincere, devout, and lofty, like the saints of the fifth century, and read his Bible as they did, and essayed a high religious life; but he was stern, gloomy, and austere, emaciated by fasts and self-denial. He had, however, those passive virtues which Mediæval piety ever enjoined,—yea, which Christ himself preached upon the Mount, and which Protestantism, in the arrogance of reason, is in danger of losing sight of,—humility, submission, and contempt of material gains. He won the admiration of his superiors for his attainments and his piety, being equally versed in Aristotle and the Holy Scriptures. He delighted most in the Old Testament heroes and prophets, and caught their sternness and invective.

He was not so much interested in dogmas as he was in morals. He had not, indeed, a turn of mind for theology, like Anselm and Calvin; but he took a practical view of the evils of society. At thirty years of age he began to preach in Ferrara and Florence, but was not very successful. His sermons at first created but little interest, and he sometimes preached to as few as twenty-five people. Probably he was too rough and vehement to suit the fastidious ears of the most refined city in Italy. People will not ordinarily bear uncouthness from preachers, however gifted, until they have earned a reputation; they prefer pretty and polished young men with nothing but platitudes or extravagances to utter. Savonarola seems to have been discouraged and humiliated at his failure, and was sent to preach to the rustic villagers, amid the mountains near Sienna. Among these people he probably felt more at home; and he gave vent to the fire within him and electrified all who heard him, winning even the admiration of the celebrated Prince of Mirandola. From this time his fame spread rapidly, he was recalled to Florence, 1490, and his great career commenced. In the following year such crowds pressed to hear him that the church of St. Mark, connected with the Dominican convent to which he was attached, could not contain the people, and he repaired to the cathedral. And even that spacious church was filled with eager listeners, — more moved than delighted. So great was his popularity, that his influence correspondingly increased and he was chosen prior of his famous convent.

He now wielded power as well as influence, and became the most marked man of the city. He was not only the most eloquent preacher in Italy, probably in the world, but his eloquence was marked by boldness, earnestness, almost fierceness. Like an ancient prophet, he was terrible in his denunciation of vices. He spared no one, and he feared no one. He resembled Chrysostom at Constantinople, when he denounced the vanity of Eudoxia and the venality of Eutropius. Lorenzo de' Medici, the absolute lord of Florence, sent for him, and expostulated and remonstrated with the unsparing preacher, — all to no effect. And when the usurper of his country's liberties was dying, the preacher was again sent for, this time to grant an absolution. But Savonarola would grant no absolution unless Lorenzo would restore the liberties which he and his family had taken away. The dying tyrant was not prepared to accede to so haughty a demand, and, collecting his strength, rolled over on his bed without saying a word, and the austere monk wended his way back to his convent, unmolested and determined.

The premature death of this magnificent prince made a great sensation throughout Italy, and produced a change in the politics of Florence, for the people began to see their political degradation. The popular discontents were increased when his successor, Pietro, proved himself incapable and tyrannical, abandoned himself to orgies, and insulted the leading citizens by an overwhelming pride. Savonarola took the side of the people, and fanned the discontents. He became the recognized leader of opposition to the Medici, and virtually ruled the city.

The Prior of St. Mark now appeared in a double light, — as a political leader and as a popular preacher. Let us first consider him in his secular aspect, as a revolutionist and statesman, — for the admirable constitution he had a principal hand in framing entitles him to the dignity of statesman rather than politician. If his cause had not been good, and if he had not appealed to both enlightened and patriotic sentiments, he would have been a demagogue; for a demagogue and a mere politician are synonymous, and a clerical demagogue is hideous.

Savonarola began his political career with terrible denunciations, from his cathedral pulpit, of the political evils of his day, not merely in Florence but throughout Italy. He detested tyrants and usurpers, and sought to conserve such liberties as the Florentines had once enjoyed. He was not only the preacher, he was also the patriot. Things temporal were mixed up with things spiritual in his discourses. In his detestation of the tyranny of the Medici, and his zeal to recover for the Florentines their lost liberties, he even hailed the French armies of Charles VIII. as deliverers, although they had crossed the Alps to invade and conquer Italy. If the gates of Florence were open to them, they would expel the Medici. So he stimulated the people to league with foreign enemies in order to recover their liberties. This would have been high treason in Richelieu's time, — as when the Huguenots encouraged the invasion of the English on the soil of France. Savonarola was a zealot, and carried the same spirit into politics that he did into religion, — such as when he made a bonfire of what he called vanities. He had an end to carry: he would use any means. There is apt to be a spirit of Jesuitism in all men consumed with zeal, determined on success. To the eye of the Florentine reformer, the expulsion of the Medici seemed the supremest necessity; and if it could be done in no other way than by opening the gates of his city to the French invaders, he would open the gates. Whatever he commanded from the pulpit was done by the people, for he seemed to have supreme control over them, gained by his eloquence as a preacher. But he did not abuse his power. When the Medici were expelled, he prevented violence; blood did not flow in the streets; order and law were preserved. The people looked up to him as their leader, temporal as well as spiritual

So he assembled them in the great hall of the city, where they formally held a *parlemento*, and reinstated the ancient magistrates. But these were men without experience. They had no capacity to govern, and they were selected without wisdom on the part of the people. The people, in fact, had not the ability to select their best and wisest men for rulers. That is an evil inherent in all popular governments. Does San Francisco or New York send its greatest men to Congress? Do not our cities elect such rulers as the demagogues point out? Do not the few rule, even in a Congregational church? If some commanding genius, unscrupulous or wise or eloquent or full of tricks, controls elections with us, much more easily could such a man as Savonarola rule in Florence, where there were no political organizations, no caucuses, no wirepullers, no other man of commanding ability. The only opinion-maker was this preacher, who indicated the general policy to be pursued. He left elections to the people; and when these proved a failure, a new constitution became a necessity. But where were the men capable of framing a constitution for the republic? Two generations of political slavery had destroyed political experience. The citizens were as incapable of framing a new constitution as the legislators of France after they had decimated the nobility, confiscated the Church lands, and cut off the head of the king. The lawyers disputed in the town hall, but accomplished nothing.

Their science amounted only to an analysis of human passion. All wanted a government entirely free from tyranny; all expected impossibilities. Some were in favor of a Venetian aristocracy, and others of a pure democracy; yet none would yield to compromise, without which no permanent political institution can ever be framed. How could the inexperienced citizens of Florence comprehend the complicated relations of governments? To make a constitution that the world respects requires the highest maturity of human wisdom. It is the supremest labor of great men. It took the ablest man ever born among the Jews to give to them a national polity. The Roman constitution was the fruit of five hundred years' experience. Our constitution was made by the wisest, most dignified, most enlightened body of statesmen that this country has yet seen, and even they could not have made it without great mutual concessions. No *one* man could have made a constitution, however great his talents and experience,— not even a Jefferson or a Hamilton, — which the nation would have accepted. It would have been as full of defects as the legislation of Solon or Lycurgus or the Abbé Sieyès. But one man gave a constitution to the Florentines, which they not only accepted, but which has been generally admired for its wisdom; and that man was our Dominican monk. The hand he had in shaping that constitution not only proved him to have been a man of great wisdom, but entitled him to the gratitude of his countrymen as a benefactor. He saw the vanity of political science as it then existed, the incapacity of popular leaders, and the sadness of a people drifting into anarchy and confusion; and, strong in his own will and his sense of right, he rose superior to himself, and directed the stormy elements of passion and fear. And this he did by his sermons from the pulpit, — for he did not descend, in person, into the stormy arena of contending passions and interests. He did not himself attend the deliberations in the town hall; he was too wise and dignified a man for that. But he preached those principles and measures which he wished to see adopted; and so great was the reverence for him that the people listened to his instructions, and afterward deliberated and acted among themselves. He did not write out a code, but he told the people what they should put into it. He was the animating genius of the city; his voice was obeyed. He unfolded the theory that the government of one man, in their circumstances, would become tyrannical; and he taught the doctrine, then new, that the people were the only source of power, — that they alone had the right to elect their magistrates. He therefore recommended a general government, which should include all citizens who had intelligence, experience, and position, — not all the people, but such as had been magistrates, or their fathers before them. Accordingly, a grand council was formed of three thousand citizens, out of a population of ninety thousand who had reached the age of twenty-nine. These three thousand citizens were divided into three equal bodies, each of which should constitute a council for six months; and no meeting was legal unless two-thirds of the members were present. This grand council appointed the magistrates. But another council was also recommended and adopted, of only eighty citizens not under forty years of age, — picked men, to be changed every six months, whom the magistrates were bound to consult weekly, and to whom was confided the appointment of some of the higher officers of the State, like ambassadors to neighboring States. All laws proposed by the magistrates, or seigniory, had to be ratified by this higher and selecter council. The higher council was a sort of Senate, the lower council were more like Representatives. But there was no universal suffrage. The clerical legislator knew well enough that only the better and more intelligent part of the people were fit to vote, even in the election of magistrates. He seems to have foreseen the fatal rock on which all popular institutions are in danger of being wrecked, — that no government is safe and respected when the people who make it are ignorant and lawless. So the constitution which Savonarola gave was neither aristocratic nor democratic. It resembled that of Venice more than that of Athens, that of England more than that of the United States. Strictly universal suffrage is a Utopian dream wherever a majority of the people are wicked and degraded. Sooner or later it threatens to plunge any nation, as nations now are, into a whirlpool of dangers, even if Divine Providence may not permit a nation to be stranded and wrecked altogether. In the politics of Savonarola we see great wisdom, and yet great sympathy for freedom. He would give the people all that they were fit for. He would make all offices elective, but only by the suffrages of the better part of the people.

But the Prior of St. Mark did not confine himself to constitutional questions and issues alone. He would remove all political abuses; he would tax property, and put an end to forced loans and arbitrary imposts; he would bring about a general pacification, and grant a general amnesty for political offences; he would guard against the extortions of the rich, and the usury of the Jews, who lent money at thirty-three per cent, with compound interest; he secured the establishment of a bank for charitable loans; he sought to make the people good citizens, and to advance their temporal as well as spiritual interests. All his reforms, political or social, were advocated, however, from the pulpit; so that he was doubtless a political priest. We, in this country and in these times, have no very great liking to this union of spiritual and temporal authority: we would separate and divide this authority. Protestants would make the functions of the ruler and the priest forever distinct. But at that time the popes themselves were secular rulers, as well as spiritual dignitaries. All bishops and abbots had the charge of political interests. Courts of law were presided over by priests. Priests were ambassadors to foreign powers; they were ministers of kings; they had the control of innumerable secular affairs, now intrusted to laymen. So their interference with politics did not shock the people of Florence, or the opinions of the age. It was indeed imperatively called for, since the clergy were the most learned and influential men of those times, even in affairs of state. I doubt if the Catholic Church has ever abrogated or ignored her old right to meddle in the politics of a state or nation. I do not know, but apprehend, that the Catholic clergy even in this country take it upon themselves to instruct the people in their political duties. No enlightened Protestant congregation would endure this interference. No Protestant minister dares ever to discuss direct political issues from the pulpit, except perhaps on Thanksgiving Day, or in some rare exigency in public affairs. Still less would he venture to tell his parishioners how they should vote in town-meetings. In imitation of ancient saints and apostles, he is wisely constrained from interference in secular and political affairs. But in the Middle Ages, and the Catholic Church, the priest could be political in his preaching, since many of his duties were secular. Savonarola usurped no prerogatives. He refrained from meeting men in secular vocations. Even in his politics he confined himself to his sphere in the pulpit. He did not attend the public debates; he simply preached. He ruled by wisdom, eloquence, and sanctity; and as he was an oracle, his utterances became a law.

But while he instructed the people in political duties, he paid far more attention to public morals. He would break up luxury, extravagance, ostentatious living, unseemly dresses in the house of God. He was the foe of all levities, all frivolities, all insidious pleasures. Bad men found no favor in his eyes, and he exposed their hypocrisies and crimes. He denounced sin, in high places and low. He did not confine himself to the sins of his own people alone, but censured those of princes and of other cities. He embraced all Italy in his glance. He invoked the Lord to take the Church out of the hands of the Devil, to pour out his wrath on guilty cities. He throws down a gauntlet of defiance to all corrupt potentates; he predicts the near approach of calamities; he foretells the certainty of divine judgment upon all sin; he clothes himself with the thunders of the Jewish prophets; he seems to invoke woe, desolation, and destruction. He ascribes the very invasion of the French to the justice of retribution. "Thy crimes, O Florence! thy crimes, O Rome! thy crimes, O Italy! are the causes of these chastisements." And so terrible are his denunciations that the whole city quakes with fear. Mirandola relates that as Savonarola's voice sounded like a clap of thunder in the cathedral, packed to its utmost capacity with the trembling people, a cold shiver ran through all his bones and the hairs of his head stood on end. "O Rome!" exclaimed the preacher, "thou shalt be put to the sword, since thou wilt not be converted. O Italy! confusion upon confusion shall overtake thee; the confusion of war shall follow thy sins, and famine and pestilence shall follow after war." Then he denounces Rome: "O harlot Church! thou hast made thy deformity apparent to all the world; thou hast multiplied thy fornications in Italy, in France, in Spain, in every country. Behold, saith the Lord, I will stretch forth my hand upon thee; I will deliver thee into the hands of those that hate thee." The burden of his soul is sin, — sin everywhere, even in the bosom of the Church, — and the necessity of repentance, of turning to the Lord. He is more than an Elijah, — he is a John the Baptist. His sermons are chiefly drawn from the Old Testament, especially from the prophets in their denunciation of woes; like them, he is stern, awful, sublime. He does not attack the polity or the constitution of the Church, but its corruptions. He does not call the Pope a usurper, a fraud, an impostor; he does not attack the office; but if the Pope is a bad man he denounces his crimes. He is still the Dominican monk, owning his allegiance, but demanding the reformation of the head of the Church, to whom God has given the keys of Saint Peter. Neither does he meddle with the doctrines of the Church; he does not take much interest in dogmas. He is not a theologian, but he would change the habits and manners of the people of Florence. He would urge throughout Italy a reformation of morals. He sees only the degeneracy in life; he threatens eternal penalties if sin be persisted in. He alarms the fears of the people, so that women part with their ornaments, dress with more simplicity, and walk more demurely; licentious young men become modest and devout; instead of the songs of the carnival, religious hymns are sung; tradesmen forsake their shops for the churches; alms are more freely given; great scholars become monks; even children bring their offerings to the Church; a pyramid of "vanities" is burned on the public square.

And no wonder. A man had appeared at a great crisis in wickedness, and yet while the people were still susceptible of grand sentiments; and this man — venerated, austere, impassioned, like an ancient prophet, like one risen from the dead — denounces woes with such awful tones, such majestic fervor, such terrible emphasis, as to break through all apathy, all delusions, and fill the people with remorse, astonish them by his revelations, and make them really feel that the supernal powers, armed with the terrors of Omnipotence, would hurl them into hell unless they repented.

No man in Europe at the time had a more lively and impressive sense of the necessity of a general reformation than the monk of St. Mark; but it was a reform in morals, not of doctrine. He saw the evils of the day — yea, of the Church itself — with perfect clearness, and demanded redress. He is as sad in view of these acknowledged evils as Jeremiah was in view of the apostasy of the Jews; he is as austere in his own life as Elijah or John the Baptist was. He would not abolish monastic institutions, but he would reform the lives of the monks, — cure them of gluttony and sensuality, not shut up their monasteries. He would not rebel against the authority of the Pope, for even Savonarola supposed that prelate to be the successor of Saint Peter; but he would prevent the Pope's nepotism and luxury and worldly spirit, — make him once more a true "servant of the servants of God," even when clothed with the insignia of universal authority. He would not give up auricular confession, or masses for the dead, or prayers to the Virgin Mary, for these were indorsed by venerated ages; but he would rebuke a priest if found in unseemly places. Whatever was a sin, when measured by the laws of immutable morality, he would denounce, whoever was guilty of it; whatever would elevate the public morals he would advocate, whoever opposed. His morality was measured by the declaration of Christ and the Apostles, not by the standard of a corrupt age. He revered the Scriptures, and incessantly pondered them, and exalted their authority, holding them to be the ultimate rule of holy living, the everlasting handbook of travellers to the heavenly Jerusalem. In all respects he was a good man,— a beautiful type of Christian piety, with fewer faults than Luther or Calvin had, and as great an enemy as they to corruptions in State and Church, which he denounced even more fiercely and passionately. Not even Erasmus pointed out the vices of the day with more freedom or earnestness. He covered up nothing; he shut his eyes to nothing.

The difference between Savonarola and Luther was that the Saxon reformer attacked the root of the corruption; not merely outward and tangible and patent sins which everybody knew, but also and more earnestly those false principles of theology and morals which sustained them, and which logically pushed out would necessarily have produced them. For instance, he not merely attacked indulgences, then a crying evil, as peddled by Tetzel and others like him, and all to get money to support the temporal power of the popes or build St. Peter's church; but he would show that penance, on which indulgences are based, is antagonistic to the doctrine which Paul so forcibly expounded respecting the forgiveness of sins and the grounds of justification. And Luther saw that all the evils which good men lamented would continue so long as the false principles from which they logically sprung were the creed of the Church. So he directed his giant energies to reform doctrines rather than morals. His great idea of justification could be defended only by an appeal to the Scriptures, not to the authority of councils and learned men. So he made the Scriptures the sole source of theological doctrine. Savonarola also accepted the Scriptures, but Luther would put them in the hands of everybody, of peasants even,—and thus instituted private judgment, which is the basal pillar of Protestantism. The Catholic theologians never recognized this right in the sense that Luther understood it, and to which he was pushed by inexorable logic. The Church was to remain the interpreter of the doctrinal and disputed points of the Scriptures.

Savonarola was a churchman. He was not a fearless theological doctor, going wherever logic and the Bible carried him. Hence, he did not stimulate thought and inquiry as Luther did, nor inaugurate a great revolutionary movement, which would gradually undermine papal authority and many institutions which the Catholic Church indorsed. Had he been a great genius, with his progressive proclivities, he might have headed a rebellion against papal authority, which upheld doctrines that logically supported the very evils he denounced. But he was contented to lop off branches; he did not dig up the roots. Luther went to the roots, as Calvin did; as Saint Augustine would have done had there been a necessity in his day, for the theology of Saint Augustine and Calvin is essentially the same. It was from Saint Augustine that Calvin drew his inspiration next after Saint Paul. But Savonarola cared very little for the discussion of doctrines; he probably hated all theological speculations, all metaphysical divinity. Yet there is a closer resemblance between doctrines and morals than most people are aware of. As a man thinketh, so is he. Hence, the reforms of Savonarola were temporary, and were not widely extended; for he did not kindle the intelligence of the age, as did Luther and those associated with him. There can be no great and lasting reform without an appeal to reason, without the assistance of logic, without conviction. The house that had been swept and garnished was re-entered by devils, and the last state was worse than the first. To have effected a radical and lasting reform, Savonarola should have gone deeper. He should have exposed the foundations on which the superstructure of sin was built; he should have undermined them, and appealed to the reason of the world. He did no such thing. He simply rebuked the evils, which must needs be, so long as the root of them is left untouched. And so long as his influence remained, so long as his voice was listened to, he was mighty in the reforms at which he aimed, — a reformation of the morals of those to whom he preached. But when his voice was hushed, the evils he detested returned, since he had not created those convictions which bind men together in association; he had not fanned that spirit of inquiry which is hostile to ecclesiastical despotism, and which, logically projected, would subvert the papal throne. The reformation of Luther was a grand protest against spiritual tyranny. It not only aimed at a purer life, but it opposed the bondage of the Middle Ages, and all the superstitions and puerilities and fables which were born and nurtured in that dark and gloomy period and to which the clergy clung as a means of power or wealth. Luther called out the intellect of Germany, exalted liberty of conscience, and appealed to the dignity of reason. He showed the necessity of learning, in order to unravel and explain the truths of revelation. He made piety more exalted by giving it an intelligent stimulus. He looked to the future rather than the past. He would make use, in his interpretation of the Bible, of all that literature, science, and art could contribute. Hence his writings had a wider influence than could be produced by the fascination of personal eloquence, on which Savonarola relied, but which Luther made only accessory.

Again, the sermons of the Florentine reformer do not impress us as they did those to whom they were addressed. They are not logical, nor doctrinal, nor learned, — not rich in thought, like the sermons of those divines whom the Reformation produced. They are vehement denunciations of sin; are eloquent appeals to the heart, to religious fears and hopes. He would indeed create faith in the world, not by the dissertations of Paul, but by the agonies of the dying Christ. He does not instruct; he does not reason. He is dogmatic and practical. He is too earnest to be metaphysical, or even theological. He takes it for granted that his hearers know all the truths necessary for salvation. He enforces the truths with which they are familiar, not those to be developed by reason and learning. He appeals, he urges, he threatens; he even prophesies; he dwells on divine wrath and judgment. He is an Isaiah foretelling what will happen, rather than a Peter at the Day of Pentecost.

Savonarola was transcendent in his oratorical gifts, the like of which has never before nor since been witnessed in Italy. He was a born orator; as vehement as Demosthenes, as passionate as Chrysostom, as electrical as Bernard. Nothing could withstand him; he was a torrent that bore everything before him. His voice was musical, his attitude commanding, his gestures superb. He was all alive with his subject. He was terribly in earnest, as if he believed everything he said, and that what he said were most momentous truths. He fastened his burning eyes upon his hearers, who listened with breathless attention, and inspired them with his sentiments; he made them feel that they were in the very jaws of destruction, and that there was no hope but in immediate repentance. His whole frame quivered with emotion, and he sat down utterly exhausted. His language was intense, not clothing new thoughts, but riveting old ideas,— the ideas of the Middle Ages; the fear of hell, the judgments of Almighty God. Who could resist such fiery earnestness, such a convulsed frame, such quivering tones, such burning eyes, such dreadful threatenings, such awful appeals? He was not artistic in the use of words and phrases like Bourdaloue, but he reached the conscience and the heart like Whitefield. He never sought to amuse; he would not stoop to any trifling. He told no stories; he made no witticisms; he used no tricks.

He fell back on truths, no matter whether his hearers relished them or not; no matter whether they were amused or not. He was the messenger of God urging men to flee as for their lives, like Lot when he escaped from Sodom.

Savonarola's manner was as effective as his matter. He was a kind of Peter the Hermit, preaching a crusade, arousing emotions and passions, and making everybody feel as he felt. It was life more than thought which marked his eloquence,—his voice as well as his ideas, his wonderful electricity, which every preacher must have, or he preaches to stones. It was himself, even more than his truths, which made people listen, admire, and quake. All real orators impress themselves—their own individuality—on their auditors. They are not actors, who represent other people, and whom we admire in proportion to their artistic skill in producing deception. These artists excite admiration, make us forget where we are and what we are, but kindle no permanent emotions, and teach no abiding lessons. The eloquent preacher of momentous truths and interests makes us realize them, in proportion as he feels them himself. They would fall dead upon us, if ever so grand, unless intensified by passion, fervor, sincerity, earnestness. Even a voice has power, when electrical, musical, impassioned, although it may utter platitudes. But when the impassioned voice rings with trumpet notes through a vast audience, appealing to what is dearest to the human soul, lifting the mind to the contemplation of the sublimest truths and most momentous interests, then there is *real* eloquence, such as is never heard in the theatre, interested as spectators may be in the triumphs of dramatic art.

But I have dwelt too long on the characteristics of that eloquence which produced such a great effect on the people of Florence in the latter part of the fifteenth century. That ardent, intense, and lofty monk, world-deep like Dante, not world-wide like Shakspeare, who filled the cathedral church with eager listeners, was not destined to uninterrupted triumphs. His career was short; he could not even retain his influence. As the English people wearied of the yoke of a Puritan Protector, and hankered for their old pleasures, so the Florentines remembered the sports and spectacles and *fêtes* of the old Medicean rule. Savonarola had arrayed against himself the enemies of popular liberty, the patrons of demoralizing excitements, the partisans of the banished Medici, and even the friends and counsellors of the Pope. The dreadful denunciation of sin in high places was as offensive to the Pope as the exposure of a tyrannical usurpation was to the family of the old lords of Florence; and his enemies took counsel together, and schemed for his overthrow. If the irritating questions and mockeries of Socrates could not be endured at

Athens, how could the bitter invectives and denunciations of Savonarola find favor at Florence? The fate of prophets is to be stoned. Martyrdom and persecution, in some form or other, are as inevitable to the man who sails against the stream, as a broken constitution and a diseased body are to a sensualist, a glutton, or a drunkard. Impatience under rebuke is as certain as the operation of natural law.

The bitterest and most powerful enemy of the Prior of St. Mark was the Pope himself, — Alexander VI., of the infamous family of the Borgias, — since his private vices were exposed, and by one whose order had been especially devoted to the papal empire. In the eyes of the wicked Pope, the Florentine reformer was a traitor and conspirator, disloyal and dangerous. At first he wished to silence him by soft and deceitful letters and tempting bribes, offering to him a cardinal's hat, and inviting him to Rome. But Savonarola refused alike the bribe and the invitation. His Lenten sermons became more violent and daring. "If I have preached and written anything heretical," said this intrepid monk, "I am willing to make a public recantation. I have always shown obedience to my church; but it is my duty to obey God rather than man." This sounds like Luther at the Diet of Worms; but he was more defenceless than Luther, since the Saxon reformer was protected by powerful princes, and was backed by the enthusiasm of Northern Germans. Yet the Florentine preacher boldly continued his attacks on all hypocritical religion, and on the vices of Rome, not as incidental to the system, but extraneous, — the faults of a man or age. The Pope became furious, to be thus balked by a Dominican monk, and in one of the cities of Italy, — a city that had not rebelled against his authority. He complained bitterly to the Florentine ambassador, of the haughty friar who rebuked and defied him. He summoned a consistory of fourteen eminent Dominican theologians, to inquire into his conduct and opinions, and issued a brief forbidding him to preach, under penalty of excommunication. Yet Savonarola continued to preach, and more violently than ever. He renewed his charges against Rome. He even called her a harlot Church, against whom heaven and earth, angels and devils, equally brought charges. The Pope then seized the old thunderbolts of the Gregories and the Clements, and excommunicated the daring monk and preacher, and threatened the like punishment on all who should befriend him. And yet Savonarola continued to preach. All Rome and Italy talked of the audacity of the man. And it was not until Florence itself was threatened with an interdict for shielding such a man, that the magistrates of the city were compelled to forbid his preaching.

The great orator mounted his pulpit March 18, 1498,

now four hundred years ago, and took an affectionate farewell of the people whom he had led, and appealed to Christ himself as the head of the Church. It was not till the preacher was silenced by the magistrates of his own city, that he seems to have rebelled against the papal authority; and then not so much against the authority of Rome as against the wicked shepherd himself, who had usurped the fold. He now writes letters to all the prominent kings and princes of Europe, to assemble a general council; for the general council of Constance had passed a resolution that the Pope must call a general council every ten years, and that, should he neglect to assemble it, the sovereign powers of the various states and empires were themselves empowered to collect the scattered members of the universal Church, to deliberate on its affairs. In his letters to the kings of France, England, Spain, and Hungary, and the Emperor of Germany, he denounced the Pope as simoniacal, as guilty of all the vices, as a disgrace to the station which he held. These letters seem to have been directed against the man, not against the system. He aimed at the Pope's ejectment from office, rather than at the subversion of the office itself,—another mark of the difference between Savonarola and Luther, since the latter waged an uncompromising war against Rome herself, against the whole *régime* and government and institutions and dogmas of the Catholic Church; and that is the reason why Catholics hate Luther so bitterly, and deny to him either virtues or graces, and represent even his deathbed as a scene of torment and despair, — an instance of that pursuing hatred which goes beyond the grave; like that of the zealots of the Revolution in France, who dug up the bones of the ancient kings from those vaults where they had reposed for centuries, and scattered their ashes to the winds.

Savonarola hoped the Christian world would come to his rescue; but his letters were intercepted, and reached the eye of Alexander VI., who now bent the whole force of the papal empire to destroy that bold reformer who had assailed his throne. And it seems that a change took place in Florence itself in popular sentiment. The Medicean party obtained the ascendency in the government. The people — the fickle people — began to desert Savonarola; and especially when he refused to undergo the ordeal of fire, — one of the relics of Mediæval superstition, — the people felt that they had been cheated out of their amusement, for they had waited impatiently the whole day in the public square to see the spectacle. He finally consented to undergo the ordeal, provided he might carry the crucifix. To this his enemies would not consent. He then laid aside the crucifix, but insisted on entering the fire with the sacrament in his hand. His persecutors would not allow this either, and the ordeal did not take place.

At last his martyrdom approaches: he is led to prison. The magistrates of the city send to Rome for absolution for having allowed the Prior to preach. His enemies busy themselves in collecting evidence against him, — for what I know not, except that he had denounced corruption and sin, and had predicted woe. His two friends are imprisoned and interrogated with him, Fra Domenico da Pescia and Fra Silvestro Maruffi, who are willing to die for him. He and they are now subjected to most cruel tortures. As the result of bodily agony his mind begins to waver. His answers are incoherent; he implores his tormentors to end his agonies; he cries out, with a voice enough to melt a heart of stone, "Take, oh, take my life!" Yet he confessed nothing to criminate himself. What they wished him especially to confess was that he had pretended to be a prophet, since he had predicted calamities. But all men are prophets, in one sense, when they declare the certain penalties of sin, from which no one can escape, though he take the wings of the morning and fly to the uttermost parts of the sea.

Savonarola thus far had remained firm, but renewed examinations and fresh tortures took place. For a whole month his torments were continuous. In one day he was drawn up by a rope fourteen times, and then suddenly dropped, until all his muscles quivered with anguish. Had he been surrounded by loving disciples, like Latimer at the burning pile, he might have summoned more strength; but alone, in a dark inquisitorial prison, subjected to increasing torture among bitter foes, he did not fully defend his visions and prophecies; and then his extorted confessions were diabolically altered. But that was all they could get out of him, — that he had prophesied. In all matters of faith he was sound. The inquisitors were obliged to bring their examination to an end. They could find no fault with him, and yet they were determined on his death. The Government of Florence consented to it and hastened it, for a Medici again held the highest office of the State.

Nothing remained to the imprisoned and tortured friar but to prepare for his execution. In his supreme trial he turned to the God in whom he believed. In the words of the dying Xavier, on the Island of Sancian, he exclaimed, *In te domine speravi, non confundar in eternum.* "O Lord," he prays, "a thousand times hast thou wiped out my iniquity. I do not rely on my own justification, but on thy mercy." His few remaining days in prison were passed in holy meditation.

At last the officers of the papal commission arrive. The tortures are renewed, and also the examinations, with the same result. No fault could be found with his doctrines. "But a dead enemy," said they, "fights no more." He is condemned to execution. The messengers of death arrive at his cell, and find him on his knees. He is overpowered by his sufferings and vigils, and can with difficulty be kept from sleep. But he arouses himself, and passes the night in prayer, and administers the elements of redemption to his doomed companions, and closes with this prayer: "Lord, I know thou art that perfect Trinity, — Father, Son, and Holy Ghost; I know that thou art the eternal Word; that thou didst descend from heaven into the bosom of Mary; that thou didst ascend upon the cross to shed thy blood for our sins. I pray thee that by that blood I may have remission for my sins." The simple faith of Paul, of Augustine, of Pascal! He then partook of the communion, and descended to the public square, while the crowd gazed silently and with trepidation, and was led with his companions to the first tribunal, where he was disrobed of his ecclesiastical dress. Then they were led to another tribunal, and delivered to the secular arm; then to another, where sentence of death was read; and then to the place of execution,—not a burning funeral pyre, but a scaffold, which mounting, composed, calm, absorbed, Savonarola submitted his neck to the hangman, in the forty-fifth year of his life: a martyr to the cause of Christ, not for an attack on the Church, or its doctrines, or its institutions, but for having denounced the corruption and vices of those who ruled it, — for having preached against sin.

Thus died one of the greatest and best men of his age, one of the truest and purest whom the Catholic Church has produced in any age. He was stern, uncompromising, austere, but a reformer and a saint; a man who was merciful and generous in the possession of power; an enlightened statesman, a sound theologian, and a fearless preacher of that righteousness which exalteth a nation. He had no vices, no striking defects. He lived according to the rules of the convent he governed with the same wisdom that he governed a city, and he died in the faith of the primitive apostles. His piety was monastic, but his spirit was progressive, sympathizing with liberty, advocating public morality. He was unselfish, disinterested, and true to his Church, his conscience, and his cause, — a noble specimen both of a man and Christian, whose deeds and example form part of the inheritance of an admiring posterity. We pity his closing days, after such a career of power and influence; but we may as well compassionate Socrates or Paul. The greatest lights of the world have gone out in martyrdom, to be extinguished, however, only for a time, and then to loom up again in another age, and burn with inextinguishable brightness to remotest generations, as examples of the power of faith and truth in this wicked and rebellious world,—a world to be finally redeemed by the labors and religion of just such men, whose days are days of sadness, protest, and suffering, and whose hours of triumph and exaltation are not like those of conquerors, nor like those whose eyes stand out with fatness, but few and far between. "I have loved righteousness, I have hated iniquity," said the great champion of the Mediæval Church, "and therefore I die in exile."

In ten years after this ignominious execution, Raphael painted the martyr among the sainted doctors of the Church in the halls of the Vatican, and future popes did justice to his memory, for he inaugurated that reform movement in the Catholic Church itself which took place within fifty years after his death. In one sense he was the precursor of Loyola, of Xavier, and of Aquaviva,—those illustrious men who headed the counter-reformation; Jesuits, indeed, but ardent in piety, and enlightened by the spirit of a progressive age. "He was the first," says Villari, "in the fifteenth century, to make men feel that a new light had awakened the human race; and thus he was a prophet of a new civilization,—the forerunner of Luther, of Bacon, of Descartes. Hence the drama of his life became, after his death, the drama of Europe. In the course of a single generation after Luther had declared his mission, the spirit of the Church of Rome underwent a change.

From the halls of the Vatican to the secluded hermitages of the Apennines this revival was felt. Instead of a Borgia there reigned a Caraffa." And it is remarkable that from the day that the counter-reformation in the Catholic Church was headed by the early Jesuits, Protestantism gained no new victories, and in two centuries so far declined in piety and zeal that the cities which witnessed the noblest triumphs of Luther and Calvin were disgraced by a boasting rationalism, to be succeeded again in our times by an arrogance of scepticism which has had no parallel since the days of Democritus and Lucretius. "It was the desire of Savonarola that reason, religion, and liberty might meet in harmonious union, but he did not think a new system of religious doctrines was necessary."

The influence of such a man cannot pass away, and has not passed away, for it cannot be doubted that his views have been embraced by enlightened Catholics from his day to ours,— by such men as Pascal, Fénelon, and Lacordaire, and thousands like them, who prefer ritualism and auricular confession, and penance, monasticism, and an ecclesiastical monarch, and all the machinery of a complicated hierarchy, with all the evils growing out of papal domination, to rationalism, sectarian dissensions, irreverence, license, want of unity, want of government, and even dispensation from the marriage vow. Which is worse, the physical arm of the beast, or the maniac soul of a lying prophet? Which is worse, the superstition and narrowness which excludes the Bible from schools, or that unbounded toleration which smiles on those audacious infidels who cloak their cruel attacks on the faith of Christians with the name of a progressive civilization? — and so far advanced that one of these new lights, ignorant, perhaps, of everything except of the fossils and shells and bugs and gases of the hole he has bored in, assumes to know more of the mysteries of creation and the laws of the universe than Moses and David and Paul, and all the Bacons and Newtons that ever lived? Names are nothing; it is the spirit, the *animus,* which is everything. It is the soul which permeates a system, that I look at. It is the Devil from which I would flee, whatever be his name, and though he assume the form of an angel of light, or cunningly try to persuade me, and ingeniously argue, that there is no God. True and good Catholics and true and good Protestants have ever been united in one thing, — *in this belief,* that there is a God who made the heaven and the earth, and that there is a Christ who made atonement for the sins of the world. It is good morals, faith, and love to which both Catholics and Protestants are exhorted by the Apostles. When either Catholics or Protestants accept the one faith and the one Lord which Christianity alone reveals, then they equally belong to the grand army of spiritual warriors under the banner of the Cross, though they may march under different generals and in different divisions; and they will receive the same consolations in this world, and the same rewards in the world to come.

AUTHORITIES.

Villari's Life of Savonarola; Biographie Universelle; Ranke's History of the Popes. There is much in "Romola," by George Eliot. Life of Savonarola, by the Prince of Mirandola.

MICHAEL ANGELO.

A. D. 1475–1564.

THE REVIVAL OF ART.

MICHAEL ANGELO.

THE REVIVAL OF ART.

MICHAEL ANGELO BUONARROTI — one of the Great Lights of the new civilization — may stand as the most fitting representative of reviving art in Europe; also as an illustrious example of those virtues which dignify intellectual pre-eminence. He was superior, in all that is sterling and grand in character, to any man of his age, — certainly in Italy; exhibiting a rugged, stern greatness which reminds us of Dante, and of other great benefactors; nurtured in the school of sorrow and disappointment, leading a checkered life, doomed to envy, ingratitude, and neglect; rarely understood, and never fully appreciated even by those who employed and honored him. He was an isolated man; grave, abstracted, lonely, yet not unhappy, since his world was that of glorious and exalting ideas, even those of grace, beauty, majesty, and harmony, — the world which Plato lived in, and in which all great men live who seek to rise above the transient, the false, and puerile in common life. He was also an original genius, remarkable in everything he attempted, whether as sculptor, painter, or architect, and even as poet. He saw the archetypes of everything beautiful and grand, which are invisible except to those who are almost divinely gifted; and he had the practical skill to embody them in permanent forms, so that all ages may study those forms, and rise through them to the realms in which his soul lived.

Michael Angelo not only created, but he reproduced. He reproduced the glories of Grecian and Roman art. He restored the old civilization in his pictures, his statues, and his grand edifices. He revived a taste for what is imperishable in antiquity. As such he is justly regarded as an immortal benefactor; for it is art which gives to nations culture, refinement, and the enjoyment of the beautiful. Art diverts the mind from low and commonplace pursuits, exalts the imagination, and makes its votary indifferent to the evils of life. It raises the soul into regions of peace and bliss.

But art is most ennobling when it is inspired by lofty and consecrated sentiments, — like those of religion, patriotism, and love. Now ancient art was consecrated to Paganism. Of course there were noble exceptions; but as a general rule temples were erected in honor of heathen deities. Statues represented mere physical strength and beauty and grace. Pictures portrayed the charms of an unsanctified humanity. Hence ancient art did very little to arrest human degeneracy; facilitated rather than retarded the ruin of states and empires, since it did not stimulate the virtues on which the strength of man is based: it did not check those depraved tastes and habits which are based on egotism.

Now the restorers of ancient art cannot be said to have contributed to the moral elevation of the new races, unless they avoided the sensualism of Greece and Rome, and appealed purely to those eternal ideas which the human mind, even under Pagan influences, sometimes conceived, and which do not conflict with Christianity itself.

In considering the life and labors of Michael Angelo, then, we are to examine whether, in the classical glories of antiquity which he substituted for the Gothic and Mediæval, he advanced civilization in the noblest sense; and moreover, whether he carried art to a higher degree than was ever attained by the Greeks and Romans, and hence became a benefactor of the world.

In considering these points I shall not attempt a minute criticism of his works. I can only seize on the great outlines, the salient points of those productions which have given him immortality. No lecture can be exhaustive. If it only prove suggestive, it has reached its end.

Michael Angelo stands out in history in the three aspects of sculptor, painter, and architect; and that too in a country devoted to art, and in an age when Italy won all her modern glories, arising from the matchless works which that age produced. Indeed, those works will probably never be surpassed, since all the energies of a great nation were concentrated upon their production, even as our own age confines itself chiefly to mechanical inventions and scientific research and speculation. What railroads and telegraphs and spindles and chemical tests and compounds are to us; what philosophy was to the Greeks; what government and jurisprudence were to the Romans; what cathedrals and metaphysical subtilties were to the Middle Ages; what theological inquiries were to the divines of the seventeenth century; what social urbanities and refinements were to the French in the eighteenth century,— the fine arts were to the Italians in the sixteenth century: a fact too commonplace to dwell upon, and which will be conceded when we bear in mind that no age has been distinguished for everything, and that nations can try satisfactorily but one experiment at a time, and are not likely to repeat it with the same enthusiasm. As the mind is unbounded in its capacities, and our world affords inexhaustible fields of enterprise, the progress of the race is to be seen in the new developments which successively appear, but in which only a certain limit has thus far been reached. Not in absolute perfection in any particular sphere is this progress seen, but rather in the variety of the experiments. It may be doubted whether any Grecian edifice will ever surpass the Parthenon in beauty of proportion or fitness of ornament; or any nude statue show grace of form more impressive than the Venus de Milo or the Apollo Belvedere; or any system of jurisprudence be more completely codified than that systematized by Justinian; or any Gothic church rival the lofty expression of Cologne cathedral; or any painting surpass the holy serenity and ethereal love depicted in Raphael's madonnas; or any court witness such a brilliant assemblage of wits and beauties as met at Versailles to render homage to Louis XIV.; or any theological discussion excite such a national interest as when Luther confronted Doctor Eck in the great hall of the Electoral Palace at Leipsic; or any theatrical excitement such as was produced on cultivated intellects when Garrick and Siddons represented the sublime conceptions of the myriad-minded Shakspeare. These glories may reappear, but never will they shine as they did before. No more Olympian games, no more Roman triumphs, no more Dodona oracles, no more Flavian amphitheatres, no more Mediæval cathedrals, no more councils of Nice or Trent, no more spectacles of kings holding the stirrups of popes, no more Fields of the Cloth of Gold, no more reigns of court mistresses in such palaces as Versailles and Fontainbleau, — ah! I wish I could add, no more such battlefields as Marengo and Waterloo, — only copies and imitations of these, and without the older charm. The world is moving on and perpetually changing, nor can we tell what new vanity will next arise, — vanity or glory, according to our varying notions of the dignity and destiny of man. We may predict that it will not be any mechanical improvement, for ere long the limit will be reached, — and it will be reached when the great mass cannot find work to do, for the everlasting destiny of man is toil and labor. But it will be some sublime wonders of which we cannot now conceive, and which in time will pass away for other wonders and novelties, until the great circle is completed; and all human experiments shall verify the moral wisdom of the eternal revelation. Then all that man has done, all that man can do, in his own boastful thought, will be seen, in the light of the celestial verities, to be indeed a vanity and a failure, not of human ingenuity and power, but to realize the happiness which is only promised as the result of supernatural, not mortal, strength, yet which the soul in its restless aspirations never ceases its efforts to secure, — everlasting Babel-building to reach the unattainable on earth.

Now the revival of art in Italy was one of the great movements in the series of human development. It peculiarly characterized the fifteenth and sixteenth centuries. It was an age of artistic wonders, of great creations.

Italy, especially, was glorious when Michael Angelo was born, 1474; when the rest of Europe was comparatively rude, and when no great works in art, in poetry, in history, or philosophy had yet appeared. He was descended from an illustrious family, and was destined to one of the learned professions; but he could not give up his mind to anything but drawing, — as annoying to his father as Galileo's experiments were to his parent; as unmeaning to him as Gibbon's History was to George III., — "Scribble, scribble, scribble; Mr. Gibbon, I perceive, sir, you are always a-scribbling." No perception of a new power, no sympathy with the abandonment to a specialty not indorsed by fashions and traditions, but without which abandonment genius cannot easily be developed. At last the father yielded, and the son was apprenticed to a painter, — a degradation in the eyes of Mediæval aristocracy.

The celebrated Lorenzo de' Medici was then in the height of power and fame in Florence, adored by Roscoe as the patron of artists and poets, although he subverted the liberties of his country. This overlauded prince, heir of the fortunes of a great family of merchants, wishing to establish a school for sculpture, filled a garden with statues, and freely admitted to it young scholars in art. Michael Angelo was one of the most frequent and enthusiastic visitors to this garden, where in due time he attracted the attention of the magnificent Lord of Florence by a head chiselled so remarkably that he became an inmate of the palace, sat at the table of Lorenzo, and at last was regularly adopted as one of the Prince's family, with every facility for prosecuting his studies. Before he was eighteen the youth had sculptured the battle of Hercules with the Centaurs, which he would never part with, and which still remains in his family; so well done that he himself, at the age of eighty, regretted that he had not given up his whole life to sculpture.

It was then as a sculptor that Michael Angelo first appears to the historical student, — about the year 1492, when Columbus was crossing the great unknown ocean to realize his belief in a western passage to India. Thus commercial enterprise began with the revival of art, and was destined never to be separated in its alliance with it, since commerce brings wealth, and wealth seeks to ornament the palaces and gardens which it has created or purchased. The sculptor's art was not born until piety had already edifices in which to worship God, or pride the monuments in which it sought the glories of a name; but it made rapid progress as wealth increased and taste became refined; as the need was felt for ornaments and symbols to adorn naked walls and empty spaces, especially statuary, grouped or single, of men or animals, — a marble history to interpret or reproduce consecrated associations. Churches might do without them; the glass stained in every color of the rainbow, the altar shining with gold and silver and precious stones, the pillars multiplied and diversified, and rich in foliated circles, mullions, mouldings, groins, and bosses, and bearing aloft the arched and ponderous roof, — one scene of dazzling magnificence, — these could do without them; but the palaces and halls and houses of the rich required the image of man, — and of man not emaciated and worn and monstrous, but of man as he appeared to the classical Greeks, in the perfection of form and physical beauty. So the artists who arose with the revival of commerce, with the multiplication of human wants and the study of antiquity, sought to restore the buried statues with the long-neglected literature and laws. It was in sculptured marbles that enthusiasm was most marked. These were found in abundance in various parts of Italy whenever the vast débris of the ancient magnificence was removed, and were universally admired and prized by popes, cardinals, and princes, and formed the nucleus of great museums.

The works of Michael Angelo as a sculptor were not

numerous, but in sublimity they have never been surpassed,— *non multa, sed multum*. His unfinished monument of Julius II., begun at that pontiff's request as a mausoleum, is perhaps his greatest work; and the statue of Moses, which formed a part of it, has been admired for three hundred years. In this, as in his other masterpieces, grandeur and majesty are his characteristics. It may have been a reproduction, and yet it is not a copy. He made character and moral force the first consideration, and form subservient to expression. And here he differed, it is said by great critics, from the ancients, who thought more of form than of moral expression, — as may be seen in the faces of the Venus de Medici and the Apollo Belvedere, matchless and inimitable as these statues are in grace and beauty. The Laocoön and the Dying Gladiator are indeed exceptions, for it is character which constitutes their chief merit, — the expression of pain, despair, and agony. But there is almost no intellectual or moral expression in the faces of other famous and remarkable antique statues, only beauty and variety of form, such as Powers exhibited in his Greek Slave, — an inferior excellence, since it is much easier to copy the beautiful in the nude statues which people Italy, than to express such intellectual majesty as Michael Angelo conceived — that intellectual expression which Story has succeeded in giving to his African Sibyl. Thus while the great

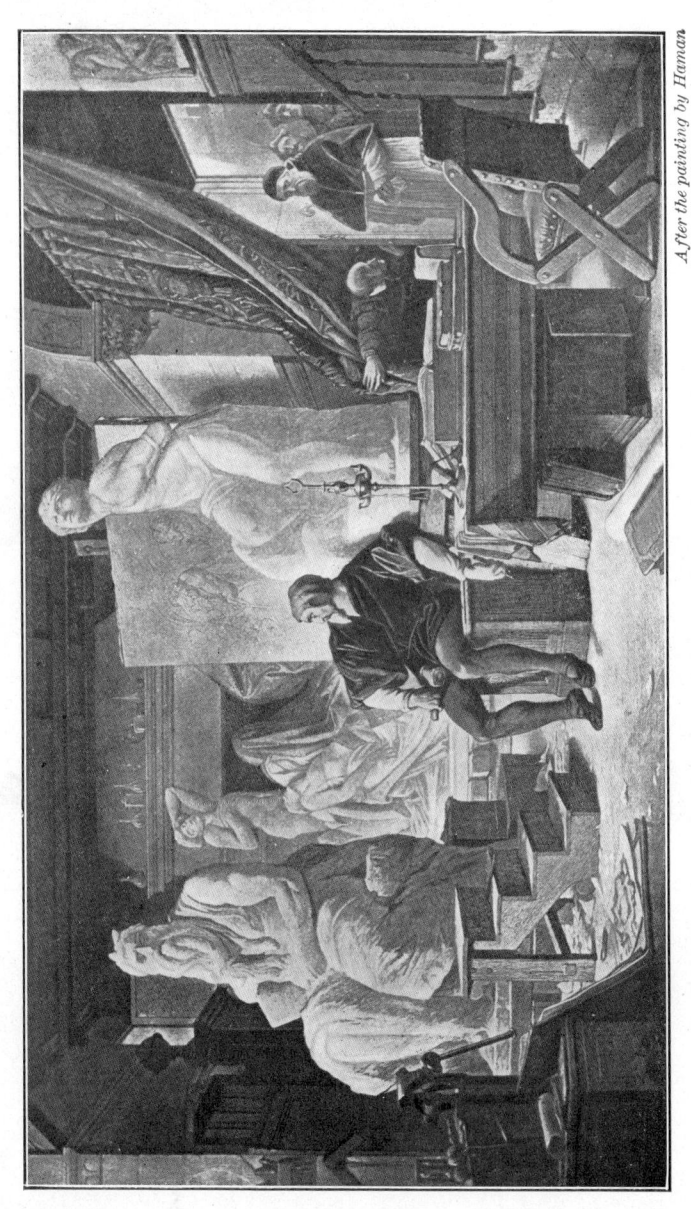

MICHAEL ANGELO IN HIS STUDIO VISITED BY POPE JULIUS II.

After the painting by Haman

artist retained the antique, he superadded a loftiness such as the ancients rarely produced; and sculpture became in his hands, not demoralizing and Pagan, resplendent in sensual charms, but instructive and exalting, — instructive for the marvellous display of anatomical knowledge, and exalting from grand conceptions of dignity and power. His knowledge of anatomy was so remarkable that he could work without models. Our artists, in these days, must always have before their eyes some nude figure to copy.

The same peculiarities which have given him fame as a sculptor he carried out into painting, in which he is even more remarkable; for the artists of Italy at this period often combined a skill for all the fine arts. In sculpture they were much indebted to the ancients, but painting seems to have been purely a development. In the Middle Ages it was comparatively rude. No noted painter arose until Cimabue, in the middle of the thirteenth century. Before him, painting was a lifeless imitation of models afforded by Greek workers in mosaics; but Cimabue abandoned this servile copying, and gave a new expression to heads, and grouped his figures. Under Giotto, who was contemporary with Dante, drawing became still more correct, and coloring softer. After him, painting was rapidly advanced. Pietro della Francesca was the father of perspective; Domenico painted in oil, discovered by Van Eyck in Flanders, in 1410; Masaccio studied anatomy; gilding disappeared as a background around pictures. In the fifteenth century the enthusiasm for painting became intense; even monks became painters, and every convent and church and palace was deemed incomplete without pictures. But ideal beauty and harmony in coloring were still wanting, as well as freedom of the pencil. Then arose Da Vinci and Michael Angelo, who practised the immutable principles by which art could be advanced; and rapidly following in their steps, Fra Bartolommeo, Fra Angelico, Rossi, and Andrea del Sarto made the age an era in painting, until the art culminated in Raphael and Corregio and Titian. And divers cities of Italy — Bologna, Milan, Parma, and Venice — disputed with Rome and Florence for the empire of art; as also did many other cities which might be mentioned, each of which has a history, each of which is hallowed by poetic associations; so that all men who have lived in Italy, or even visited it, feel a peculiar interest in these cities, — an interest which they can feel in no others, even if they be such capitals as London and Paris. I excuse this extravagant admiration for the wonderful masterpieces produced in that age, making marble and canvas eloquent with the most inspiring sentiments, because, wrapt in the joys which they excite, the cultivated and imaginative man forgets — and

THE REVIVAL OF ART. 195

rejoices that he can forget—the priests and beggars, the dirty hotels, filthy friars, superstition, unthrift, Jesuitism, which stare ordinary tourists in the face, and all the other disgusting realities which philanthropists deplore so loudly in that degenerate but classical and ever-to-be-hallowed land. For, come what will, in spite of popes and despots it has been the scene of the highest glories of antiquity, calling to our minds saints and martyrs, as well as conquerors and emperors, and revealing at every turn their tombs and broken monuments, and all the hoary remnants of unsurpassed magnificence, as well as preserving in churches and palaces those wonders which were created when Italy once again lived in the noble aspiration of making herself the centre and the pride of the new civilization.

Da Vinci, the oldest of the great masters who immortalized that era, died in 1519, in the arms of Francis I. of France, and Michael Angelo received his mantle. The young sculptor was taken away from his chisel to paint, for Pope Julius II., the ceiling of the Sistine Chapel. After the death of his patron Lorenzo, he had studied and done famous work in marble at Bologna, at Rome, and again at Florence. He had also painted some, and with such immediate success that he had been invited to assist Da Vinci in decorating a hall in the ducal palace at Florence. But sculpture was his chosen art, and when called to paint the Sistine Chapel, he implored the Pope that he might be allowed to finish the mausoleum which he had begun, and that Raphael, then dazzling the whole city by his unprecedented talents, might be substituted for him in that great work. But the Pope was inflexible; and the great artist began his task, assisted by other painters; however, he soon got disgusted with them and sent them away, and worked alone. For twenty months he toiled, rarely seen, living abstemiously, absorbed utterly in his work of creation; and the greater portion of the compartments in the vast ceiling was finished before any other voice than his, except the admiring voice of the Pope, pronounced it good.

It would be useless to attempt to describe those celebrated frescos. Their subjects were taken from the Book of Genesis, with great figures of sibyls and prophets. They are now half-concealed by the accumulated dust and smoke of three hundred years, and can be surveyed only by reclining at full length on the back. We see enough, however, to be impressed with the boldness, the majesty, and the originality of the figures, — their fidelity to nature, the knowledge of anatomy displayed, and the disdain of inferior arts; especially the noble disdain of appealing to false and perverted taste, as if he painted from an exalted ideal in his own mind, which ideal is ever associated with creative power.

It is this creative power which places Michael Angelo at the head of the artists of his great age; and not merely the power to create but the power of realizing the most exalted conceptions. Raphael was doubtless superior to him in grace and beauty, even as Titian afterwards surpassed him in coloring. He delighted, like Dante, in the awful and the terrible. This grandeur of conception was especially seen in his Last Judgment, executed thirty years afterwards, in completion of the Sistine Chapel, the work on which had been suspended at the death of Julius. This vast fresco is nearly seventy feet in height, painted upon the wall at the end of the chapel, as an altar-piece. No subject could have been better adapted to his genius than this — the day of supernal terrors (*dies iræ, dies illa*), when, according to the sentiments of the Middle Ages, the doomed were subjected to every variety of physical suffering, and when this agony of pain, rather than agony of remorse, was expressed in tortured limbs and in faces writhing with demoniacal despair. Such was the variety of tortures which he expressed, showing an unexampled richness in imaginative powers, that people came to see it from the remotest parts of Italy. It made a great sensation, like the appearance of an immortal poem, and was magnificently rewarded; for the painter received a pension of twelve hundred golden crowns a year,— a great sum in that age.

But Michael Angelo did not paint many pieces; he confined himself chiefly to cartoons and designs, which, scattered far and wide, were reproduced by other artists. His most famous cartoon was the Battle of Pisa, the one executed for the ducal palace of Florence, as pendant to one by Leonardo da Vinci, then in the height of his fame. This picture was so remarkable for the accuracy of drawing, and the variety and form of expression, that Raphael came to Florence on purpose to study it; and it was the power of giving boldness and dignity and variety to the human figure, as shown in this painting, which constitutes his great originality and transcendent excellence. The great creations of the painters, in modern times as well as in the ancient, are those which represent the human figure in its ideal excellence, — which of course implies what is most perfect, not in any one man or woman, but in men and women collectively. Hence the greatest of painters rarely have stooped to landscape painting, since no imaginary landscape can surpass what everybody has seen in nature. You cannot improve on the colors of the rainbow, or the gilded clouds of sunset, or the shadows of the mountain, or the graceful form of trees, or the varied tints of leaves and flowers;

but you can represent the figure of a man or woman more beautiful than any one man or woman that has ever appeared. What mortal woman ever expressed the ethereal beauty depicted in a Madonna of Raphael or Murillo? And what man ever had such a sublimity of aspect and figure as the creations of Michael Angelo? Why, "a beggar," says one of his greatest critics, "arose from his hand the patriarch of poverty; the hump of his dwarf is impressed with dignity; his infants are men, and his men are giants." And, says another critic, "he is the inventor of epic painting, in that sublime circle of the Sistine Chapel which exhibits the origin, progress, and final dispensation of the theocracy. He has personified motion in the cartoon of Pisa, portrayed meditation in the prophets and sibyls of the Sistine Chapel and in the Last Judgment, traced every attitude which varies the human body, with every passion which sways the human soul." His supremacy is in the mighty soaring of his intellectual conceptions. Marvellous as a creator, like Shakspeare; profound and solemn, like Dante; representing power even in repose, and giving to the Cyclopean forms which he has called into being a charm of moral excellence which secures our sympathy; a firm believer in a supreme and personal God; disciplined in worldly trials, and glowing in lofty conceptions of justice, — he delights in portraying the stern prophets of Israel, surrounded with an atmosphere of holiness, yet breathing compassion on those whom they denounce; august in dignity, yet melting with tenderness; solemn, sad, profound. Thus was his influence pure and exalted in an art which has too often been prostituted to please the perverted taste of a sensual age. The most refined and expressive of all the arts,—as it sometimes is, and always should be,—is the one which oftenest appeals to that which Christianity teaches us to shun. You may say, "Evil to him who evil thinks," especially ye pure and immaculate persons who have walked uncorrupted amid the galleries of Paris, Dresden, Florence, and Rome; but I fancy that pictures, like books, are what we choose to make them, and that the more exquisite the art by which vice is divested of its grossness, but not of its subtle poisons,—like the New Héloïse of Rousseau or the Wilhelm Meister of Goethe,—the more fatally will it lead astray by the insidious entrance of an evil spirit in the guise of an angel of light. Art, like literature, is neither good nor evil abstractly, but may become a savor of death unto death, as well as of life unto life. You cannot extinguish it without destroying one of the noblest developments of civilization; but you cannot have civilization without multiplying the temptations of human society, and hence must be guarded from those destructive cankers which, as in old Rome, eat out the virtues on which the strength of man is based. The old apostles, and other great benefactors of the world, attached more value to the truths which elevate than to the arts which soften. It was the noble direction which Michael Angelo gave to art which made him a great benefactor not only of civilization, but also of art, by linking with it the eternal ideas of majesty and dignity, as well as the truths which are taught by divine inspiration, — another illustration of the profound reverence which the great master minds of the world, like Augustine, Pascal, and Bacon, have ever expressed for the ideas which were revealed by Christianity and the old prophets of Jehovah; ideas which many bright but inferior intellects, in their egotistical arrogance, have sought to subvert.

Yet it was neither as sculptor nor painter that Michael Angelo left the most enduring influence, but as architect. Painting and sculpture are the exclusive ornaments and possession of the rich and favored. But architecture concerns all men, and most men have something to do with it in the course of their lives. What boots it that a man pays two thousand pounds for a picture to be shut up in his library, and probably more valued for its rarity, or from the caprices of fashion, than for its real merits? But it is something when a nation pays a million for a ridiculous building, without regard to the object for which it is intended, — to be observed and criticised by everybody and for succeeding generations. A good picture is the admiration of a few; a magnificent edifice is the pride of thousands. A picture necessarily cultivates the taste of a family circle; a public edifice educates the minds of millions. Even the Moses of Michael Angelo is a mere object of interest to those who visit the church of San Pietro in Vincoli; but St. Peter's is a monument to be seen by large populations from generation to generation. All London contemplates St. Paul's Church or the Palace of Westminster, but the National Gallery may be visited by a small fraction of the people only once a year. Of the thousands who stand before the Tuileries or the Madeleine not one in a hundred has visited the gallery of the Louvre. What material works of man so grand as those hoary monuments of piety or pride erected three thousand years ago, and still magnificent in their very ruins! How imposing are the pyramids, the Coliseum, and the Gothic cathedrals of the Middle Ages! And even when architecture does not rear vaulted roofs and arches and pinnacles, or tower to dazzling heights, or inspire reverential awe from the associations which cluster around it, how interesting are even its minor triumphs! Who does not stop to admire a beautiful window, or porch, or portico? Who does not criticise his neighbor's house, its proportions, its general effect, its adaptation to the uses designed? Architecture never wearies us, for its wonders are inexhaustible; they appeal to the common eye, and have reference to the necessities of man, and sometimes express the consecrated sentiments of an age or a nation. Nor can it be prostituted, like painting and sculpture; it never corrupts the mind, and sometimes inspires it; and if it makes an appeal to the senses or the imagination, it is to kindle perceptions of the severe beauty of geometrical forms.

Whoever, then, has done anything in architecture has contributed to the necessities of man, and stimulated an admiration for what is venerable and magnificent. Now Michael Angelo was not only the architect of numerous palaces and churches, but also one of the principal architects of that great edifice which is, on the whole, the noblest church in Christendom, — a perpetual marvel and study; not faultless, but so imposing that it will long remain, like the old temple of Ephesus, one of the wonders of the world. He completed the church without great deviation from the plan of the first architect, Bramante, whom he regarded as the greatest architect that had lived, — altering Bramante's plans from a Latin to a Greek cross, the former of which was retained after Michael Angelo's death. But it is the interior, rather than the exterior of St. Peter's, which shows its vast superiority over all other churches for splendor and effect, and surprises all who are even fresh from Cologne and Milan and Westminster. It impresses us like a wonder of nature rather than as the work of man, — a great work of engineering as well as a marvel of majesty and beauty. We are surprised to see so vast a structure, covering nearly five acres, so elaborately finished, nothing neglected; the lofty walls covered with precious marbles, the side chapels filled with statues and monuments, the altars ornamented with pictures, — and those pictures not painted in oil, but copied in mosaic, so that they will neither decay nor fade, but last till destroyed by violence. What feelings overpower the poetic mind when the glories of that interior first blaze upon the brain; what a world of brightness, softness, and richness; what grandeur, solidity, and strength; what unnumbered treasures around the altars; what grand mosaics relieve the height of the wondrous dome, — larger than .the Pantheon, rising two hundred feet from the intersection of those lofty and massive piers which divide transept from choir and nave; what effect of magnitude after the eye gets accustomed to the vast proportions! Oh, what silence reigns around! How difficult, even for the sonorous chants of choristers and priests to disturb that silence, — to be more than echoes of a distant music which seems to come from the very courts of heaven itself: to some a holy sanctuary, where one may meditate among crowds and feel alone; where one breathes an atmosphere which changes not with heat or cold; and where the ever-burning lamps and clouds of incense diffusing the fragrance of the East, and the rich dresses of the mitred priests, and the unnumbered symbols, suggest the ritualism of that imposing worship when Solomon dedicated to Jehovah the grandest temple of antiquity!

Truly was St. Peter's Church the last great achievement of the popes, the crowning demonstration of their temporal dominion; suggestive of their wealth and power, a marble history of pride and pomp, a fitting emblem of that worship which appeals to sense rather than to God. And singular it was, when the great artist reared that gigantic pile, even though it symbolized the cross, he really gave a vital wound to that cause to which he consecrated his noblest energies; for its lofty dome could not be completed without the contributions of Christendom, and those contributions could not be made without an appeal to false principles which entered into Mediæval Catholicism,— even penance and self-expiation, which stirred the holy indignation of a man who knew and declared on what different ground justification should be based. Thus was Luther, in one sense, called into action by the labors of Michael Angelo; thus was the erection of St. Peter's Church overruled in the preaching of reformers, who would show that the money obtained by the sale of indulgences for sin could never purchase an acceptable offering to God, even though the monument were filled with Christian emblems, and consecrated by those prayers and anthems which had been the life of blessed saints and martyrs for more than a thousand years.

St. Peter's is not Gothic, it is a restoration of the Greek; it belongs to what artists call the Renaissance, — a style of architecture marked by a return to the classical models of antiquity. Michael Angelo brought back to civilization the old ideas of Grecian grace and Roman majesty,— typical of the original inspirations of the men who lived in the quiet admiration of eternal beauty and grace; the men who built the Parthenon, and who shaped pillars and capitals and entablatures in the severest proportions, and fitted them with ornaments drawn from the living world,— plants and animals, especially images of God's highest work, even of man; and of man not worn and macerated and dismal and monstrous, but of man when most resplendent in the perfections of the primeval strength and beauty. He returned to a style which classical antiquity carried to great perfection, but which had been neglected by the new Teutonic nations.

Nor is there evidence that Michael Angelo disdained the creations especially seen in those Gothic monuments which are still the objects of our admiration. Who does not admire the church architecture of the

Middle Ages? Of its kind it has never been surpassed. Geometry and art — the true and the beautiful — meet. Nothing ever erected by the hand of man surpasses the more famous cathedrals of the twelfth and thirteenth centuries, in the richness and variety of their symbolic decorations. They typify the great ideas of Christianity; they inspire feelings of awe and reverence; they are astonishing structures, in their magnitude and in their effect. Monuments are they of religious zeal and poetical inspiration, — the creations of great artists, although we scarcely know their names; adapted to the uses designed; the expression of consecrated sentiments; the marble history of the ages in which they were erected, — now heavy and sombre when society was enslaved and mournful; and then cheerful and lofty when Christianity was joyful and triumphant. Who ever was satisfied in contemplating the diversified wonders of those venerable structures? Who would lose the impression which almost overwhelmed the mind when York minster, or Cologne, or Milan, or Amiens was first beheld, with their lofty spires and towers, their sculptured pinnacles, their flying buttresses, their vaulted roofs, their long arcades, their purple windows, their holy altars, their symbolic carvings, their majestic outlines, their grand proportions!

But beautiful, imposing, poetical, and venerable as are these hoary piles, they are not the all in all of art.

Suppose all the buildings of Europe the last four hundred years had been modelled from these churches, how gloomy would be our streets, how dark and dingy our shops, how dismal our dwellings, how inconvenient our hotels! A new style was needed, at least as a supplement of the old, — as lances and shields were giving place to fire-arms, and the line and the plummet for the mariner's compass; as a new civilization was creating new wants and developing the material necessities of man.

So Michael Angelo arose, and revived the imperishable models of the classical ages, — to be applied not merely to churches but to palaces, civic halls, theatres, libraries, museums, banks, — all of which have mundane purposes. The material world had need of conveniences, as much as the Mediæval age had need of shrines. Humanity was to be developed as well as the Deity to be worshipped. The artist took the broadest views, looking upon Gothic architecture as but one division of art, — even as truth is greater than any system, and Christianity wider than any sect. O, how this Shakspeare of art would have smiled on the vague and transcendental panegyrics of Michelet or Ruskin, and other sentimental admirers of an age which never can return! And how he might have laughed at some modern enthusiasts, who trace religion to the disposition of stones and arches, forgetting that religion is an inspiration which comes from God, and never from the work of man's hands, which can be only a form of idolatry.

Michael Angelo found that the ornamentations of the ancient temples were as rich and varied as those of Mediæval churches. Mouldings were discovered of incomparable elegance; the figures on entablatures were found to be chiselled accurately from nature; the pillars were of matchless proportions, the capitals of graceful curvatures. He saw beauty in the horizontal lines of the Parthenon, as much as in the vertical lines of Cologne. He would not pull down the venerable monuments of religious zeal, but he would add to them. "Because the pointed arch was sacred, he would not despise the humble office of the lintel." And in southern climates especially there was no need of those steep Gothic roofs which were intended to prevent a great weight of rain and snow, and where the graceful portico of the Greeks was more appropriate than the heavy tower of the Lombards. He would seize on everything that the genius of past ages had indorsed, even as Christianity itself appropriates everything human, — science, art, music, poetry, eloquence, literature, — sanctifies it, and dedicates it to the Lord; not for the pride of priests, but for the improvement of humanity. Civilization may exist with Paganism, but only performs its highest uses when tributary to Christianity. And Christianity accepts the tribute which even Pagan civilization offers for the adornment of our race, — expelled from Paradise, and doomed to hard and bitter toils, — without abdicating her more glorious office of raising the soul to heaven.

Nor was Michael Angelo responsible for the vile mongrel architecture which followed the Renaissance, and which disfigures the modern capitals of Europe, any more than for the perversion of painting in the hands of Titian. But the indiscriminate adoption of pillars for humble houses, shops with Roman arches, spires and towers erected on Grecian porticoes, are no worse than schoolhouses built like convents, and chapels designed for preaching as much as for choral chants made dark and gloomy, where the voice of the preacher is lost and wasted amid vaulted roofs and useless pillars. Michael Angelo encouraged no incongruities; he himself conceived the beautiful and the true, and admired it wherever found, even amid the excavations of ruined cities. He may have overrated the buried monuments of ancient art, but how was he to escape the universal enthusiasm of his age for the remains of a glorious and forgotten civilization? Perhaps his mind was wearied with the Middle Ages, from which he had nothing more to learn, and sought a greater fulness and a more perfect unity in the expanding forces of a new and grander era than was ever seen by Pagan heroes or by Gothic saints.

But I need not expatiate on the new ideas which Michael Angelo accepted, or the impulse he gave to art in all its forms, and to the revival of which civilization is so much indebted. Let us turn and give a parting look at the man, — that great creative genius who had no superior in his day and generation. Like the greatest of all Italians, he is interesting for his grave experiences, his dreary isolations, his vast attainments, his creative imagination, and his lofty moral sentiments. Like Dante, he stands apart from, and superior to, all other men of his age. He never could sport with jesters, or laugh with buffoons, or chat with fools; and because of this he seemed to be haughty and disdainful. Like Luther, he had no time for frivolities, and looked upon himself as commissioned to do important work. He rejoiced in labor, and knew no rest until he was eighty-nine. He ate that he might live, not lived that he might eat. For seventeen years after he was seventy-two he worked on St. Peter's church; worked without pay, that he might render to God his last earthly tribute without alloy,— as religious as those unknown artists who erected Rheims and Westminster. He was modest and patient, yet could not submit to the insolence of little men in power. He even left the papal palace in disdain when he found his labors unappreciated. Julius II. was forced to bend to the stern artist, not the artist to the Pope. Yet when Leo X. sent him to quarry marbles for nine years, he submitted without complaint. He had no craving for riches like Rubens, no love of luxury like Raphael, no envy like Da Vinci. He never over-tasked his brain, or suffered himself, like Raphael, — who died exhausted at thirty-seven, — to crowd three days into one, knowing that over-work exhausts the nervous energies and shortens life. He never attempted to open the doors which Providence had plainly shut against him, but waited patiently for his day, knowing it would come; yet whether it came or not, it was all the same to him, — a man with all the holy rapture of a Kepler, and all the glorious self-reliance of a Newton. He was indeed jealous of his fame, but he was not greedy of admiration. He worked without the stimulus of praise, — one of the rarest things, — urged on purely by love of art. He loved art for its own sake, as good men love virtue, as Palestrina loved music, as Bacon loved truth, as Kant loved philosophy, — satisfied with itself as its own reward. He disliked to be patronized, but always remembered benefits, and loved the tribute of respect and admiration, even as he scorned the empty flatterer of fashion. He was the soul of sincerity as well as of magnanimity; and hence had great capacity for friendship, as well as great power of self-sacrifice

His friendship with Vittoria Colonna is as memorable as that of Jerome and Paula, or that of Hildebrand and the Countess Matilda. He was a great patriot, and clung to his native Florence with peculiar affection. Living in habits of intimacy with princes and cardinals, he never addressed them in adulatory language, but talked and acted like a nobleman of nature, whose inborn and superior greatness could be tested only by the ages. He placed art on the highest pinnacle of the temple of humanity, but dedicated that temple to the God of heaven in whom he believed. His person was not commanding, but intelligence radiated from his features, and his earnest nature commanded respect. In childhood he was feeble, but temperance made him strong. He believed that no bodily decay was incompatible with intellectual improvement. He continued his studies until he died, and felt that he had mastered nothing. He was always dissatisfied with his own productions. *Excelsior* was his motto, as Alp on Alp arose upon his view. His studies were diversified and vast. He wrote poetry as well as carved stone, his sonnets especially holding a high rank. He was engineer as well as architect, and fortified Florence against her enemies. When old he showed all the fire of youth, and his eye, like that of Moses, never became dim, since his strength and his beauty were of the soul, — ever expanding, ever adoring. His temper was stern, but affectionate. He had no mercy on a fool or a dunce, and turned in disgust from those who loved trifles and lies. He was guilty of no immoralities like Raphael and Titian, being universally venerated for his stern integrity and allegiance to duty, — as one who believes that there really is a God to whom he is personally responsible. He gave away his riches, like Ambrose and Gregory, valuing money only as a means of usefulness. Sickened with the world, he still labored for the world, and died in 1564, over eighty-nine years of age, in the full assurance of eternal blessedness in heaven.

His marbles may crumble down, in spite of all that we can do to preserve them as models of hopeless imitation; but the exalted ideas he sought to represent by them, are imperishable and divine, and will be subjects of contemplation when

> "Seas shall waste, the skies to smoke decay,
> Rocks fall to dust, and mountains melt away."

AUTHORITIES.

Grimm's Life of Michael Angelo; Vasari's Lives of the Most Excellent Painters, Sculptors and Architects; Duppa's Life of Michael Angelo; Bayle's Histoire de la Peinture en Italie.

MARTIN LUTHER.

A. D. 1483–1546.

THE PROTESTANT REFORMATION.

MARTIN LUTHER.

THE PROTESTANT REFORMATION.

AMONG great benefactors, Martin Luther is one of the most illustrious. He headed the Protestant Reformation. This movement is so completely interlinked with the literature, the religion, the education, the prosperity — yea, even the political history — of Europe, that it is the most important and interesting of all modern historical changes. It is a subject of such amazing magnitude that no one can claim to be well informed who does not know its leading issues and developments, as it spread from Germany to Switzerland, France, Holland, Sweden, England, and Scotland.

The central and prominent figure in the movement is Luther; but the way was prepared for him by a host of illustrious men, in different countries, — by Savonarola in Italy, by Huss and Jerome in Bohemia, by Erasmus in Holland, by Wyclif in England, and by sundry others, who detested the corruptions they ridiculed and lamented, but could not remove.

How flagrant those evils! Who can deny them? The papal despotism, and the frauds on which it was based; monastic corruptions; penance, and indulgences for sin, and the sale of them, more shameful still; the secular character of the clergy; the pomp, wealth, and arrogance of bishops; auricular confession; celibacy of the clergy, their idle and dissolute lives, their ignorance and superstition; the worship of the images of saints, and masses for the dead; the gorgeous ritualism of the mass; the substitution of legends for the Scriptures, which were not translated, or read by the people; pilgrimages, processions, idle pomps, and the multiplication of holy days; above all, the grinding spiritual despotism exercised by priests, with their inquisitions and excommunications, all centring in the terrible usurpation of the popes, keeping the human mind in bondage, and suppressing all intellectual independence, — these evils prevailed everywhere. I say nothing here of the massacres, the poisonings, the assassinations, the fornications, the abominations of which history accuses many of the pontiffs who sat on papal thrones. Such evils did not stare the German and English in the face, as they did the Italians in the fifteenth century. In Germany the vices were mediæval and monkish, not the unblushing infidelity and levities of the Renaissance, which made a radical reformation in Italy impossible. In Germany and England there was left among the

THE PROTESTANT REFORMATION. 219

people the power of conscience, a rough earnestness of character, the sense of moral accountability, and a fear of divine judgment.

Luther was just the man for his work. Sprung from the people, poor, popular, fervent; educated amid privations, religious by nature, yet with exuberant animal spirits; dogmatic, boisterous, intrepid, with a great insight into realities; practical, untiring, learned, generally cheerful and hopeful; emancipated from the terrors of the Middle Ages, scorning the Middle Ages; progressive in his spirit, lofty in his character, earnest in his piety, believing in the future and in God,—such was the great leader of this emancipating movement. He was not so learned as Erasmus, nor so logical as Calvin, nor so scholarly as Melancthon, nor so broad as Cranmer. He was not a polished man; he was often offensively rude and brusque, and lavish of epithets. Nor was he what we call a modest and humble man; he was intellectually proud, disdainful, and sometimes, when irritated, abusive. None of his pictures represent him as a refined-looking man, scarcely intellectual, but coarse and sensual rather, as Socrates seemed to the Athenians. But with these defects and drawbacks he had just such traits and gifts as fitted him to lead a great popular movement,—bold, audacious, with deep convictions and rapid intellectual processes; prompt, decided, kind-hearted, generous, brave; in sympathy with the people, eloquent, Herculean in energies, with an amazing power of work; electrical in his smile and in his words, and always ready for contingencies. Had he been more polished, more of a gentleman, more fastidious, more scrupulous, more ascetic, more modest, he would have shrunk from his tasks; he would have lost the elasticity of his mind,—he would have been discouraged. Even Saint Augustine, a broader and more catholic man than Luther, could not have done his work. He was a sort of converted Mirabeau. He loved the storms of battle; he impersonated revolutionary ideas. But he was a man of thought, as well as of action.

Luther's origin was of the humblest. Born in Eisleben, Nov. 10, 1483, the son of a poor peasant, his childhood was spent in penury. He was religious from a boy. He was religious when he sang hymns for a living, from house to house, before the people of Mansfield while at school there, and also at the schools of Magdeburg and Eisenach, where he still earned his bread by his voice. His devotional character and his music gained for him a friend who helped him through his studies, till at the age of eighteen he entered the University at Erfurt, where he distinguished himself in the classics and the Mediæval philosophy. And here his religious meditations led him to enter the Augustinian monastery: he entered that strict retreat, as others did, to lead a religious life. The great question of all time pressed upon his mind with peculiar force, "What shall a man give in exchange for his soul?" And it shows that religious life in Germany still burned in many a heart, in spite of the corruptions of the Church, that a young man like Luther should seek the shades of monastic seclusion, for meditation and study. He was a monk, like other monks; but it seems he had religious doubts and fears more than ordinary monks. At first he conformed to the customary ways of men seeking salvation. He walked in the beaten road, like Saint Dominic and Saint Francis; he accepted the great ideas of the Middle Ages, which he was afterwards to repudiate,—he was not beyond them, or greater than they were, at first; he fasted like monks, and tormented his body with austerities, as they did from the time of Benedict; he sang in the choir from early morn, and practised the usual severities. But his doubts and fears remained. He did not, like other monks, find peace and consolation; he did not become seraphic, like Saint Francis, or Bonaventura, or Loyola. Perhaps his nature repelled asceticism; perhaps his inquiring and original mind wanted something better and surer to rest upon than the dreams and visions of a traditionary piety. Had he been satisfied with the ordinary mode of propitiating the Deity, he would never have emerged from his retreat.

To a scholar the monastery had great attractions, even in that age. It was still invested with poetic associations and consecrated usages; it was indorsed by the venerable Fathers of the Church; it was favorable to study, and free from the noisy turmoil of the world. But with all these advantages Luther was miserable. He felt the agonies of an unforgiven soul in quest of peace with God; he could not get rid of them, they pursued him into the immensity of an intolerable night. He was in despair. What could austerities do for *him?* He hungered and thirsted after the truth, like Saint Augustine in Milan. He had no taste for philosophy, but he wanted the repose that philosophers pretended to teach. He was then too narrow to read Plato or Boethius. He was a self-tormented monk without relief; he suffered all that Saint Paul suffered at Tarsus. In some respects this monastic pietism resembled the pharisaism of Saul, in the schools of Tarsus, — a technical, rigid, and painful adherence to rules, fastings, obtrusive prayers, and petty ritualisms, which form the essence and substance of all pharisaism and all monastic life; based on the enormous error that man deserves heaven by external practices, in which, however, he can never perfect himself, though he were to live, like Simeon Stylites, on the top of a pillar for twenty years without once descending; an eternal unrest, because perfection cannot be attained; the most terrible slavery to which a man can be conscientiously doomed, verging into hypocrisy and fanaticism.

It was then that a kind and enlightened friend visited him, and recommended him to read the Bible. The Bible never has been a sealed book to monks; it was ever highly prized; no convent was without it: but it was read with the spectacles of the Middle Ages. Repentance meant penance. In Saint Paul's Epistles Luther discovers the true ground of justification, — not works, but faith; for Paul had passed through similar experiences. Works are good, but faith is the gift of God. Works are imperfect with the best of men, even the highest form of works, to a Mediæval eye, — self-expiation and penance; but faith is infinite, radiating from divine love; faith is a boundless joy, — salvation by the grace of God, his everlasting and precious boon to people who cannot climb to heaven on their hands and knees, the highest gift which God ever bestowed on men, — eternal life.

Luther is thus emancipated from the ideas of the Middle Ages and of the old Syriac monks and of the Jewish Pharisees. In his deliverance he has new hopes and aspirations; he becomes cheerful, and devotes himself to his studies. Nothing can make a man more cheerful and joyful than the cordial reception of a gift which is infinite, a blessing which is too priceless to be bought. The pharisee, the monk, the ritualist, is gloomy, ascetic, severe, intolerant; for he is not quite sure of his salvation. A man who accepts heaven as a gift is full of divine enthusiasm, like Saint Augustine. Luther now comprehends Augustine, the great doctor of the Church, embraces his philosophy and sees how much it has been misunderstood. The rare attainments and interesting character of Luther are at last recognized; he is made a professor of divinity in the new university, which the Elector of Saxony has endowed, at Wittenberg. He becomes a favorite with the students; he enters into the life of the people. He preaches with wonderful power, for he is popular, earnest, original, fresh, electrical. He is a monk still, but the monk is merged in the learned doctor and eloquent preacher. He does not yet even dream of attacking monastic institutions, or the Pope; he is a good Catholic in his obedience to authorities; but he hates the Middle Ages, and all their ghostly, funereal, burdensome, and technical religious customs. He is human, almost convivial, — fond of music, of poetry, of society, of friends, and of the good cheer of the social circle. The people love Luther, for he has a broad humanity. They never did love monks, only feared their maledictions.

About this time the Pope was in great need of money: this was Leo X. He not only squandered his vast revenues in pleasures and pomps, like any secular monarch; he not only collected pictures and statues,— but he wanted to complete St. Peter's Church. It was the crowning glory of papal magnificence. Where was he to get money except from the contributions of Christendom? But kings and princes and bishops and abbots were getting tired of this everlasting drain of money to Rome, in the shape of annats and taxes; so Leo revived an old custom of the Dark Ages, — he would sell indulgences for sin; and he sent his agents to peddle them in every country.

The agent in Saxony was a very vulgar, boisterous, noisy, bullying Dominican, by the name of Tetzel. Luther abhorred him, not so much because he was vulgar and noisy, but because his infamous business derogated from the majesty of God and religion. In wrathful indignation he preached against Tetzel and his practices, — the abominable traffic of indulgences. Only God can forgive sins. It seemed to him to be an insult to the human understanding that any man, even a pope, should grant an absolution for crime. These indulgences were the very worst form of penance, since they made a mockery of virtue. And it was useless to preach against them so long as the principles on which they were based were not assailed. Everybody believed in penance; everybody believed that this, in some form, would insure salvation. It consisted in a temporal penalty or punishment inflicted on the sinner after confession to the priest, as a condition of his receiving absolution or an authoritative pardon of his sin by the Church as God's representative. And the indulgence was originally an official remission of this penalty, to be gained by offerings of money to the Church for its sacred uses. However ingenious this theory, the practice inevitably ran into corruption. The people who bought, the agents who sold, the popes who dispensed, these indulgences used them for the vilest purposes.

Fortunately, in those times in Germany everybody felt he had a soul to save. Neither the popes nor the Church ever lost that idea. The clergy ruled by its force, — by stimulating fears of divine wrath, whereby the wretched sinner would be physically tormented forever, unless he escaped by a propitiation of the Deity, — the common form of which was penance, deeds of supererogation, donations to the Church, self-expiation, works of fear and penitence, which commended themselves to the piety of the age; and this piety Luther now believed to be unenlightened, not the kind enjoined by Christ or Paul.

So, to instruct his students and the people as to the true ground of justification, which he had worked out from the study of the Bible and Saint Augustine amid the agonies of a tormented conscience, Luther prepared his theses, — those celebrated ninety-five propositions, which he affixed to the gates of the church of Wittenberg, and which excited a great sensation throughout Northern Germany, reaching even the eyes of the Pope himself, who did not comprehend their tendency, but was struck with their power. "This Doctor Luther," said he, "is a man of fine genius." The students of the university, and the people generally, were kindled as if by Pentecostal fires. The new invention of printing scattered those theses everywhere, far and near; they reached the humble hamlet as well as the palaces of bishops and princes. They excited immediate and immense enthusiasm: there was freshness in them, originality, and great ideas. We cannot wonder at the enthusiasm which those religious ideas excited nearly four hundred years ago when we reflect that they were not cant words then, not worn-out platitudes, not dead dogmas, but full of life and exciting interest, — even as were the watchwords of Rousseau — "Liberty, Fraternity, Equality" — to Frenchmen, on the outbreak of their political revolution. And as those watchwords — abstractly true — roused the dormant energies of the French to a terrible conflict against feudalism and royalty, so those theses of Luther kindled Germany into a living flame. And why? Because they presented more cheerful and comforting grounds of justification than had been preached for one thousand years, — faith rather than penance; for works hinged on penance. The underlying principle of those propositions was *grace*, — divine grace to save the world, — the principle of Paul and Saint Augustine; therefore not new, but forgotten; a mighty comfort to miserable people, mocked and cheated and robbed by a venal and a gluttonous clergy. Even Taine admits that this doctrine of grace is the foundation stone of Protestantism as it spread over Europe in the sixteenth century. In those places where Protestantism is dead, —where rationalism or Pelagian speculations have taken its place, — this fact may be denied; but the history of Northern Europe blazes with it, — a fact which no historian of any honesty can deny.

Very likely those who are not in sympathy with this great idea of Luther, Augustine, and Paul may ignore the fact, — even as Caleb Cushing once declared to me, that the Reformation sprang from the desire of Luther to marry Catherine Bora; and that learned and ingenious sophist overwhelmed me with his citations from infidel and ribald Catholic writers like Audin. Greater men than he deny that grace underlies the whole original movement of the reformers, and they talk of the Reformation as a mere revolt from Rome, as a war against papal corruption, as a protest against monkery and the dark ages, brought about by the spirit of a new age, the onward march of humanity, the necessary progress of society. I admit the secondary causes of the Reformation, which are very important, — the awakened spirit of inquiry in the sixteenth century, the revival of poetry and literature and art, the breaking up of feudalism, fortunate discoveries, the introduction of Greek literature, the Renaissance, the disgusts of Christendom, the voice of martyrs calling aloud from their funeral pyres; yea, the friendly hand of princes and scholars deploring the evils of a corrupted Church. But how much had Savonarola, or Erasmus, or John Huss, or the Lollards aroused the enthusiasm of Europe, great and noble as were their angry and indignant protests? The genius of the Reformation in its early stages was a *religious* movement, not a political or a moral one, although it became both political and moral. Its strength and fervor were in the new ideas of salvation, — the same that gave power to the early preachers of Christianity, — not denunciations of imperialism and slavery, and ten thousand evils which disgraced the empire, but the proclamation of the ideas of Paul as to the grounds of hope when the soul should leave the body; the salvation of the Lord, declared to a world in bondage. Luther kindled the same religious life among the masses that the apostles did; the same that Wyclif did, and by the same means, — the declaration of salvation by belief in the incarnate Son of God, shedding his blood in infinite love. Why, see how this idea spread through Germany, Switzerland, and France. and took possession of the minds of the English and Scotch yeomanry, with all their stern and earnest ruggedness. See how it was elaborately expanded by Calvin, how it gave birth to a new and strong theology, how it entered into the very life of the people, especially among the Puritans, — into the souls of even Cromwell's soldiers. What made "The Pilgrim's Progress" the most popular book ever published in England? Because it reflected the theology of the age, the religion of the people, all based on Luther's theses,— the revival of those old doctrines which converted the Roman provinces from Paganism. I do not care if these statements are denied by Catholics, or rationalists, or progressive savants. What is it to me that the old views have become unfashionable, or are derided, or are dead, in the absorbing materialism of this Epicurean yet brilliant age? I know this, that I am true to history when I declare that the glorious Reformation in which we all profess to rejoice, and which is the greatest movement, and the best, of our modern time, — susceptible of indefinite application, interlinked with the literature and the progress of England and America, — took its first great spiritual start from the ideas of Luther as to justification. This was the voice of heaven's messenger proclaiming aloud, so that the heavens re-echoed to the glorious and triumphant annunciation, and the earth heard and rejoiced with exceeding joy, "Behold, I send tidings of salvation: it is grace, divine grace, which shall undermine the throne of popes and pagans, and reconcile a fallen world to God!"

Yes, it was a Christian philosopher, a theologian, — a doctor of divinity, working out in his cell and study, through terrible internal storm and anguish, and against the whole teaching of monks and bishops and popes and universities, from the time of Charlemagne, the same truth which Augustine learned in his wonderful experiences, — who started the Reformation in the right direction; who became the greatest benefactor of these modern times, because he based his work on everlasting and positive ideas, which had life in them, and hope, and the sanction of divine authority; thus virtually invoking the aid of God Almighty to bring about and restore the true glory of his Church on earth, — a glory forever to be identified with the death of his Son. I see no law of progress here, no natural and necessary development of nations; I see only the light and power of individual genius, brushing away the cobwebs and sophistries and frauds of the Middle Ages, and bringing out to the gaze of Europe the vital truth which, with supernatural aid, made in old times the day of Pentecost. And I think I hear the emancipated people of Saxony exclaim, from the Elector downwards, "If these ideas of Doctor Luther are true, and we feel them to be, then all our penances have been worse than wasted, — we have been **Pagans.** Away with our miserable efforts to scale the heavens! Let us accept what we cannot buy; let us make our palaces and our cottages alike vocal with the praises of Him whom we now accept as our Deliverer, our King, and our Eternal Lord."

Thus was born the first great idea of the Reformation, out of Luther's brain, out of his agonized soul, and sent forth to conquer, and produce changes most marvellous to behold.

It is not my object to discuss the truth or error of this fundamental doctrine. There are many who deny it, even among Protestants. I am not a controversialist, or a theologian: I am simply an historian. I wish to show what is historically true and clear; and I defy all the scholars and critics of the world to prove that this doctrine is not the basal pillar of the Reformation of Luther. I wish to make emphatic the statement that *justification by faith* was, as an historical fact, the great primal idea of Luther; not new, but new to him and to his age.

I have now to show how this idea led to others; how they became connected together; how they produced not only a spiritual movement, but political, moral, and intellectual forces, until all Europe was in a blaze.

Thus far the agitation under Luther had been chiefly theological. It was not a movement against popes **or** institutions, it was not even the vehement denunciation against sin in high places, which inflamed the anger of the Pope against Savonarola. To some it doubtless seemed like the old controversy between Augustine and Pelagius, like the contentions between Dominican and Franciscan monks. But it was too important to escape the attention of even Leo X., although at first he gave it no thought. It was a dangerous agitation; it had become popular; there was no telling where it would end, or what it might not assail. It was deemed necessary to stop the mouth of this bold and intellectual Saxon theologian.

So the voluptuous, infidel, elegant Pope — accomplished in manners and pagan arts and literature — sent one of the most learned men of the Church which called him Father, to argue with Doctor Luther, confute him, conquer him, — deeming this an easy task. But the doctor could not be silenced. His convictions were grounded on the rock; not on Peter, but on the rock from which Peter derived his name. All the papal legates and cardinals in the world could neither convince nor frighten him. He courted argument; he challenged the whole Church to refute him.

Then the schools took up the controversy. All that was imposing in names, in authority, in traditions, in associations, was arrayed against him. They came down upon him with the whole array of scholastic learning. The great Goliath of controversy in that day was Doctor Eck, who challenged the Saxon monk to a public disputation at Leipsic. All Germany was interested. The question at issue stirred the nation to its very depths.

The disputants met in the great hall of the palace of the Elector. Never before was seen in Germany such an array of doctors and theologians and dignitaries. It rivalled in importance and dignity the Council of Nice, when the great Constantine presided, to settle the Trinitarian controversy. The combatants were as great as Athanasius and Arius, — as vehement, as earnest, though not so fierce. Doctor Eck was superior to Luther in reputation, in dialectical skill, in scholastic learning. He was the pride of the universities. Luther, however, had deeper convictions, more genius, greater eloquence, and at that time he was modest.

The champion of the schools, of sophistries and authorities, of dead-letter literature, of quibbles, refinements, and words, soon overwhelmed the Saxon monk with his citations, decrees of councils, opinions of eminent ecclesiastics, the literature of the Church, its mighty authority. He was on the eve of triumph. Had the question been settled, as Doctor Eck supposed, by authorities, as lawyers and pedants would settle the question, Luther would have been beaten. But his genius came to his aid, and the consciousness of truth.

He swept away the premises of the argument. He denied the supreme authority of popes and councils and universities. He appealed to the Scriptures, as the only ultimate ground of authority. He did not deny authority, but appealed to it in its highest form. This was unexpected ground. The Church was not prepared openly to deny the authority of Saint Paul or Saint Peter; and Luther, if he did not gain his case, was far from being beaten, and — what was of vital importance to his success — he had the Elector and the people with him.

Thus was born the second great idea of the Reformation, — the *supreme authority of the Scriptures,* to which Protestants of every denomination have since professed to cling. They may differ in the interpretation of texts, — and thus sects and parties gradually arose, who quarrelled about their meaning, — but none of them deny their supreme authority. All the issues of Protestants have been on the meaning of texts, on the interpretation of the Scriptures, — to be settled by learning and reason. It was not until rationalism arose, and rejected plain and obvious declarations of Scripture, as inconsistent with reason, as interpolations, as uninspired, that the authority of the Scriptures was weakened; and these rationalists — and the land of Luther became full of them — have gone infinitely beyond the Catholics in undermining the Bible.

The Catholics never have taken such bold ground as the rationalists respecting the Scriptures. The Catholic Church still accepts the Bible, but explains away the meaning of many of its doctrines; the rationalists would sweep away its divine authority, extinguish faith, and leave the world in night. Satan came into the theological school of the Protestants, disguised in the robes of learned doctors searching for truth, and took away the props of religious faith. This was worse than baptizing repentance with the name of penance. Better have irrational fears of hell than no fears at all, for this latter is Paganism. Pagan culture and Pagan philosophy could not keep society together in the old Roman world; but Mediæval appeals to the fears of men did keep them from crimes and force upon them virtues.

The triumph of Luther at Leipsic was, however, incomplete. The Catholics rallied after their stunning blow. They said, in substance: "We, too, accept the Scriptures; we even put them above Augustine and Thomas Aquinas and the councils. But who can interpret them? Can peasants and women, or even merchants and nobles? The Bible, though inspired, is full of difficulties; there are contradictory texts. It is a sealed book, except to the learned; only the Church can reconcile its difficulties. And what we mean by the Church is the clergy,—the learned clergy, acknowledging allegiance to their spiritual head, who in matters of faith is also infallible. We can accept nothing which is not indorsed by popes and councils. No matter how plain the Scriptures seem to be, on certain disputed points only the authority of the Church can enlighten and instruct us. We distrust reason, — that is, what you call reason, — for reason can twist anything, and pervert it; but what the Church says, is true, — its collective intelligence is our supreme law [thus putting papal dogmas above reason, above the literal and plain declarations of Scripture]. Moreover, since the Scriptures are to be interpreted only by priests, it is not a safe book for the people. We, the priests, will keep it out of their hands. They will get notions from it fatal to our authority; they will become fanatics; they will, in their conceit, defy us."

Then Luther rose, more powerful, more eloquent, more majestic than before; he rose superior to himself. "What," said he, "keep the light of life from the people; take away their guide to heaven; keep them in ignorance of what is most precious and most exalting; deprive them of the blessed consolations which sustain the soul in trial and in death; deny the most palpable truths, because your dignitaries put on them a construction to bolster up their power! What an abomination! what treachery to heaven! what peril to the souls of men! Besides, your authorities differ. Augustine takes different ground from Pelagius; Bernard from Abélard; Thomas Aquinas from Dun Scotus. Have not your grand councils given contradictory decisions? Whom shall we believe? Yea, the popes themselves, your infallible guides, — have they not at different times rendered different decisions? What would Gregory I. say to the verdicts of Gregory VII.?

"No, the Scriptures are the legacy of the early Church to universal humanity; they are the equal and treasured inheritance of all nations and tribes and kindreds upon the face of the earth, and will be till the day of judgment. It was intended that they should be diffused, and that every one should read them, and interpret them each for himself; for he has a soul to save, and he dare not intrust such a precious thing as his soul into the keeping of selfish and ambitious priests. Take away the Bible from a peasant, or a woman, or any layman, and cannot the priest, armed with the terrors and the frauds of the Middle Ages, shut up his soul in a gloomy dungeon, as noisome and funereal as your Mediæval crypts? And will you, ye boasted intellectual guides of the people, extinguish reason in this world in reference to the most momentous interests? What other guide has a man but his reason? And you would prevent this very reason from being enlightened by the Gospel! You would obscure reason itself by your traditions, O ye blind leaders of the blind! O ye legal and technical men, obscuring the light of truth! O ye miserable Pharisees, ye bigots, ye selfish priests, tenacious of your power, your inventions, your traditions, — will ye withhold the free redemption, God's greatest boon, salvation by the blood of Christ, offered to all the world? Yea, will you suffer the people to perish, soul and body, because you fear that, instructed by God himself, they will rebel against your accursed despotism? Have you considered what a mighty crime you thus commit against God, against man? Ye rule by an infernal appeal to the superstitious fears of men; but how shall ye yourselves, for such crimes, escape the damnation of that hell into which you would push your victims unless they obey *you?*

"No, I say, let the Scriptures be put into the hands of everybody; let every one interpret them for himself, according to the light he has; let there be private judgment; let spiritual liberty be revived, as in Apostolic days. Then only will the people be emancipated from the Middle Ages, and arise in their power and majesty, and obey the voice of enlightened conscience, and be true to their convictions, and practise the virtues which Christianity commands, and obey God rather than man, and defy all sorts of persecution and martyrdom, having a serene faith in those blessed promises which the Gospel unfolds. Then will the people become great, after the conflicts of generations, and put under their feet the mockeries and lies and despotisms which grind them to despair."

Thus was born the third great idea of the Reformation, out of Luther's brain, a logical sequence from the first idea, — *the right of private judgment*, religious liberty, call it what you will; a great inspiration which in after times was destined to march triumphantly over battle-fields, and give dignity and power to the people, and lead to the reception of great truths obscured by priests for one thousand years; the motive of an irresistible popular progress, planting England with Puritans, and Scotland with heroes, and France with martyrs, and North America with colonists; yea, kindling a fervid religious life; creating such men as Knox and Latimer and Taylor and Baxter and Howe, who owed their greatness to the study of the Scriptures, — at last put into every hand, and scattered far and wide, even to India and China. Can anybody doubt the marvellous progress of Protestant nations in consequence of the translation and circulation of the Scriptures? How these are bound up with their national life, and all their social habits, and all their religious aspirations; how they have elevated the people, ten hundred millions of times more than the boasted Renaissance which sprang from apostate and infidel and

Pagan Italy, when she dug up the buried statues of Greece and Rome, and revived the literature and arts which soften, but do not save! — for private judgment and religious liberty mean nothing more and nothing less than the unrestricted perusal of the Scriptures as the guide of life.

This right of private judgment, on which Luther was among the first to insist, and of which certainly he was the first great champion in Europe, was in that age a very bold idea, as well as original. It flattered as well as stimulated the intellect of the people, and gave them dignity; it gave to the Reformation its popular character; it appealed to the mind and heart of Christendom. It gave consolation to the peasantry of Europe; for no family was too poor to possess a Bible, the greatest possible boon and treasure, — read and pondered in the evening, after hard labors and bitter insults; read aloud to the family circle, with its inexhaustible store of moral wealth, its beautiful and touching narratives, its glorious poetry, its awful prophecies, its supernal counsels, its consoling and emancipating truths, — so tender and yet so exalting, raising the soul above the grim trials of toil and poverty into the realms of seraphic peace and boundless joy. The Bible even gave hope to heretics. All sects and parties could take shelter under it; all could stand on the broad platform of religion, and survey from it the wonders and glories of God. At last men might even differ on important points of doctrine and worship, and yet be Protestants. Religious liberty became as wide in its application as the unity of the Church. It might create sects, but those sects would be all united as to the value of the Scriptures and their cardinal declarations. On this broad basis John Milton could shake hands with John Knox, and John Locke with Richard Baxter, and Oliver Cromwell with Queen Elizabeth, and Lord Bacon with William Penn, and Bishop Butler with John Wesley, and Jonathan Edwards with Doctor Channing.

This idea of private judgment is what separates the Catholics from the Protestants; not most ostensibly, but most vitally. Many are the Catholics who would accept Luther's idea of grace, since it is the idea of Saint Augustine; and of the supreme authority of the Scriptures, since they were so highly valued by the Fathers: but few of the Catholic clergy have ever tolerated religious liberty, — that is, the interpretation of the Scriptures by the people, — for it is a vital blow to their supremacy, their hierarchy, and their institutions. They will no more readily accept it than William the Conqueror would have accepted the Magna Charta; for the free circulation and free interpretation of the Scriptures are the charter of human liberties fought for at Leipsic by Gustavus

LUTHER PREACHING AT WARTBURG

From the painting by Hugo Vogel

Adolphus, at Ivry by Henry IV. This right of worshipping God according to the dictates of conscience, enlightened by the free reading of the Scriptures, is just what the "invincible armada" was sent by Philip II. to crush; just what Alva, dictated by Rome, sought to crush in Holland; just what Louis XIV., instructed by the Jesuits, did crush out in France, by the revocation of the Edict of Nantes. The Satanic hatred of this right was the cause of most of the martyrdoms and persecutions of the sixteenth and seventeenth centuries. It was the declaration of this right which emancipated Europe from the dogmas of the Middle Ages, the thraldom of Rome, and the reign of priests. Why should not Protestants of every shade cherish and defend this sacred right? This is what made Luther the idol and oracle of Germany, the admiration of half Europe, the pride and boast of succeeding ages, the eternal hatred of Rome; not his religious experiences, not his doctrine of justification by faith, but the emancipation he gave to the mind of the world. This is what peculiarly stamps Luther as a man of genius, and of that surprising audacity and boldness which only great geniuses evince when they follow out the logical sequence of their ideas, and penetrate at a blow the hardened steel of vulcanic armor beneath which the adversary boasts.

Great was the first Leo, when from his rifled palace

on one of the devastated hills of Rome he looked out upon the Christian world, pillaged, sacked, overrun with barbarians, full of untold calamities, — order and law crushed; literature and art prostrate; justice a byword; murders and assassinations unavenged; central power destroyed; vice, in all its enormities, vulgarities, and obscenities, rampant and multiplying itself; false opinions gaining ground; soldiers turned into banditti, and senators into slaves; women shrieking in terror; bishops praying in despair; barbarism everywhere, paganism in danger of being revived; a world disordered, forlorn, and dismal; Pandemonium let loose, with howling and shouting and screaming, in view of the desolation predicted alike by Jeremy the prophet and the Cumæan sybil; — great was that Leo, when in view of all this he said, with old patrician heroism, "I will revive government once more upon this earth; not by bringing back the Cæsars, but by declaring a new theocracy, by making myself the vicegerent of Christ, by virtue of the promise made to Peter, whose successor I am, in order to restore law, punish crime, head off heresy, encourage genius, conserve peace, heal dissensions, protect learning; appealing to love, but ruling by fear. Who but the Church can do this? A theocracy will create a new civilization. Not a diadem, but a tiara will I wear, the symbol of universal sovereignty, before which barbarism shall flee away, and happiness be restored once more." As he sent out his legates, he fulminated his bulls and established tribunals of appeal; he made a net-work of ecclesiastical machinery, and proclaimed the dangers of eternal fire, and brought kings and princes before him on their knees. The barbaric world was saved.

But greater than Leo was Luther, when — outraged by the corruptions of this spiritual despotism, and all the false and Pagan notions which had crept into theology, obscuring the light of faith and creating an intolerable bondage, and opposing the new spirit of progress which science and art and industry and wealth had invoked — he courageously yet modestly comes forward as the champion of a new civilization, and declares, with trumpet tones, " Let there be private judgment; liberty of conscience; the right to read and interpret Scripture, in spite of priests! so that men may think for themselves, not only on the doctrines of eternal salvation but on all the questions to be deduced from them, or interlinked with the past or present or future institutions of the world. Then shall arise a new creation from dreaded destruction, and emancipated millions shall be filled with an unknown enthusiasm, and advance with the new weapons of reason and truth from conquering to conquer, until all the strongholds of sin and Satan shall be subdued, and laid triumphantly at the foot of His throne whose right it is to reign."

Thus far Luther has appeared as a theologian, a philosopher, a man of ideas, a man of study and reflection, whom the Catholic Church distrusts and fears, as she always has distrusted genius and manly independence; but he is henceforth to appear as a reformer, a warrior, to carry out his ideas, and also to defend himself against the wrath he has provoked; impelled step by step to still bolder aggressions, until he attacks those venerable institutions which he once respected, — all the frauds and inventions of Mediæval despotism, all the machinery by which Europe had been governed for one thousand years; yea, the very throne of the Pope himself, whom he defies, whom he insults, and against whom he urges Christendom to rebel. As a combatant, a warrior, a reformer, his person and character somewhat change. He is coarser, he is more sensual-looking, he drinks more beer, he tells more stories, he uses harder names; he becomes arrogant, dogmatic; he dictates and commands; he quarrels with his friends; he is imperious; he fears nobody, and is scornful of old usages; he marries a nun; he feels that he is a great leader and general, and wields new powers; he is an executive and administrative man, for which his courage and insight and will and Herculean physical strength wonderfully fit him,— the man for the times, the man to head a new movement, the forces of an age of protest and rebellion and conquest.

How can I compress into a few sentences the demolitions and destructions which this indignant and irritated reformer now makes in Germany, where he is protected by the Elector from Papal vengeance? Before the reconstruction, the old rubbish must be cleared away, and Augean stables must be cleansed. He is now at issue with the whole Catholic régime, and the whole Catholic world abuse him. They call him a glutton, a wine-bibber, an adulterer, a scoffer, an atheist, an imp of Satan; and he calls the Pope the scarlet mother of abominations, Antichrist, Babylon. That age is prodigal in offensive epithets; kings and prelates and doctors alike use hard words. They are like angry children and women and pugilists; their vocabulary of abuse is amusing and inexhaustible. See how prodigal Shakspeare and Ben Jonson are in the language of vituperation. But they were all defiant and fierce, for the age was rough and earnest. The Pope, in wrath, hurls the old weapons of the Gregorys and the Clements. But they are impotent as the darts of Priam; Luther laughs at them, and burns the Papal bull before a huge concourse of excited students and shopkeepers and enthusiastic women. He severs himself completely from Rome, and declares an unextinguishable warfare. He destroys and breaks up the ceremonies of the Mass; he pulls down the consecrated altars, with their candles and smoking incense and vessels of silver and gold, since they are the emblems of Jewish and Pagan worship; he tears off the vestments of priests, with their embroideries and their gildings and their millineries and their laces, since these are made to impose on the imagination and appeal to the sense; he breaks up monasteries and convents, since they are dens of infamy, cages of unclean birds, nurseries of idleness and pleasure, abodes at the best of narrow-minded, ascetic Asiatic recluses, who rejoice in penance and self-expiation and other modes of propitiating the Deity, like soofists and fakirs and Braminical devotees. In defiance of the most sacred of the institutions of the Middle Ages, he openly marries Catherine Bora and sets up a hilarious household, and yet a household of prayer and singing. He abolishes the old Gregorian service; and for Mediæval chants, monotonous and gloomy, he prepares hymns and songs, — not for boys and priests to intone in the distant choir, but for the whole congregation to sing, inspired by the melodies of David and the exulting praises of a Saviour who redeems from darkness into light. How grand that hymn of his, —

> "A mighty fortress is our God,
> A bulwark never failing."

He makes worship more heartfelt, and revives apostolic usages: preaching and exhortation and instruction from the pulpit, — a forgotten power. He appeals to reason rather than sense; denounces superstitions, while he rebukes sins; and kindles a profound fervor, based on the recognition of new truths. He is not fully emancipated from the traditions of the past; for he retains the doctrine of transubstantiation, and keeps up the holidays of the Church, and allows recreation on the Sabbath. But what he thinks the most of is the circulation of the Scriptures among plain people. So he translates them into German, — a gigantic task; and this work, almost single-handed, is done so well that it becomes the standard of the German language, as the Bible of Tindale helped to form the English tongue; and not only so, but it has remained the common version in use throughout Germany, even as the authorized King James version, made nearly a century later by the labor of many scholars and divines, has remained the standard English Bible. Moreover, he finds time to make liturgies and creeds and hymns, and to write letters to all parts of Christendom, — a Jerome, a Chrysostom, and an Augustine united; a kind of Protestant pope, to whom everybody looks for advice and consolation. What a wonderful man! No wonder the Germans are so fond of him and so proud of him, — a Briareus with a hundred arms; a marvel, a wonder, a prodigy of nature; the most gifted, versatile, hard-working man of his century or nation!

At last, this great theologian, this daring innovator, is

summoned by imperial, not papal, authority before the Diet of the empire at Worms, where the Emperor, the great Charles V., presides, amid bishops, princes, cardinals, legates, generals, and dignitaries. Thither Luther must go,—yet under imperial safe conduct,—and consummate his protests, and perhaps offer up his life. Painters, poets, historians, have made that scene familiar,—the most memorable in the life of Luther, as well as one of the grandest spectacles of the age. I need not dwell on that exciting scene, where, in the presence of all that was illustrious and powerful in Germany, this defenceless doctor dares to say to supremest temporal and spiritual authority, "Unless you confute me by arguments drawn from Scripture, I cannot and will not recant anything . . . Here I stand; I cannot otherwise: God help me! Amen." How superior to Galileo and other scientific martyrs! He is not afraid of those who can kill only the body; he is afraid only of Him who hath power to cast both soul and body into hell. So he stands as firm as the eternal pillars of justice, and his cause is gained. What if he did not live long enough to accomplish all he designed! What if he made mistakes, and showed in his career many of the infirmities of human nature! What if he cared very little for pictures and statues,—the revived arts of Greece and Rome, the Pagan Renaissance in which he only sees infidelity, levities, and luxuries, and other abominations which excited his disgust and abhorrence when he visited Italy! *He* seeks, not to amuse and adorn the Papal empire, but to reform it; as Paul before him sought to plant new sentiments and ideas in the Roman world, indifferent to the arts of Greece, and even the beauties of nature, in his absorbing desire to convert men to Christ. And who, since Paul, has rendered greater service to humanity than Luther? The whole race should be proud that such a man has lived.

We will not follow the great reformer to the decline of his years; we will not dwell on his subsequent struggles and dangers, his marvellous preservation, his personal habits, his friendships and his hatreds, his joys and sorrows, his bitter alienations, his vexations, his disappointments, his gloomy anticipations of approaching strife, his sickened yet exultant soul, his last days of honor and of victory, his final illness, and his triumphant death in the town where he was born. It is his legacy that we are concerned in, the inheritance he left to succeeding generations, — the perpetuated ideas of the Reformation, which he worked out in anguish and in study, and which we will not let die, but will cherish in our memories and our hearts, as among the most precious of the heirlooms of genius, susceptible of boundless application. And it is destined to grow brighter and richer, in spite of counter-reformation and

Jesuitism, of Pagan levities and Pagan lies, of boastful science and Epicurean pleasures, of material glories, of dissensions and sects and parties, as the might and majesty of ages coursing round the world regenerates institutions and nations, and proclaims the sovereignty of intelligence, the glory and the power of God.

AUTHORITIES.

Ranke's Reformation in Germany; D'Aubigné's History of the Reformation; Luther's Letters; Mosheim's History of the Church; Melancthon's Life of Luther: Erasmi Epistolæ; Encyclopædia Britannica.

THOMAS CRANMER.

A. D. 1489–1556.

THE ENGLISH REFORMATION.

THOMAS CRANMER.

THE ENGLISH REFORMATION.

AS the great interest of the Middle Ages, in an historical point of view, centres around the throne of the popes, so the most prominent subject of historical interest in our modern times is the revolt from their almost unlimited domination. The Protestant Reformation, in its various relations, was a movement of transcendent importance. The history of Christendom, in a moral, a political, a religious, a literary, and a social point of view, for the last three hundred years, cannot be studied or comprehended without primary reference to that memorable revolution.

We have seen how that great insurrection of human intelligence was headed in Germany by Luther, and we shall shortly consider it in Switzerland and France under Calvin. We have now to contemplate the movement in England.

The most striking figure in it was doubtless Thomas Cranmer, Archbishop of Canterbury, although he does not represent the English Reformation in all its phases. He was neither so prominent nor so great a man as Luther or Calvin, or even Knox. But, taking him all in all, he was the most illustrious of the English reformers; and he, more than any other man, gave direction to the spirit of reform, which had been quietly working ever since the time of Wyclif, especially among the humbler classes.

The English Reformation — the way to which had been long preparing — began in the reign of Henry VIII.; and this unscrupulous and tyrannical monarch, without being a religious man, gave the first great impulse to an outbreak the remote consequences of which he did not anticipate, and with which he had no sympathy. He rebelled against the authority of the Pope, without abjuring the Roman Catholic religion, either as to dogmas or forms. In fact, the first great step towards reform was made, not by Cranmer, but by Thomas Cromwell, Earl of Essex, as the prime minister of Henry VIII., — a man of whom we really know the least of all the very great statesmen of English history. It was he who demolished the monasteries, and made war on the whole monastic system, and undermined the papal power in England, and swept away many of the most glaring of those abuses which disgraced the Papal Empire. Armed with the powers which Wolsey had wielded, he directed them into a totally different channel, so far as the religious welfare of the nation is considered, although in his principles of government he was as absolute as Richelieu. Like the great French statesman, he exalted the throne; but, unlike him, he promoted the personal reign of the sovereign he served with remarkable ability and devotion.

Thomas Cromwell, the prime minister of Henry VIII., after the fall of Wolsey, was born in humble ranks, and was in early life a common soldier in the wars of Italy, then a clerk in a mercantile house in Antwerp, then a wool merchant in Middleborough, then a member of Parliament, and was employed by Wolsey in suppressing some of the smaller monasteries. His fidelity to his patron Wolsey, at the time of that great cardinal's fall, attracted the special notice of the King, who made him royal secretary in the House of Commons. He made his fortune by advising Henry to declare himself Head of the English Church, when he was entangled in the difficulties growing out of the divorce of Catharine. This advice was given with the patriotic view of making the royal authority superior to that of the Pope in Church patronage, and of making England independent of Rome.

The great scandal of the times was the immoral lives of the clergy, especially of the monks, and the immunities they enjoyed. They were a hindrance to the royal authority, and weakened the resources of the country by the excessive drain of gold and silver sent to Rome to replenish the papal treasury. Cromwell would make the clergy dependent on the King and not on the Pope for their investitures and promotions; and he abominated the idle and vagabond lives of the monks, who had degenerated in England, perhaps more than in any other country in Europe, in consequence of the great wealth of their monasteries. He was able to render his master and the kingdom a great service, from the powers lavished upon him. He presided at convocations as the King's vicegerent; controlled the House of Commons, and was inquisitor-general of the monasteries; he was foreign and home secretary, vicar-general, and president of the star-chamber or privy-council. The proud Nevilles, the powerful Percies, and the noble Courtenays all bowed before this plebeian son of a mechanic, who had arisen by force of genius and lucky accidents,— too wise to build a palace like Hampton Court, but not ecclesiastical enough in his sympathies to found a college like Christ's Church as Wolsey did. He was a man simple in his tastes, and hard-working like Colbert, — the great finance minister of France under Louis XIV., — whom he resembled in his habits and policy.

His great task, as well as his great public service, was the visitation and suppression of monasteries. He perceived that they had fulfilled their mission; that they were no longer needed; that they had become corrupt, and too corrupt to be reformed; that they were no longer abodes of piety, or beehives of industry, or nurseries of art, or retreats of learning; that their wealth was squandered; that they upheld the arm of a foreign power; that they shielded offenders against the laws; that they encouraged vagrancy and extortion; that, in short, they were nests of unclean birds.

The monks and friars opposed the new learning now extending from Italy to France, to Germany, and to England. Colet came back from Italy, not to teach Platonic mysticism, but to unlock the Scriptures in the original,— the centre of a group of scholars at Oxford, of whom Erasmus and Thomas More stood in the foremost rank. Before the close of the fifteenth century, it is said that ten thousand editions of various books had been printed in different parts of Europe. All the Latin authors, and some of the Greek, were accessible to students. Tunstall and Latimer were sent to Padua to complete their studies. Fox, bishop of Winchester, established a Greek professorship at Oxford. It was an age of enthusiasm for reviving literature, — which, however, received in Germany, through the influence chiefly of Luther, a different direction from what it received in Italy, and which extended from Germany to England. But to this awakened spirit the monks presented obstacles and discouragements. They had no sympathy with progress; they belonged to the Dark Ages; they were hostile to the circulation of the Scriptures; they were pedlers of indulgences and relics; impostors, frauds, vagabonds, gluttons, worldly, sensual, and avaricious.

So notoriously corrupt had monasteries become that repeated attempts had been made to reform them, but without success. As early as 1489, Innocent VII. had issued a commission for a general investigation. The monks were accused of dilapidating public property, of frequenting infamous places, of stealing jewels from consecrated shrines. In 1511, Archbishop Warham instituted another visitation. In 1523 Cardinal Wolsey himself undertook the task of reform. At last the Parliament, in 1535, appointed Cromwell vicar or visitor-general, issued a commission, and intrusted it to lawyers, not priests, who found that the worst had not been told. It was found that two thirds of the monks of England were living in concubinage; that their lands were wasted and mortgaged, and their houses falling into ruins. They found the Abbot of Fountains surrounded with more women than Mohammed allowed his followers, and the nuns of Litchfield scandalously immoral.

On this report, the Lords and Commons — deliberately, not rashly — decreed the suppression of all monasteries the income of which was less than two hundred pounds a year, and the sequestration of their lands to the King. About two hundred of the lesser convents were thus suppressed, and the monks turned adrift, yet not entirely without support. This spoliation may have been a violation of the rights of property, but the monks had betrayed their trusts. The next Parliament completed the work. In 1539 all the religious houses were suppressed, both great and small. Such venerable and princely retreats as St. Albans, Glastonbury, Reading, Bury St. Edmunds, and Westminster, which had flourished one thousand years, — founded long before the Conquest, — shared the common ruin. These probably would have been spared, had not the first suppression filled the country with traitors. The great insurrection in Lincolnshire which shook the foundation of the throne, the intrigues of Cardinal Pole, the Cornish conspiracy in which the great house of Neville was implicated, and various other agitations, were all fomented by the angry monks.

Rapacity was not the leading motive of Henry or his minister, but the public welfare. The measure of suppression and sequestration was violent, but called for. Cromwell put forth no such sophistical pleas as those revolutionists who robbed the French clergy, — that their property belonged to the nation. In France the clergy were despoiled, not because they were infamous, but because they were rich. In England the monks may have suffered injustice from the severity of their punishment, but no one now doubts that punishment was deserved. Nor did Henry retain all the spoils himself: he gave away the abbey lands with a prodigality equal to his rapacity. He gave them to those who upheld his throne, as a reward for service or loyalty. They were given to a new class of statesmen, who led the popular party,— like the Fitzwilliams, the Russells, the Dudleys, and the Seymours,— and thus became the foundation of their great estates. They were also distributed to many merchants and manufacturers who had been loyal to the government. From one-third to two-thirds of the landed property of the kingdom,— as variously estimated,— thus changed hands. It was an enormous confiscation,— nearly as great as that made by William the Conqueror in favor of his army of invaders. It must have produced an immense impression on the mind of Europe. It was almost as great a calamity to the Catholic Church of England as the emancipation of slaves was to their Southern masters in our late war. Such a spoliation of the Church had not before taken place in any country of Europe. How great an evil the monastic system must have been regarded by Parliament to warrant such an act! Had it not been popular, there would have been discontents amounting to a general hostility to the throne.

It must also be borne in mind that this dissolution of the monasteries, this attack on the monastic system, was not a religious movement fanned by reformers, but an act of Parliament, at the instance of a royal minister. It was not done under the direction of a Protestant king,— for Henry was never a Protestant, — but as a public measure in behalf of morality and for reasons of State. It is true that Henry had, by his marriage with Anne Boleyn and the divorce of his virtuous queen, defied the Pope and separated England from Rome, so far as appointments to ecclesiastical benefices are concerned. But in offending the Pope he also equally offended Charles V. The results of his separation from Rome, during his life, were purely political. The King did not give up the Mass or the Roman communion or Roman dogmas of faith; he only prepared the way for reform in the next reign. He only intensified the hatred between the old conservative party and the party of reform and progress.

How far Cromwell himself was a Protestant it is difficult to tell. Doubtless he sympathized with the new religious spirit of the age, but he did not openly avow the faith of Luther. He was the able and unscrupulous minister of an absolute monarch, bent on sweeping away abuses of all kinds, but with the idea of enlarging the royal authority as much, perhaps, as promoting the prosperity of the realm.

He therefore turned his attention to the ecclesiastical courts, which from the time of Becket had been antagonistic to royal encroachments. The war between the civil power and these courts had begun before the fall of Wolsey, and had resulted in the curtailment of probate duties, legacies, and mortuaries, by which the clergy had been enriched. A limitation of pluralities and enforcement of residence had also been effected. But a still greater blow to the privileges of the clergy was struck by the Parliament under the influence of Cromwell, who had elevated it in order to give legality to the despotic measures of the Crown; and in this way a law was passed that no one under the rank of a subdeacon, if convicted of felony, should be allowed to plead his "benefit of clergy," but should be punished like ordinary criminals, — thus re-establishing the constitutions of Clarendon in the time of Becket. Another act also was passed, by which no one could be summoned, as aforetime, to the archbishop's court out of his own diocese, — a very beneficent act, since the people had been needlessly subject to great expense and injustice in being obliged to travel considerable distances. It was moreover enacted that men could not burden their estates beyond twenty years by providing priests to sing masses for their souls. The Parliament likewise abolished annats, — a custom which had long prevailed in Europe, which required one year's income to be sent to the Pope on any new preferment; a great burden to the clergy; a sort of tribute to a foreign power. Within fifty years, one hundred and sixty thousand pounds had thus been sent from England to Rome, from this one source of papal revenue alone, — equal to three million pounds at the present time, or fifteen millions of dollars, from a country of only three millions of people. It was the passage of that act which induced Sir Thomas More (a devoted Catholic, but a just and able and incorruptible judge) to resign the seals which he had so long and so honorably held, — the most prominent man in England after Cromwell and Cranmer; and it was the execution of this lofty character, because he held out against the imperious demands of Henry, which is the greatest stain upon this monarch's reign. Parliament also called the clergy to account for excessive acts of despotism, and subjected them to the penalty of a premunire (the offence of bringing a foreign authority into England), from which they were freed only by enormous fines.

Thus it would seem that many abuses were removed by Cromwell and the Parliament during the reign of Henry VIII. which may almost be considered as reforms of the Church itself. The authority of the Church was not attacked, still less its doctrines, but only abuses and privileges the restraint of which was of public benefit, and which tended to reduce the power of the clergy. It was this reduction of clerical usurpations and privileges which is the main feature in the legislation of Henry VIII., so far as it pertained to the Church. It was wresting away the power which the clergy had enjoyed from the days of Alfred and Ina, — a reform which Henry II. and Edward I., and other sovereigns, had failed to effect. This was the great work of Cromwell, and in it he had the support of his royal master, since it was a transfer of power from the clergy to the throne; and Henry VIII. was hated and anathematized by Rome as Henry IV. of Germany was, without ceasing to be a Catholic. He even retained the title of Defender of the Faith, which had been conferred upon him by the Pope for his opposition to the theological doctrines of Luther, which he never accepted, and which he always detested.

Cromwell did not long survive the great services he rendered to his king and the nation. In the height of his power he made a fatal mistake. He deceived the King in regard to Anne of Cleves, whose marriage he favored from motives of expediency and a manifest desire to promote the Protestant cause. He palmed upon the King a woman who could not speak a word of English, — a woman without graces or accomplishments, who was absolutely hateful to him. Henry's disappointment was bitter, and his vengeance was unrelenting. The enemies of Cromwell soon took advantage of this mistake. The great Duke of Norfolk, head of the Catholic party, accused him at the council-board of high treason. Two years before, such a charge would have received no attention; but Henry now hated him, and was resolved to punish him for the wreck of his domestic happiness.

Cromwell was hurried to that gloomy fortress whose outlet was generally the scaffold. He was denied even the form of trial. A bill of attainder was hastily passed by the Parliament he had ruled. Only one person in the realm had the courage to intercede for him, and this was Cranmer, Archbishop of Canterbury; but his entreaties were futile. The fallen minister had no chance of life, and no one knew it so well as himself. Even a trial would have availed nothing; nothing could have availed him,—he was a doomed man. So he bade his foes make quick work of it; and quick work was made. In eighteen days from his arrest, Thomas Cromwell, Earl of Essex, Knight of the Garter, Grand Chamberlain, Lord Privy Seal, Vicar-General, and Master of the Wards, ascended the scaffold on which had been shed the blood of a queen,—making no protestation of innocence, but simply committing his soul to Jesus Christ, in whom he believed. Like Wolsey, he arose from an humble station to the most exalted position the King could give; and, like Wolsey, he saw the vanity of delegated power as soon as he offended the source of power.

> "He who ascends the mountain-tops shall find
> The loftiest peak most wrapped in clouds and storms.
> Though high above the sun of glory shines,
> And far beneath the earth and ocean spread,
> Round *him* are icy rocks, and loudly blow
> Contending tempests on his naked head."

On the disappearance of Cromwell from the stage, Cranmer came forward more prominently. He was a learned doctor in that university which has ever sent forth the apostles of great emancipating movements. He was born in 1489, and was therefore twenty years of age on the accession of Henry VIII. in 1509, and was twenty-eight when Luther published his theses. He early sympathized with the reform doctrines, but was too politic to take an active part in their discussion. He was a moderate, calm, scholarly man, not a great genius or great preacher. He had none of those bold and dazzling qualities which attract the gaze of the world. We behold in him no fearless and impetuous Luther,—attacking with passionate earnestness the corruptions of Rome; bracing himself up to revolutionary assaults, undaunted before kings and councils, and giving no rest to his hands or slumber to his eyes until he had consummated his protests,— a man of the people, yet a dictator to princes. We see no severely logical Calvin,

— pushing out his metaphysical deductions until he had chained the intellect of his party to a system of incomparable grandeur and yet of repulsive austerity, exacting all the while the same allegiance to doctrines which he deduced from the writings of Paul as he did to the direct declarations of Christ; next to Thomas Aquinas, the acutest logician the Church has known; a system-maker, like the great Dominican schoolmen, and their common master and oracle, Saint Augustine of Hippo. We see in Cranmer no uncompromising and aggressive reformer like Knox,— controlling by a stern dogmatism both a turbulent nobility and an uneducated people, and filling all classes alike with inextinguishable hatred of everything that even reminded them of Rome. Nor do we find in Cranmer the outspoken and hearty eloquence of Latimer, — appealing to the people at St. Paul's Cross to shake off all the trappings of the "Scarlet Mother," who had so long bewitched the world with her sorceries.

Cranmer, if less eloquent, less fearless, less logical, less able than these, was probably broader, more comprehensive in his views, — adapting his reforms to the circumstances of the age and country, and to the genius of the English mind. Hence his reforms, if less brilliant, were more permanent. He framed the creed that finally was known as the Thirty-nine Articles, and was the true founder of the English Church, as that

Church has existed for more than three centuries,—neither Roman nor Puritan, but "half-way between Rome and Geneva;" a compromise, and yet a Church of great vitality, and endeared to the hearts of the English people. Northern Germany — the scene of the stupendous triumphs of Luther — is and has been, since the time of Frederick the Great, the hot-bed of rationalistic inquiries; and the Genevan as well as the French and Swiss churches which Calvin controlled have become cold, with a dreary and formal Protestantism, without poetry or life. But the Church of England has survived two revolutions and all the changes of human thought, and is still a mighty power, decorous, beautiful, conservative, yet open to all the liberalizing influences of an age of science and philosophy. Cranmer, though a scholastic, seems to have perceived that nothing is more misleading and uncertain and unsatisfactory than any truth pushed out to its severest logical conclusions without reference to other truths which have for their support the same divine authority. It is not logic which has built up the most enduring institutions, but common-sense and plain truths, and appeals to human consciousness, — the *cogito, ergo sum*, without whose approval most systems have perished. *In mediis tutissimus ibis*, is not indeed an agreeable maxim to zealots and partisans and dialectical logicians, but it seems to be induced from the varied experiences of human life and the history of different ages and nations, and applies to all the mixed sciences, like government and political economy, as well as to church institutions.

As Cromwell made his fortune by advising the King to assume the headship of the Church in England, so Cranmer's rise is to be traced to his advice to Henry to appeal to the decision of universities whether or not he could be legally divorced from Catharine, since the Pope — true to the traditions of the Catholic Church, or from fear of Charles V. — would not grant a dispensation. All this business was a miserable quibble, a tissue of scholastic technicalities. But it answered the ends of Cranmer. The schools decided for the King, and a great injustice and heartless cruelty was done to a worthy and loyal woman, and a great insult offered to the Church and to the Emperor Charles of Germany, who was a nephew of the Spanish Princess and English Queen. This scandal resulted in a separation from Rome, as was foreseen both by Cromwell and Cranmer; and the latter became Archbishop of Canterbury, a prelate whose power and dignity were greater then than at the present day, exalted as the post is even now, — the highest in dignity and rank to which a subject can aspire, — higher even than the Lord High Chancellorship; both of which, however, pale before the position of a Prime Minister so far as power is concerned.

The separation from Rome, the suppression of the monasteries, and the curtailment of the powers of the spiritual courts were the only reforms of note during the reign of Henry VIII., unless we name also the new translation of the Bible, authorized through Cranmer's influence, and the teaching of the creed, the commandments, and the Lord's prayer in English. The King died in 1547. Cranmer was now fifty-seven, and was left to prosecute reforms in his own way as president of the council of regency, Edward VI. being but nine years old, — "a learned boy," as Macaulay calls him, but still a boy in the hands of the great noblemen who composed the regency, and who belonged to the progressive school.

I do not think the career of Cranmer during the life of Henry is sufficiently appreciated. He must have shown at least extraordinary tact and wisdom, — with his reforming tendencies and enlightened views, — not to come in conflict with his sovereign as Becket did with Henry II. He had to deal with the most capricious and jealous of tyrants; cruel and unscrupulous when crossed; a man who rarely retained a friendship or remembered a service; who never forgave an injury or forgot an affront; a glutton and a sensualist; although prodigal with his gifts, social in his temper, enlightened in his government, and with very respectable abilities and very considerable theological knowl-

After the painting by Hans Holbein, Windsor Castle, England
HENRY VIII. OF ENGLAND

edge. This hard and exacting master Cranmer had to serve, without exciting his suspicions or coming in conflict with him; so that he seemed politic and vacillating, for which he would not be excused were it not for his subsequent services, and his undoubted sincerity and devotion to the Protestant cause. During the life of Henry we can scarcely call Cranmer a reformer. The most noted reformer of the day was old Hugh Latimer, the King's chaplain, who declaimed against sin with the zeal and fire of Savonarola, and aimed to create a religious life among the people, from whom he sprung and whom he loved, — a rough, hearty, honest, conscientious man, with deep convictions and lofty soul.

In the reforms thus far carried on we perceive that, though popular, they emanated from princes and not from the people. The people had no hand in the changes made, as at Geneva, only the ministers of kings and great public functionaries. And in the reforms subsequently effected, which really constitute the English Reformation, they were made by the council of regency, under the leadership of Cranmer and the protectorship of Somerset.

The first thing which the Government did after the accession of Edward VI. was to remove images from the churches, as a form of idolatry, — much to the wrath of Gardiner, Bishop of Winchester, the ablest man of the old conservative and papal party. But Ridley, afterwards Bishop of Rochester, preached against all forms of papal superstition with so much ability and zeal that the churches were soon cleared of these "helps to devotion."

Cranmer, now unchecked, turned his attention to other reforms, but proceeded slowly and cautiously, not wishing to hazard much at the outset. First communion of both kinds, heretofore restricted to the clergy, was appointed; and, closely connected with it, Masses were put down. Then a law was passed by Parliament that the appointment of bishops should vest in the Crown alone, and not, as formerly, be confirmed by the Pope. The next great thing to which the reformers directed their attention was the preparation of a new liturgy in the public worship of God, which gave rise to considerable discussion. They did not seek to sweep away the old form, for it was prepared by the sainted doctors of the Church of all ages; but they would purge it of all superstitions, and retain what was most beautiful and expressive in the old prayers. The Ten Commandments, the Lord's Prayer, and the early creeds of course were retained, as well as whatever was in harmony with primitive usages. These changes called out letters from Calvin at Geneva, who was now recognized as a great oracle among the Protestants: he encouraged the work, but advised a more complete reformation, and complained of the coldness of the clergy, as well as of the general vices of the times. Martin Bucer of Strasburg, at this time professor at Cambridge, also wrote letters to the same effect; but the time had not come for more radical reforms. Then Parliament, controlled by the Government, passed an act allowing the clergy to marry,—opposed, of course, by many bishops in allegiance to Rome. This was a great step in reform, and removed many popular scandals; it struck a heavy blow at the superstitions of the Middle Ages, and showed that celibacy sprung from no law of God, but was Oriental in its origin, encouraged by the popes to cement their throne. And this act concerning the marriage of the clergy was soon followed by the celebrated Forty-two Articles, framed by Cranmer and Ridley, which are the bases of the English Church, — a theological creed, slightly amended afterwards in the reign of Elizabeth; evangelical but not Calvinistic, affirming the great ideas of Augustine and Luther as to grace, justification by faith, and original sin, and repudiating purgatory, pardons, the worship and invocation of saints and images; a larger creed than the Nicene or Athanasian, and comprehensive,—such as most Protestants might accept. Both this and the book of Common Prayer were written with consummate taste, were the work of great scholars,—moderate, broad, enlightened, conciliatory.

The reformers then gave their attention to an alteration of ecclesiastical laws in reference to matters which had always been decided in ecclesiastical courts. The commissioners — the ablest men in England, thirty-two in number — had scarcely completed their work before the young King died, and Mary ascended the throne.

We cannot too highly praise the moderation with which the reforms had been made, especially when we remember the violence of the age. There were only two or three capital executions for heresy. Gardiner and Bonner, who opposed the reformation with unparalleled bitterness were only deprived of their sees and sent to the Tower. The execution of Somerset was the work of politicians, of great noblemen jealous of his ascendency. It does not belong to the reformation, nor do the executions of a few other noblemen.

Cranmer himself was a statesman rather than a preacher. He left but few sermons, and these commonplace, without learning, or wit, or zeal, — ordinary exhortations to a virtuous life. The chief thing, outside of the reforms I have mentioned, was the publication of a few homilies for the use of the clergy, — too ignorant to write sermons, — which homilies were practical and orthodox, but containing nothing to stir up an ardent religious life. The Bible was also given a greater scope; everybody could read it if he wished. Public prayer was restored to the people in a language which they could understand, and a few preachers arose who appealed to conscience and reason, — like Latimer and Ridley, and Hooper and Taylor; but most of them were formal and cold. There must have been great religious apathy, or else these reforms would have excited more opposition on the part of the clergy, who generally acquiesced in the changes. But the Reformation thus far was official; it was not popular. It repressed vice and superstition, but kindled no great enthusiasm. It was necessary for the English reformers and sincere Protestants to go through a great trial; to be persecuted, to submit to martyrdom for the sake of their opinions. The school of heroes and saints has ever been among blazing fires and scaffolds. It was martyrdom which first gave form and power to early Christianity. The first chapter in the history of the early Church is the torments of the martyrs. The English Reformation had no great dignity or life until the funeral pyres were lighted. Men had placidly accepted new opinions, and had Bibles to instruct them; but it was to be seen how far they would make sacrifices to maintain them.

This test was afforded by the accession of Mary, daughter of Catharine the Spaniard, — an affectionate and kind-hearted woman enough in ordinary times, but a fiend of bigotry, like Catherine de' Medicis, when called upon to suppress the Reformation, although on her accession she declared that she would force no man's conscience. But the first thing she does is to restore the popish bishops, — for so they were called then by historians; and the next thing she does is to restore the Mass, and the third to shut up Cranmer and Latimer in the Tower, attaint and execute them, with sundry others like Ridley and Hooper, as well as those great nobles who favored the claims of the Lady Jane Grey and the religious reforms of Edward VI. She reconciles herself with Rome, and accepts its legate at her court; she receives Spanish spies and Jesuit confessors; she marries the son of Charles V., afterwards Philip II.; she executes the Lady Jane Grey; she keeps the strictest watch on the Princess Elizabeth, who learns in her retirement the art of dissimulation and lying; she forms an alliance with Spain; she makes Cardinal Pole Archbishop of Canterbury; she gives almost unlimited power to Gardiner and Bonner, who begin a series of diabolical persecutions, burning such people as John Rogers, Sanders, Doctor Taylor of Hadley, William Hunter, and Stephen Harwood, ferreting out all suspected of heresy, and confining them in the foulest jails, — burning even little children. Mary even takes measures to introduce the Inquisition and restore the monasteries. Everywhere are scaffolds and burnings. In three years nearly three hundred people were burned alive, often with green wood, — a small number compared with those who were executed and assassinated in France, about this time, by Catherine de' Medicis, the Guises, and Charles IX.

In those dreadful persecutions which began with the accession of Mary, it was impossible that Cranmer should escape. In spite of his dignity, rank, age, and services, he could hope for no favor or indulgence from that morose woman in whose sapless bosom no compassion for the Protestants ever found admission, and still less from those cruel, mercenary, bigoted prelates whom she selected for her ministers. It was not customary in that age for the Roman Church to spare heretics, whether high or low. Would it forgive him who had overturned the consecrated altars, displaced the ritual of a thousand years, and revolted from the authority of the supreme head of the Christian world? Would Mary suffer him to pass unpunished who had displaced her mother from the nuptial bed, and pronounced her own birth to be stained with an ignominious blot, and who had exalted a rival to the throne? And Gardiner and Bonner, too, those bigoted prelates and ministers who would have sent to the flames an unoffending woman if she denied the authority of the Pope, were not the men to suffer him to escape who had not only overturned the papal power in England, but had deprived them of their sees and sent them to the Tower. No matter how decent the forms of law or respectful the agents of the crown, Cranmer had not the shadow of a hope; and hence he was certainly weak to say the least, to trust to any deceitful promises made to him. What his enemies were bent upon was his recantation, as preliminary to his execution; and he should have been firm, both for his cause, and because his martyrdom was sure. In an evil hour he listened to the voice of the seducer. Both life and dignities were promised if he would recant. "Confounded, heart-broken, old," the love of life and the fear of death were stronger for a time than the power of conscience or dignity of character. Six several times was he induced to recant the doctrines he had preached, and profess an allegiance which could only be a solemn mockery.

True, Cranmer came to himself; he perceived that he was mocked, and felt both grief and shame in view of his apostasy. His last hours were glorious. Never did a good man more splendidly redeem his memory from shame. Being permitted to address the people before his execution,—with the hope on the part of his tormentors that he would publicly confirm his recantation,—he first supplicated the mercy and forgiveness of Almighty God, and concluded his speech with these memorable words: "And now I come to the great thing that troubleth my conscience more than anything I ever did or said, even the set-

CRANMER AT THE TRAITOR'S GATE

From the painting by Frederick Goodall

ting forth of writings contrary to the truth, which I now renounce and refuse, — those things written with my own hand contrary to the truth I thought in my heart, and writ for fear of death and to save my life. And forasmuch as my hand offended in writing contrary to my heart, therefore my hand shall first be punished; for if I come to the fire, it shall first be burned. As for the Pope, I denounce him as Christ's enemy and Antichrist, with all his false doctrines." Then he was carried away, and a great multitude ran after him, exhorting him, while time was, to remember himself. "Coming to the stake," says the Catholic eye-witness, "with a cheerful countenance and willing mind, he took off his garments in haste and stood upright in his shirt. Fire being applied, he stretched forth his right hand and thrust it into the flame, before the fire came to any other part of his body; when his hand was to be seen sensibly burning, he cried with a loud voice, 'This hand hath offended.'"

Thus died Cranmer, in the sixty-seventh year of his age, after presiding over the Church of England above twenty years, and having bequeathed a legacy to his countrymen of which they continue to be proud. He had not the intrepidity of Latimer; he was supple to Henry VIII.; he was weak in his recantation; he was not an original genius, — but he was a man of great breadth of views, conciliating wise, temperate in reform, and discharged his great trust with conscientious adherence to the truth as he understood it; the friend of Calvin, and revered by the Protestant world.

Queen Mary reigned, fortunately, but five years, and the persecutions she encouraged and indorsed proved the seed of a higher morality and a loftier religious life.

> "For thus spake aged Latimer:
> I tarry by the stake,
> Not trusting in my own weak heart,
> But for the Saviour's sake.
> Why speak of life or death to me,
> Whose days are but a span?
> Our crown is yonder,—Ridley, see!
> Be strong and play the man!
> God helping, such a torch this day
> We 'll light on English land,
> That Rome, with all her cardinals,
> Shall never quench the brand!"

The triumphs of Gardiner and Bonner too were short. Mary died with a bruised heart and a crushed ambition. On her death, and the accession of her sister Elizabeth, exiles returned from Geneva and Frankfort to advocate more radical changes in government and doctrine. Popular enthusiasm was kindled, never afterwards to be repressed.

The great ideas of the Reformation began now to agitate the mind of England,—not so much the logical doctrines of Calvin as the emancipating ideas of Luther.

The Renaissance had begun, and the two movements were incorporated, — the religious one of Germany and the Pagan one of Italy, both favoring liberality of mind, a freer style of literature, restless inquiries, enterprise, the revival of learning and art, an intense spirit of progress, and disgust for the Dark Ages and all the dogmas of scholasticism. With this spirit of progress and moderate Protestantism Elizabeth herself, the best educated woman in England, warmly sympathized, as did also the illustrious men she drew to her court, to whom she gave the great offices of state. I cannot call her age a religious one: it was a merry one, cheerful, inquiring, untrammelled in thought, bold in speculation, eloquent, honest, fervid, courageous, hostile to the Papacy and all the bigots of Europe. It was still rough, coarse, sensual; when money was scarce and industries in their infancy, and material civilization not very attractive. But it was a great age, glorious, intellectual, brilliant; with such statesmen as Burleigh and Walsingham to head off treason and conspiracy; when great poets arose, like Jonson and Spenser and Shakspeare; and philosophers, like Bacon and Sir Thomas Browne; and lawyers, like Nicholas Bacon and Coke; and elegant courtiers, like Sidney and Raleigh and Essex; men of wit, men of enterprise, who would explore distant seas and colonize new countries; yea, great preachers, like Jeremy Taylor and Hall; and great theologians, like Hooker and Chillingworth, — giving polish and dignity to an uncouth language, and planting religious truth in the minds of men.

Elizabeth, with such a constellation around her, had no great difficulty in re-establishing Protestantism and giving it a new impetus, although she adhered to liturgies and pomps, and loved processions and fêtes and banquets and balls and expensive dresses, — a worldly woman, but progressive and enlightened.

In the religious reforms of that age you see the work of princes and statesmen still, rather than any great insurrection of human intelligence or any great religious revival, although the germs of it were springing up through the popular preachers and the influence of Genevan reformers. Calvin's writings were potent, and John Knox was on his way to Scotland.

I pass by rapidly the reforms of Elizabeth's reign, effected by the Queen and her ministers and the convocation of Protestant bishops and clergy and learned men in the universities. Oxford and Cambridge were then in their glory, — crowded with poor students from all parts of England, who came to study Greek and Latin and read theology, not to ride horses and row boats, to put on dandified airs and sneer at lectures, running away to London to attend theatres and flirt with girls and drink champagne, beggaring their fathers and ruining their own expectations and their health. In a very short time after the accession of Elizabeth, which was hailed generally as a very auspicious event, things were restored to nearly the state in which they were left by Cranmer in the preceding reign. This was not done by direct authority of the Queen, but by acts of Parliament. Even Henry VIII. ruled through the Parliament, only it was his tool and instrument. Elizabeth consulted its wishes as the representation of the nation, for she aimed to rule by the affections of her people. But she recommended the Parliament to conciliatory measures; to avoid extremes; to drop offensive epithets, like "papist" and "heretic;" to go as far as the wants of the nation required, and no farther. Though a zealous Protestant, she seemed to have no great animosities. Her particular aversion was Bonner, — the violent, blood-thirsty, narrow-minded Bishop of London, who was deprived of his see and shut up in the Tower, put out of harm's way, not cruelly treated, — he was not even deprived of his good dinners. She appointed, as her prerogative allowed, a very gentle, moderate, broad, kind-hearted man to be Archbishop of Canterbury, — Parker, who had been chaplain to her mother, and who was highly esteemed by Burleigh and Nicholas Bacon, her most influential ministers. Parliament confirmed the old act, passed during the reign of Henry VIII., making the sovereign the head of the English Church, although the title of "supreme head" was left out in the oath of allegiance, to conciliate the Catholic party. To execute this supremacy, the Court of High Commission was established, — afterwards so abused by Charles I. The Church Service was modified, and the Act of Uniformity was passed by Parliament, after considerable debate. The changes were all made in the spirit of moderation, and few suffered beyond a deprivation of their sees or livings for refusing to take the oath of supremacy.

Then followed the Thirty-nine Articles, setting forth the creed of the Established Church, — substantially the creed which Cranmer had made, — and a new translation of the Bible, and the regulation of ecclesiastical courts.

But whatever was done was in good taste, — marked by good sense and moderation, — to preserve decency and decorum, and repress all extremes of superstition and license. The clergy preached in a black gown and Genevan bands, using the surplice only in the liturgy; we see no lace or millinery. The churches were stripped of images, the pulpits became high and prominent, the altars were changed to communion-tables without candles and symbols. There was not much account made of singing, for the lyric version of the Psalms was execrable. For the first time since Chrysostom and Gregory Nazianzen, preaching became the chief duty of the clergyman; and his sermons were long, for the people were greedy of instruction, and were not critical of artistic merits. Among other things of note, the exiles were recalled, who brought back with them the learning of the Continent and the theology of Geneva, and an intense hatred for all the old forms of superstition, — images, crucifixes, lighted candles, Catholic vestments, — and a supreme regard for the authority of the Scriptures, rather than the authority of the Church.

These men, mostly learned and pious, were not contented with the restoration as effected by Elizabeth's reformers, — they wanted greater simplicity of worship and a more definite and logical creed; and they made a good deal of trouble, being very conscientious and somewhat narrow and intolerant. So that, after the re-establishment of Protestantism, the religious history of the reign is chiefly concerned with the quarrels and animosities within the Church, particularly about vestments and modes of worship, — things unessential, minute, technical, — which led to great acerbity on both sides, and to some persecution; for these quarrels provoked the Queen and her ministers, who wanted peace and uniformity. To the Government it seemed strange and absurd for these returned exiles to make such a fuss about a few externals; to these intensified Protestants it seemed harsh and cruel that Government should insist on such a rigid uniformity, and punish them for not doing as they were bidden by the bishops.

So they separated from the Established Church, and became what were called Nonconformists, — having not only disgust of the decent ritualism of the Church, but great wrath for the bishops and hierarchy and spiritual courts. They also disapproved of the holy days which the Church retained, and the prayers and the cathedral style of worship, the use of the cross in baptism, godfathers and godmothers, the confirmation of children, kneeling at the sacrament, bowing at the name of Jesus, the ring in marriage, the surplice, the divine right of bishops, and some other things which reminded them of Rome, for which they had absolute detestation, seeing in the old Catholic Church nothing but abominations and usurpations, no religion at all, only superstition and anti-Christian government and doctrine,— the reign of the beast, the mystic Babylon, the scarlet mother revelling in the sorceries of ancient Paganism. These terrible animosities against even the shadows and resemblances of what was called Popery were increased and intensified by the persecution and massacres which the Catholics about this time were committing on the Protestants in France and Germany and the Low Countries, and which filled the people of England,— especially the middle and lower classes,—- with fear, alarm, anger, and detestation.

I will not enter upon the dissensions which so early crept into the English Church, and led to a separation or a schism, whatever name it goes by, — to most people in these times not very interesting or edifying, because they were not based on any great ideas of universal application, and seeming to such minds as Bacon and Parker and Jewell rather narrow and frivolous.

The great Puritan controversy would have no dignity if it were confined to vestments and robes and forms of worship, and hatred of ceremonies and holy days, and other matters which seemed to lean to Romanism. But the grandeur and the permanence of the movement were in a return to the faith of the primitive Church and a purer national morality, and to the unrestricted study of the Bible, and the exaltation of preaching and Christian instruction over forms and liturgies and antiphonal chants; above all, the exaltation of reason and learning in the interpretation of revealed truth, and the education of the people in all matters which concern their temporal or religious interests, so that a true and rapid progress was inaugurated in civilization itself, which has peculiarly marked all Protestant countries having religious liberty. Underneath all these apparently insignificant squabbles and dissensions there were two things of immense historical importance: first, a spirit of intolerance on the part of government and of church dignitaries, — the State allied with the

Church forcing uniformity with their decrees, and severely punishing those who did not accept them, — in matters beyond all worldly authority; and, secondly, a rising spirit of religious liberty, determined to assert its glorious rights at any cost or hazard, and especially defended by the most religious and earnest part of the clergy, who were becoming Calvinistic in their creed, and were pushing the ideas of the Reformation to their utmost logical sequence. This spirit was suppressed during the reign of Elizabeth, out of general respect and love for her as a Queen, and the external dangers to which the realm was exposed from Spain and France, which diverted the national mind. But it burst out fiercely in the next reigns, under James and Charles, about the beginning of the seventeenth century. And this is the last development of the Reformation in England to which I can allude,— the great Puritan contest for liberty of worship, running, when opposed unjustly and cruelly, into a contest for civil liberty; that is, the right to change forms and institutions of civil government, even to the dethronement of kings, when it was the expressed and declared will of the people, in whom was vested the ultimate source of sovereignty.

But here I must be brief. I tread on familiar ground, made familiar by all our literature, especially by the most brilliant writer of modern times, though not the greatest philosopher: I mean that great artist and word-painter Macaulay, whose chief excellence is in making clear and interesting and vivid, by a world of illustration and practical good-sense and marvellous erudition, what was obvious to his own objective mind, and obvious also to most other enlightened people not much interested in metaphysical disquisitions. No man more than he does justice to the love of liberty which absolutely burned in the souls of the Puritans, — that glorious party which produced Milton and Cromwell, and Hampden and Bunyan, and Owen and Calamy, and Baxter and Howe.

The chief peculiarity of those Puritans — once called Nonconformists, afterwards Presbyterians and Independents — was their reception of the creed of John Calvin, the clearest and most logical intellect that the Reformation produced, though not the broadest; who reigned as a religious dictator at Geneva and in the Reformed churches of France, and who gave to John Knox the positivism and sternness and rigidity which he succeeded in impressing upon the churches of Scotland. And the peculiar doctrines which marked Calvin and his disciples were those deduced from the majesty of God and the comparative littleness of man, leading to and bound up with the impotence of the will, human dependence, the necessity of Divine grace,— Augustinian in spirit, but going beyond Augustine in the subtlety of metaphysical distinctions and dissertations on free-will.

election, and predestination, — unfathomable, but exceedingly attractive subjects to the divines of the seventeenth century, creating a metaphysical divinity, a theology of the brain rather than of the heart, a brilliant series of logical and metaphysical deductions from established truths, demanding to be received with the same unhesitating obedience as the truths, or Bible declarations, from which they are deduced. The greatness of human reason was never more forcibly shown than in these deductions; but they were carried so far as to insult reason itself and mock the consciousness of mankind; so that mankind rebelled against the very force of the highest reasonings of the human intellect, because they pushed logical sequence into absurdity, or to dreadful conclusions: *Decretum quidem horribile fateor*, said the great master himself.

The Puritans were trained in this theology, which developed the loftiest virtues and the severest self-constraints; making them both heroes and visionaries, always conscientious and sometimes repulsive; fitting them for gigantic tasks and unworthy squabbles; driving them to the Bible, and then to acrimonious discussions; creating fears almost mediæval; leading them to technical observation of religious duties, and transforming the most genial and affectionate people under the sun into austere saints, with whom the most ascetic of monks would have had but little sympathy.

I will not dwell on those peculiarities which Macaulay ridicules and Taine repeats,— the hatred of theatres and assemblies and symbolic festivals and bell-ringings, the rejection of the beautiful, the elongated features, the cropped hair, the unadorned garments, the proscription of innocent pleasures, the nasal voice, the cant phrases, the rigid decorums, the strict discipline, — these, doubtless exaggerated, were more than balanced by the observance of the Sabbath, family prayers, temperate habits, fervor of religious zeal, strict morality, allegiance to duty, and the perpetual recognition of God Almighty as the sovereign of this world, to whom we are responsible for all our acts and even our thoughts. They formed a noble material on which every emancipating idea could work; men trained by persecutions to self-sacrifice and humble duties,— making good soldiers, good farmers, good workmen in every department, honest and sturdy, patient and self-reliant, devoted to their families though not demonstrative of affection; keeping the Sunday as a day of worship rather than rest or recreation, cherishing as the dearest and most sacred of all privileges the right to worship God according to the dictates of conscience enlightened by the Bible, and willing to fight, even amid the greatest privations and sacrifices, to maintain this sacred right and transmit it to their children. Such were the men who fought the battles of civil liberty under Cromwell.

and colonized the most sterile of all American lands, making the dreary wilderness to blossom with roses, and sending out the shoots of their civilization to conserve more fruitful and favored sections of the great continent which God gave them, to try new experiments in liberty and education.

I need not enumerate the different sects into which these Puritans were divided, so soon as they felt they had the right to interpret Scripture for themselves. Nor would I detail the various and cruel persecutions to which these sects were subjected by the government and the ecclesiastical tribunals, until they rose in indignation and despair, and rebelled against the throne, and made war on the King, and cut off his head; all of which they did from fear and for self-defence, as well as from vengeance and wrath.

Nor can I describe the counter reformation, the great reaction which succeeded to the violence of the revolution. The English reformation was not consummated until constitutional liberty was heralded by the reign of William and Mary, when the nation became almost unanimously Protestant, with perfect toleration of religious opinions, although the fervor of the Puritans had passed away forever, leaving a residuum of deep-seated popular antipathy to all the institutions of Romanism and all the ideas of the Middle Ages. The English reformation began with princes, and ended with the agitations of the people. The German reformation began with the people, and ended in the wars of princes. But both movements were sublime, since they showed the force of religious ideas. Civil liberty is only one of the sequences which exalt the character and dignity of man amid the seductions and impediments of a gilded material life.

AUTHORITIES.

Todd's Life of Cranmer; Strype's Life of Cranmer; Wood's Annals of the Oxford University; Burnet's English Reformation; Doctor Lingard's History of England; Macaulay's Essays; Fuller's Church History; Gilpin's Life of Cranmer; Original Letters to Cromwell; Hook's Lives of the Archbishops of Canterbury; Butler's Book of the Roman Catholic Church; Wordsworth's Ecclesiastical Biography; **Turner's** Henry VIII.; Froude's History of England; Fox's Life of Latimer; Turner's **Reign of Mary.**

IGNATIUS LOYOLA.

A. D. 1491–1556.

RISE AND INFLUENCE OF THE JESUITS.

IGNATIUS LOYOLA.

RISE AND INFLUENCE OF THE JESUITS.

NEXT to the Protestant Reformation itself, the most memorable moral movement in the history of modern times was the counter-reformation in the Roman Catholic Church, finally effected, in no slight degree, by the Jesuits. But it has not the grandeur or historical significance of the great insurrection of human intelligence which was headed by Luther. It was a revival of the pietism of the Middle Ages, with an external reform of manners. It was not revolutionary; it did not cast off the authority of the popes, nor disband the monasteries, nor reform religious worship: it rather tended to strengthen the power of the popes, to revive monastic life, and to perpetuate the forms of worship which the Middle Ages had established. No doubt a new religious life was kindled, and many of the flagrant abuses of the papal empire were redressed, and the lives of the clergy made more decent, in accordance with the revival of intelligence. Nor did it disdain literature or art, or any form of modern civilization, but sought to combine progress with old ideas; it was an effort to adapt the Roman theocracy to changing circumstances, and was marked by expediency rather than right, by zeal rather than a profound philosophy.

This movement took place among the Latin races, — the Italians, French, and Spaniards, — having no hold on the Teutonic races except in Austria, as much Slavonic as German. It worked on a poor material, morally considered; among peoples who have not been distinguished for stamina of character, earnestness, contemplative habits, and moral elevation, — peoples long enslaved, frivolous in their pleasures, superstitious, indolent, fond of fêtes, spectacles, pictures, and Pagan reminiscences.

The doctrine of justification by faith was not unknown, even in Italy. It was embraced by many distinguished men. Contarini, an illustrious Venetian, wrote a treatise on it, which Cardinal Pole admired. Folengo ascribed justification to grace alone; and Vittoria Colonna, the friend of Michael Angelo, took a deep interest in these theological inquiries. But the doctrine did not spread; it was not understood by the people, — it was a speculation among scholars and doctors, which gave no alarm to the Pope. There was even an attempt at internal reform under Paul III. of the illustrious family of the Farnese, successor of Leo X. and Clement VII., the two renowned Medicean popes. He made cardinals of Contarini, Caraffa, Sadoleto, Pole, Giberto, — all men imbued with Protestant doctrines, and very religious; and these good men prepared a plan of reform and submitted it to the Pope, which ended, however, only in new monastic orders.

It was then that Ignatius Loyola appeared upon the stage, when Luther was in the midst of his victories, and when new ideas were shaking the pontifical throne. The desponding successor of the Gregorys and the Clements knew not where to look for aid in that crisis of peril and revolution. The monastic orders composed his regular army, but they had become so corrupted that they had lost the reverence of the people. The venerable Benedictines had ceased to be men of prayer and contemplation as in the times of Bernard and Anselm, and were revelling in their enormous wealth. The cloisters of Cluniacs and Cistercians — branches of the Benedictines — were filled with idle and dissolute monks. The famous Dominicans and Franciscans, who had rallied to the defence of the Papacy three centuries before, — those missionary orders that had filled the best pulpits and the highest chairs of philosophy in the scholastic age, — had become inexhaustible subjects of sarcasm and mockery, for they were peddling relics and indulgences, and quarrelling among themselves. They were hated as inquisitors, despised as scholastics, and deserted as preachers; the roads and taverns were filled with them. Erasmus laughed at them, Luther abused them, and the Pope reproached them. No hope from such men as these, although they had once been renowned for their missions, their zeal, their learning, and their preaching.

At this crisis Loyola and his companions volunteered their services, and offered to go wherever the Pope should send them, as preachers, or missionaries, or teachers, instantly, without discussion, conditions, or rewards. So the Pope accepted them, made them a new order of monks; and they did what the Mendicant Friars had done three hundred years before,— they fanned a new spirit, and rapidly spread over Europe, over all the countries to which Catholic adventurers had penetrated, and became the most efficient allies that the popes ever had.

This was in 1540, six years after the foundation of the Society of Jesus had been laid on the Mount of Martyrs, in the vicinity of Paris, during the pontificate of Paul III. Don Iñigo Lopez de Recalde Loyola, a Spaniard of noble blood and breeding, at first a page at the court of King Ferdinand, then a brave and chivalrous soldier, was wounded at the siege of Pampeluna. During a slow convalescence, having read all the romances he could find, he took up the " Lives of the

Saints," and became fired with religious zeal. He immediately forsook the pursuit of arms, and betook himself barefooted to a pilgrimage. He served the sick in hospitals; he dwelt alone in a cavern, practising austerities; he went as a beggar on foot to Rome and to the Holy Land, and returned at the age of thirty-three to begin a course of study. It was while completing his studies at Paris that he conceived and formed the "Society of Jesus."

From that time we date the counter-reformation. In fifty years more a wonderful change took place in the Catholic Church, wrought chiefly by the Jesuits. Yea, in sixteen years from that eventful night — when far above the star-lit city the enthusiastic Loyola had bound his six companions with irrevocable vows — he had established his Society in the confidence and affection of Catholic Europe, against the voice of universities, the fears of monarchs, and the jealousy of the other monastic orders. In sixteen years, this ridiculed and wandering Spanish fanatic had risen to a condition of great influence and dignity, second only in power to the Pope himself; animating the councils of the Vatican, moving the minds of kings, controlling the souls of a numerous fraternity, and making his influence felt in every corner of the world. Before the remembrance of his passionate eloquence, his eyes of fire, and his countenance of seraphic piety had passed away from the minds of his own generation, his disciples "had planted their missionary stations among Peruvian mines, in the marts of the African slave-trade, among the islands of the Indian Ocean, on the coasts of Hindustan, in the cities of Japan and China, in the recesses of Canadian forests, amid the wilds of the Rocky Mountains." They had the most important chairs in the universities; they were the confessors of monarchs and men of rank; they had the control of the schools of Italy, France, Austria, and Spain; and they had become the most eloquent, learned, and fashionable preachers in all Catholic countries. They had grown to be a great institution, — an organization instinct with life, a mechanism endued with energy and will; forming a body which could outwatch Argus with his hundred eyes, and outwork Briareus with his hundred arms; they had twenty thousand eyes open upon every cabinet, every palace, and every private family in Catholic Europe, and twenty thousand arms extended over the necks of every sovereign and all their subjects, — a mighty moral and spiritual power, irresponsible, irresistible, omnipresent, connected intimately with the education, the learning, and the religion of the age; yea, the prime agents in political affairs, the prop alike of absolute monarchies and of the papal throne, whose interests they made identical. This association, instinct with one will and for one purpose, has been beautifully likened by Doctor Williams to the chariot in the Prophet's vision: "The spirit of the living creatures was in the wheels; wherever the living creatures went, the wheels went with them; wherever those stood, these stood: when the living creatures were lifted up, the wheels were lifted up over against them; and their wings were full of eyes round about, and they were so high that they were dreadful. So of the institution of Ignatius,— one soul swayed the vast mass; and every pin and every cog in the machinery consented with its whole power to every movement of the one central conscience."

Luther moved Europe by ideas which emancipated the millions, and set in motion a progress which is the glory of our age; Loyola invented a machine which arrested this progress, and drove the Catholic world back again into the superstitions and despotisms of the Middle Ages, retaining however the fear of God and of Hell, which some among the Protestants care very little about.

What is the secret of such a wonderful success? Two things: first, the extraordinary virtues, abilities, and zeal of the early Jesuits; and, secondly, their wonderful machinery in adapting means to an end.

The history of society shows that no body of men ever obtained a wide-spread ascendancy, never secured general respect, unless they deserved it. Industry produces its fruits; learning and piety have their natural results. Even in the moral world natural law asserts its supremacy. Hypocrisy and fraud ultimately will be detected; no enduring reputation is built upon a lie; sincerity and earnestness will call out respect, even from foes; learning and virtue are lights which are not hid under a bushel. Enthusiasm creates enthusiasm; a lofty life will be seen and honored. Nor do people intrust their dearest interests except to those whom they venerate, — and venerate because their virtues shine like the face of a goddess. We yield to those only whom we esteem wiser than ourselves. Moses controlled the Israelites because they venerated his wisdom and courage; Paul had the confidence of the infant churches because they saw his labors; Bernard swayed his darkened age by the moral power of learning and sanctity. The mature judgments of centuries never have reversed the judgments which past ages gave in reference to their master minds. All the pedants and sophists of Germany cannot whitewash Frederic II. or Henry VIII. No man in Athens was more truly venerated than Socrates when he mocked his judges. Cicero, Augustine, Aquinas, appeared to contemporaries as they appear to us. Even Hildebrand did not juggle himself into his theocratic chair. Washington deserved all the reverence he enjoyed; and Bonaparte himself was worthy of the honors he received, so long as he was true to the interests of France.

So of the Jesuits, — there is no mystery in their success; the same causes would produce the same results again. When Catholic Europe saw men born to wealth and rank voluntarily parting with their goods and honors; devoting themselves to religious duties, often in a humble sphere; spending their days in schools and hospitals; wandering as preachers and missionaries amid privations and in fatigue; encountering perils and dangers and hardships with fresh and ever-sustained enthusiasm; and finally yielding up their lives as martyrs, to proclaim salvation to idolatrous savages, — it knew them to be heroic, and believed them to be sincere, and honored them in consequence. When parents saw that the Jesuits entered heart and soul into the work of education, winning their pupils' hearts by kindness, watching their moods, directing their minds into congenial studies, and inspiring them with generous sentiments, they did not stop to pry into their motives; and universities, when they discovered the superior culture of educated Jesuits, outstripping all their associates in learning, and shedding a light by their genius and erudition, very naturally appointed them to the highest chairs; and even the people, when they saw that the Jesuits were not stained by vulgar vices, but were hard-working, devoted to their labors, earnest, and eloquent, put themselves under their teachings; and especially when they added gentlemanly manners, good taste, and agreeable conversation to their unimpeachable morality and religious fervor, they made these men their confessors as well as preachers. Their lives stood out in glorious contrast with those of the old monks and the regular clergy, in an age of infidel levities, when the Italian renaissance was bearing its worst fruits, and men were going back to Pagan antiquity for their pleasures and opinions.

That the early Jesuits blazed with virtues and learning and piety has never been denied, although these things have been poetically exaggerated. The world was astonished at their intrepidity, zeal, and devotion. They were not at first intriguing, or ambitious, or covetous. They loved their Society; but they loved still more what they thought was the glory of God. *Ad majoram Dei gloriam* was the motto which was emblazoned on their standard when they went forth as Christian warriors to overcome the heresies of Christendom and the superstitions of idolaters. "The Jesuit missionary," says Stephen, "with his breviary under his arm, his beads at his girdle, and his crucifix in his hands, went forth without fear, to encounter the most dreaded dangers. Martyrdom was nothing to him; he knew that the altar which might stream with his blood, and the mound which might be raised over his remains, would become a cherished object of his fame and an expressive emblem of the power of his religion." "If I die," said Xavier, when about to visit the cannibal Island of Del Moro, "who knows but what all may receive the Gospel, since it is most certain it has ever fructified more abundantly in the field of Paganism by the blood of martyrs than by the labors of missionaries," — a sublime truth, revealed to him in his whole course of protracted martyrdom and active philanthropy, especially in those last hours when, on the Island of Sanshan, he expired, exclaiming, as his fading eyes rested on the crucifix, *In te Domine speravi, non confundar in eternum.* In perils, in fastings, in fatigues, was the life of this remarkable man passed, in order to convert the heathen world; and in ten years he had traversed a tract of more than twice the circumference of the earth, preaching, disputing, and baptizing, until seventy thousand converts, it is said, were the fruits of his mission."[1] "My companion," said the fearless Marquette, when exploring the prairies of the Western wilderness, "is an envoy of France to discover new countries, and I am an ambassador of God to enlighten them with the Gospel." Lalemant, when pierced with the arrows of the Iroquois, rejoiced that his martyrdom would induce others to follow his example. The missions of the early Jesuits extorted praises from Baxter and panegyric from Liebnitz.

[1] I am inclined to think that this statement is exaggerated; or, if true, that conversion was merely nominal.

And not less remarkable than these missionaries were those who labored in other spheres. Loyola himself, though visionary and monastic, had no higher wish than to infuse piety into the Catholic Church, and to strengthen the hands of him whom he regarded as God's vicegerent. Somehow or other he succeeded in securing the absolute veneration of his companions, so much so that the sainted Xavier always wrote to him on his knees. His "Spiritual Exercises" has ever remained the great text-book of the Jesuits, — a compend of fasts and penances, of visions and of ecstasies; rivalling Saint Theresa herself in the rhapsodies of a visionary piety, showing the chivalric and romantic ardor of a Spanish nobleman directed into the channel of devotion to an invisible Lord. See this wounded soldier at the siege of Pampeluna, going through all the experiences of a Syriac monk in his Manresan cave, and then turning his steps to Paris to acquire a university education; associating only with the pious and the learned, drawing to him such gifted men as Faber and Xavier, Salmeron and Lainez, Borgia and Bobadilla, and inspiring them with his ideas and his fervor; living afterwards, at Venice, with Caraffa (the future Paul IV.) in the closest intimacy, preaching at Vicenza, and forming a new monastic code, as full of genius and originality as it was of practical wisdom, which became the foundation of a system of government never surpassed in the power of its mechanism to bind the minds and wills of men. Loyola was a most extraordinary man in the practical turn he gave to religious rhapsodies; creating a legislation for his Society which made it the most potent religious organization in the world. All his companions were remarkable likewise for different traits and excellences, which yet were made to combine in sustaining the unity of this moral mechanism. Lainez had even a more comprehensive mind than Loyola. It was he who matured the Jesuit Constitution, and afterwards controlled the Council of Trent, — a convocation which settled the creed of the Catholic Church, especially in regard to justification, and which admitted the merits of Christ, but attributed justification to good works in a different sense from that understood and taught by Luther.

Aside from the personal gifts and qualities of the early Jesuits, they would not have so marvellously succeeded had it not been for their remarkable constitution, — that which bound the members of the Society together, and gave to it a peculiar unity and force. The most marked thing about it was the unbounded and unhesitating obedience required of every member to superiors, and of these superiors to the General of the Order, — so that there was but one will. This law of obedience is, as every one knows, one of the fundamental principles of all the monastic orders from the earliest times, enforced by Benedict as well as Basil. Still there was a difference in the vow of obedience. The head of a monastery in the Middle Ages was almost supreme. The Lord Abbot was obedient only to the Pope, and he sought the interests of his monastery rather than those of the Pope. But Loyola exacted obedience to the General of the Order so absolutely that a Jesuit became a slave. This may seem a harsh epithet; there is nothing gained by using offensive words, but Protestant writers have almost universally made these charges. From their interpretation of the constitutions of Loyola and Lainez and Aquaviva, a member of the Society had no will of his own; he did not belong to himself, he belonged to his General, — as in the time of Abraham a child belonged to his father and a wife to her husband; nay, even still more completely. He could not write or receive a letter that was not read by his Superior. When he entered the order, he was obliged to give away his property, but could not give it to his relatives.[1] When he made confession, he was obliged to tell his most intimate and sacred secrets. He could not aspire to any higher rank than that he held; he had no right to be ambitious, or seek his own individual interests; he was merged body and soul into the Society; he was only a pin in the machinery; he was bound to obey even his own servant, if required

[1] Ranke.

by his Superior; he was less than a private soldier in an army; he was a piece of wax to be moulded as the Superior directed, — and the Superior, in his turn, was a piece of wax in the hands of the Provincial, and he again in the hands of the General. "There were many gradations in rank, but every rank was a gradation in slavery." The Jesuit is accused of having no individual conscience. He was bound to do what he was told, right or wrong; nothing was right and nothing was wrong except as the Society pronounced. The General stood in the place of God. That man was the happiest who was most mechanical. Every novice had a monitor, and every monitor was a spy.[1] So strict was the rule of Loyola, that he kept Francis Borgia, Duke of Candia, three years out of the Society, because he refused to renounce all intercourse with his family.[2]

The Jesuit was obliged to make all natural ties subordinate to the will of the General. And this General was a king more absolute than any worldly monarch, because he reigned over the minds of his subjects. His kingdom was an *imperium in imperio;* he was chosen for life and was responsible to no one, although he ruled for the benefit of the Catholic Church. In one sense a General of the Jesuits resembled the prime minister of an absolute monarch, — say such a man as Richelieu, with unfettered power in the cause of abso-

---

[1] Steinmetz, i. p. 252.　　　　[2] Nicolini, p. 35.

lutism; and he ruled like Richelieu, through his spies, making his subordinates tools and instruments. The General appointed the presidents of colleges and of the religious houses; he admitted or dismissed, dispensed or punished, at his pleasure. There was no complaint; all obeyed his orders, and saw in him the representative of Divine Providence. Complaint was sin; resistance was ruin. It is hard for us to understand how any man could be brought voluntarily to submit to such a despotism. But the novice entering the order had to go through terrible discipline, — to be a servant, anything; to live according to rigid rules, so that his spirit was broken by mechanical duties. He had to learn all the virtues of a slave before he could be fully enrolled in the Society. He was drilled for years by spiritual sergeants more rigorously than a soldier in Napoleon's army: hence the efficiency of the body; it was a spiritual army of the highest disciplined troops. Loyola had been a soldier; he knew what military discipline could do, — how impotent an army is without it, what an awful power it is with discipline, and the severer the better. The best soldier of a modern army is he who has become an unconscious piece of machinery; and it was this unreflecting, unconditional obedience which made the Society so efficient, and the General himself, who controlled it, such an awful power for good or for evil. I am only speaking of the organization, the machinery, the *régime*, of the Jesuits, not of their character, not of their virtues or vices. This organization is to be spoken of as we speak of the discipline of an army, — wise or unwise, as it reached its end. The original aim of the Jesuits was the restoration of the Papal Church to its ancient power; and for one hundred years, as I think, the restoration of morals, higher education, greater zeal in preaching: in short, a reformation within the Church. Jesuitism was, of course, opposed to Protestantism; it hated the Protestants; it hated their religious creed and their emancipating and progressive spirit; it hated religious liberty.

I need not dwell on other things which made this order of monks so successful, — not merely their virtues and their mechanism, but their adaptation to the changing spirit of the times. They threw away the old dresses of monastic life; they quitted the cloister and places of meditation; they were preachers as well as scholars; they accommodated themselves to the circumstances of the times; they wore the ordinary dress of gentlemen; they remained men of the world, of fine manners and cultivated speech; there was nothing ascetic or repulsive about them, like other monks; they were all things to all men, like politicians, in order to accomplish their ends; they never were lazy, or profligate or luxurious. If their Order became enriched, they as individuals remained poor. The inferior members were not even ambitious; like good soldiers, they thought of nothing but the work assigned to them. Their pride and glory were the prosperity of their Order, — an intense *esprit de corps,* never equalled by any body of men. This, of course, while it gave them efficiency, made them narrow. They could see the needle on the barn-door, — they could not see the door itself. Hence there could be no agreement with them, no argument with them, except on ordinary matters; they were as zealous as Saul, seeking to make proselytes. They yielded nothing except in order to win; they never compromised their Order in their cause. Their fidelity to their head was marvellous; and so long as they confined themselves to the work of making people better, I think they deserved praise. I do not like their military organization, but I should have no more right to abuse it than the organization of some Protestant sects. That is a matter of government; all sects and all parties, Catholic and Protestant, have a right to choose their own government to carry out their ends, even as military generals have a right to organize their forces in their own way. The history of the Jesuits shows this, — that an organization of forces, or what we call discipline or government, is a great thing. A church without a government is a poor affair, so far as efficiency is concerned. All churches have something to learn from the Jesuits in the way of discipline. John Wesley learned something; the Independents learned very little.

But there is another side to the Jesuits. We have seen why they succeeded; we have to inquire how they failed. If history speaks of the virtues of the early members, and the wonderful mechanism of their Order, and their great success in consequence, it also speaks of the errors they committed, by which they lost the confidence they had gained. From being the most popular of all the adherents of the papal power, and of the ideas of the Dark Ages, they became the most unpopular; they became so odious that the Pope was obliged, by the pressure of public opinion and of the Bourbon courts of Europe, to suppress their Order. The fall of the Jesuits was as significant as their rise. I need not dwell on that fall, which is one of the best known facts of history.

Why did the Jesuits become unpopular and lose their influence?

They gained the confidence of Catholic countries because they deserved it, and they lost that confidence because they deserved to lose it, — in other words, because they became corrupt; and this seems to be the history of all institutions. It is strange, it is passing strange, that human societies and governments and institutions should degenerate as soon as they become rich and powerful; but such is the fact,— a sad commentary on the doctrine of a necessary progress of the race, or the natural tendency to good, which so many cherish, but than which nothing can be more false, as proved by experience and the Scriptures. Why were the antediluvians swept away? Why could not those races retain their primitive revelation? Why did the descendants of Noah become almost idolaters before he was dead? Why did the great Persian Empire become as effeminate as the empires it had supplanted? Why did the Jewish nation steadily retrograde after David? Why did not civilization and Christianity save the Roman world? Why did Christianity itself become corrupted in four centuries? Why did not the Middle Ages preserve the evangelical doctrines of Augustine and Jerome and Chrysostom and Ambrose? Why did the light of the glorious Reformation of Luther nearly go out in the German cities and universities? Why did the fervor of the Puritans burn out in England in one hundred years? Why have the doctrines of the Pilgrim Fathers become unfashionable in those parts of New England where they seemed to have taken the deepest root? Why have so many of the descendants of the disciples of George Fox become so liberal and advanced as to be enamoured of silk dresses and laces and diamonds and the ritualism of Episcopal churches? Is it an improvement to give up a simple life and lofty religious enthusiasm for materialistic enjoyments and epicurean display? Is there a true advance in a university, when it exchanges its theological teachings and its preparation of poor students for the Gospel Ministry, for Schools of Technology and boat-clubs and accommodations for the sons of the rich and worldly?

Now the Society of Jesus went through just such a transformation as has taken place, almost within the memory of living men, in the life and habits and ideas of the people of Boston and Philadelphia and in the teachings of their universities. Some may boldly say, "Why not? This change indicates progress." But this progress is exactly similar to that progress which the Jesuits made in the magnificence of their churches, in the wealth they had hoarded in their colleges, in the fashionable character of their professors and confessors and preachers, in the adaptation of their doctrines to the taste of the rich and powerful, in the elegance and arrogance and worldliness of their dignitaries. Father La Chaise was an elegant and most polished man of the world, and travelled in a coach with six horses. If he had not been such a man, he would not have been selected by Louis XIV. for his confidential and influential confessor. The change which took place among the Jesuits arose from the same causes as the change which has taken place among Methodists and Quakers and

Puritans. This change I would not fiercely condemn, for some think it is progress. But is it progress in that religious life which early marked these people; or a progress towards worldly and epicurean habits which they arose to resist and combat? The early Jesuits were visionary, fanatical, strict, ascetic, religious, and narrow. They sought by self-denying labors and earnest exhortations, like Savonarola at Florence, to take the Church out of the hands of the Devil; and the people reverenced them, as they always have reverenced martyrs and missionaries. The later Jesuits sought to enjoy their wealth and power and social position. They became — as rich and prosperous people generally become — proud, ambitious, avaricious, and worldly. They were as elegant, as scholarly, and as luxurious as the Fellows of Oxford University, and the occupants of stalls in the English cathedrals, — that is all: as worldly as the professors of Yale and Cambridge may become in half-a-century, if rich widows and brewers and bankers without children shall some day make those universities as well endowed as Jesuit colleges were in the eighteenth century. That is the old story of our fallen humanity. I would no more abuse the Jesuits because they became confessors to the great, and went into mercantile speculations, than I would rich and favored clergymen in Protestant countries, who prefer ten per cent for their money in California mines to four per cent in national consols.

But the prosperity which the Jesuits had earned during their first century of existence excited only envy, and destroyed the reverence of the people; it had not made them odious, detestable. It was the means they adopted to perpetuate their influence, after early virtues had passed away, which caused enlightened Catholic Europe to mistrust them, and the Protestants absolutely to hate and vilify them.

From the very first, the Society was distinguished for the *esprit de corps* of its members. Of all things which they loved best it was the power and glory of the Society,—just as Oxford Fellows love the *prestige* of their university. And this power and influence the Jesuits determined to preserve at all hazards and by any means; when virtues fled, they must find something else with which to bolster themselves up: they must not part with their power; the question was, how should they keep it?

First, they adopted the doctrine of expediency,—that the end justifies the means. They did not invent this sophistry,—it is as old as our humanity. Abraham used it when he told lies to the King of Egypt, to save the honor of his wife; Cæsar accepted it, when he vindicated imperialism as the only way to save the Roman Empire from anarchy; most politicians resort to it when they wish to gain their ends. Politicians have ever been as unscrupulous as the Jesuits, in adopting expediency rather than eternal right. It has been a primal law of government; it lies at the basis of English encroachments in India, and of the treatment of the aborigines in this country by our government. There is nothing new in the doctrine of expediency.

But the Jesuits are accused of pushing this doctrine to its remotest consequences, of being its most unscrupulous defenders,—so that *jesuitism* and *expediency* are synonymous, are convertible terms. They are accused of perverting education, of abusing the confessional, of corrupting moral and political philosophy, of conforming to the inclinations of the great. They even went so far as to inculcate mental reservation,—thus attacking truth in its most sacred citadel, the conscience of mankind,—on which Pascal was so severe. They made habit and bad example almost a sufficient exculpation from crime. Perjury was allowable, if the perjured were inwardly determined not to swear. They invented the notion of probabilities, according to which a person might follow any opinion he pleased, although he knew it to be wrong, provided authors of reputation had defended that opinion. A man might fight a duel, if by refusing to fight he would be stigmatized as a coward. They did not openly justify murder, treachery, and falsehood, but they excused the same, if plausible reasons could be urged. In their missions they aimed at *éclat;* and hence merely nominal conversions were accepted, because these swelled their numbers. They gave the crucifix, which covered up all sins; they permitted their converts to retain their ancient habits and customs. In order to be popular, Robert de Nobili, it is said, traced his lineage to Brahma; and one of their missionaries among the Indians told the savages that Christ was a warrior who scalped women and children. Anything for an outward success. Under their teachings it was seen what a light affair it was to bear the yoke of Christ. So monarchs retained in their service confessors who imposed such easy obligations. So ordinary people resorted to the guidance of such leaders, who made themselves agreeable. The Jesuit colleges were filled with casuists. Their whole moral philosophy, if we may believe Arnauld and Pascal, was a tissue of casuistry; truth was obscured in order to secure popularity; even the most diabolical persecution was justified if heretics stood in the way. Father Le Tellier rejoiced in the slaughter of Saint Bartholomew, and *Te Deums* were offered in the churches for the extinction of Protestantism by any means. If it could be shown to be expedient, the Jesuits excused the most outrageous crimes ever perpetrated on this earth.

Again, the Jesuits are accused of riveting fetters on the human mind in order to uphold their power, and to sustain the absolutism of the popes and the absolutism of kings, to which they were equally devoted. They taught in their schools the doctrine of passive obedience; they aimed to subdue the will by rigid discipline; they were hostile to bold and free inquiries; they were afraid of science; they hated such men as Galileo, Pascal, and Bacon; they detested the philosophers who prepared the way for the French Revolution; they abominated the Protestant idea of private judgment; they opposed the progress of human thought, and were enemies alike of the Jansenist movement in the seventeenth century and of the French Revolution in the eighteenth. They upheld the absolutism of Louis XIV., and combated the English Revolution; they sent their spies and agents to England to undermine the throne of Elizabeth and build up the throne of Charles I. Every emancipating idea, in politics and in religion, they detested. There were many things in their system of education to be commended; they were good classical scholars, and taught Greek and Latin admirably; they cultivated the memory; they made study pleasing, but they did not develop genius. The order never produced a great philosopher; the energies of its members were concentrated in imposing a despotic yoke.

The Jesuits are accused further of political intrigues; this is a common and notorious charge. They sought to control the cabinets of Europe; they had their spies in every country. The intrigues of Campion and Parsons in England aimed at the restoration of Catholic monarchs. Mary of Scotland was a tool in their hands, and so was Madame de Maintenon in France. La Chaise and Le Tellier were mere politicians. The Jesuits were ever political priests; the history of Europe the last three hundred years is full of their cabals. Their political influence was directed to the persecution of Protestants as well as infidels. They are accused of securing the revocation of the Edict of Nantes, — one of the greatest crimes in the history of modern times, which led to the expulsion of four hundred thousand Protestants from France, and the execution of four hundred thousand more. They incited the dragonnades of Louis XIV., who was under their influence. They are accused of the assassination of kings, of the fires of Smithfield, of the Gunpowder Plot, of the cruelties inflicted by Alva, of the Thirty Years' War, of the ferocities of the Guises, of inquisitions and massacres, of sundry other political crimes, with what justice I do not know; but certain it is they became objects of fear, and incurred the hostilities of Catholic Europe, especially of all liberal thinkers, and their downfall was demanded by the very courts of Europe. Why did they lose their popularity? Why were they so distrusted and hated? The fact that they *were* hated is most undoubted, and there must have been cause for it. It is a fact that at one time they were respected and honored, and deserved to be so: must there not have been grave reasons for the universal change in public opinion respecting them? The charges against them, to which I have alluded, must have had foundation. They did not become idle, gluttonous, ignorant, and sensual like the old monks: they became greedy of power; and in order to retain it resorted to intrigues, conspiracies, and persecutions. They corrupted philosophy and morality, abused the confessional privilege, adopted *Success* as their watchword, without regard to the means; they are charged with becoming worldly, ambitious, mercenary, unscrupulous, cruel; above all, they sought to bind the minds of men with a despotic yoke, and waged war against all liberalizing influences. They always were, from first to last, narrow, pedantic, one-sided, legal, technical, pharisaical. The best thing about them, in the days of their declining power, was that they always opposed infidel sentiments. They hated Voltaire and Rousseau and the Encyclopedists as much as they did Luther and Calvin. They detested the principles of the French Revolution, partly because those principles were godless, partly because they were emancipating.

Of course, in such an infidel and revolutionary age as that of Louis XV., when Voltaire was the oracle of Europe, — when from his château near Geneva he controlled the mind of Europe, as Calvin did two centuries earlier, — enemies would rise up, on all sides, against

After the painting by Fr. Boucher

MADAME DE POMPADOUR

the Jesuits. Their most powerful and bitter foe was a woman, — the mistress of Louis XV., the infamous Madame de Pompadour. She hated the Jesuits as Catharine de Medici hated the Calvinists in the time of Charles IX., — not because they were friends of absolutism, not because they wrote casuistic books, not because they opposed liberal principles, not because they were spies and agents of Rome, not because they perverted education, not because they were boastful and mercenary missionaries or cunning intriguers in the courts of princes, not because they had marked their course through Europe in a trail of blood, but because they were hostile to her ascendency, — a woman who exercised about the same influence in France as Jezebel did at the court of Ahab. I respect the Jesuits for the stand they took against this woman: it is the best thing in their history. But here they did not show their usual worldly wisdom, and they failed. They were judicially blinded. The instrument of their humiliation was a wicked woman. So strange are the ways of Providence! He chose Esther to save the Jewish nation, and a harlot to punish the Jesuits. She availed herself of their mistakes.

It seems that the Superior of the Jesuits at Martinique failed; for the Jesuits embarked in commercial speculations while officiating as missionaries. The angry creditors of La Valette, the Jesuit banker, demanded repayment from the Order. They refused to pay his debts. The case was carried to the courts, and the highest tribunal decided against them. That was not the worst. In the course of the legal proceedings, the mysterious "rule" of the Jesuits — that which was so carefully concealed from the public — was demanded. Then all was revealed, — all that Pascal had accused them of, — and the whole nation was indignant. A great storm was raised. The Parliament of Paris decreed the constitution of the Society to be fatal to all government. The King wished to save them, for he knew that they were the best supporters of the throne of absolutism. But he could not resist the pressure, — the torrent of public opinion, the entreaties of his mistress, the arguments of his ministers. He was compelled to demand from the Pope the abrogation of their charter. Other monarchs did the same; all the Bourbon courts in Europe, for the king of Portugal narrowly escaped assassination from a fanatical Jesuit. Had the Jesuits consented to a reform, they might not have fallen. But they would make no concessions. Said Ricci, their General, *Sint ut sunt, aut non sint.* The Pope — Clement XIV. — was obliged to part with his best soldiers. Europe, Catholic Europe, demanded the sacrifice, — the kings of Spain, of France, of Naples, of Portugal. *Compulsus feci, compulsus feci,* exclaimed the broken-hearted Pope, — the feeble and pious Gan-

ganelli. So that in 1773, by a papal decree, the Order was suppressed; 669 colleges were closed; 223 missions were abandoned, and more than 22,000 members were dispersed. I do not know what became of their property, which amounted to about two hundred millions of dollars, in the various countries of Europe.

This seems to me to have been a clear case of religious persecution, incited by jealous governments and the infidel or the progressive spirit of the age, on the eve of the French Revolution. It simply marks the hostilities which, for various reasons, they had called out. I am inclined to think that their faults were greatly exaggerated; but it is certain that so severe and high-handed a measure would not have been taken by the Pope had it not seemed to him necessary to preserve the peace of the Church. Had they been innocent, the Pope would have lost his throne sooner than commit so great a wrong on his most zealous servants. It is impossible for a Protestant to tell how far they were guilty of the charges preferred against them. I do not believe that their lives, as a general thing, were a scandal sufficient to justify so sweeping a measure; but their institution, their régime, their organization, their constitution, were deemed hostile to liberty and the progress of society. And if zealous governments — Catholic princes themselves — should feel that the Jesuits were opposed to the true progress of nations, how much more reason had Protestants to distrust them, and to rejoice in their fall!

And it was not until the French Revolution and the empire of Napoleon had passed away, not until the Bourbons had been restored nearly half a century, that the Order was re-established and again protected by the Papal court. They have now regained their ancient power, and seem to have the confidence of Catholic Europe. Some of their most flourishing seminaries are in the United States. They are certainly not a scandal in this country, although their spirit and institution are the same as ever: mistrusted and disliked and feared by the Protestants, as a matter of course, as such a powerful organization naturally would be; hostile still to the circulation of the Scriptures among the people and free inquiry and private judgment, — in short, to all the ideas of the Reformation. But whatever they are, and however much the Protestants dislike them, they have in our country, — this land of unbounded religious toleration, — the same right to their religion and their ecclesiastical government that Protestant sects have; and if Protestants would nullify their influence so far as it is bad, they must outshine them in virtues, in a religious life, in zeal, and in devotion to the spiritual interests of the people. If the Jesuits keep better schools than Protestants they will be patronized, and if they command the respect of the

Catholics for their virtues and intelligence, whatever may be the machinery of their organization, they will retain their power; and not until they interfere with elections and Protestant schools, or teach dangerous doctrines of public morality, has our Government any right to interfere with them. They will stand or fall as they win the respect or excite the wrath of enlightened nations. But the principles they are supposed to defend, — expediency, casuistry, and hostility to free inquiry and the circulation of the Scriptures in vernacular languages, — these are just causes of complaint and of unrelenting opposition among all those who accept the great ideas of the Protestant Reformation, since they are antagonistic to what we deem most precious in our institutions. So long as the contest shall last between good and evil in this world, we have a right to declaim against all encroachments on liberty and sound morality and an evangelical piety from any quarter whatever, and we are recreant to our duties unless we speak our minds. Hence, from the light I have, I pronounce judgment against the Society of Jesus as a dangerous institution, unfortunately planted among us, but which we cannot help, and can attack only with the weapons of reason and truth.

And yet I am free to say that for my part I prefer even the Jesuit discipline and doctrines, much as I dislike them, to the unblushing infidelity which has lately been propagated by those who call themselves *savans*,—and which seems to have reached and even permeated many of the schools of science, the newspapers, periodicals, clubs, and even pulpits of this materialistic though progressive country. I make war on the slavery of the will and a religion of formal technicalities; but I prefer these evils to a godless rationalism and the extinction of the light of faith.

AUTHORITIES.

Secreta Monita; Steinmetz's History of the Jesuits; Ranke's History of the Popes; Spiritual Exercises; Encyclopædia Britannica; Biographie Universelle; Fall of the Jesuits, by St. Priest; Lives of Ignatius Loyola, Aquiviva, Lainez, Salmeron, Borgia, Xavier, Bobadilla; Pascal's Provincial Letters; Bonhours' Crétineau; Lingard's History of England; Tierney; Lettres Ædificantes; Jesuit Missions; Mémoires Sécrètes du Cardinal Dubois; Tanner's Societas Jesu; Dodd's Church History.

JOHN CALVIN.

A. D. 1509–1564.

PROTESTANT THEOLOGY.

JOHN CALVIN.

PROTESTANT THEOLOGY.

JOHN CALVIN was pre-eminently the theologian of the Reformation, and stamped his genius on the thinking of his age, — equally an authority with the Swiss, the Dutch, the Huguenots, and the Puritans. His vast influence extends to our own times. His fame as a benefactor of mind is immortal, although it cannot be said that he is as much admired and extolled now as he was fifty years ago. Nor was he ever a favorite with the English Church. He has been even grossly misrepresented by theological opponents; but no critic or historian has ever questioned his genius, his learning, or his piety. No one denies that he has exerted a great influence on Protestant countries. As a theologian he ranks with Saint Augustine and Thomas Aquinas, — maintaining essentially the same views as those held by these great lights, and being distinguished for the same logical power; reigning like them as an intellectual dictator in the schools, but not so interesting as they were as men. And he was more than a theologian; he was a reformer and legislator, laying down rules of government, organizing church discipline, and carrying on reforms in the worship of God,—second only to Luther. His labors were prodigious as theologian, commentator, and ecclesiastical legislator; and we are surprised that a man with so feeble a body could have done so much work.

Calvin was born in Picardy in 1509,—the year that Henry VIII. ascended the British throne, and the year that Luther began to preach at Wittenberg. He was not a peasant's son, like Luther, but belonged to what the world calls a good family. Intellectually he was precocious, and received an excellent education at a college in Paris, being destined for the law by his father, who sent him to the University of Orleans and then to Bourges, where he studied under eminent jurists, and made the acquaintance of many distinguished men. His conversion took place about the year 1529, when he was twenty; and this gave a new direction to his studies and his life. He was a pale-faced young man, with sparkling eyes, sedate and earnest beyond his years. He was twenty-three when he published the books of Seneca on Clemency, with learned commentaries. At the age of twenty-three he was in communion with the reformers of Germany, and was acknowledged to be, even at that early age, the head of the reform party in France. In 1533 he went to Paris, then as always the centre of the national life, where the new ideas were creating great commotion in scholarly and ecclesiastical circles, and even in the court itself. Giving offence to the doctors of the Sorbonne for his evangelical views as to Justification, he was obliged to seek refuge with the Queen of Navarre, whose castle at Pau was the resort of persecuted reformers. After leading rather a fugitive life in different parts of France, he retreated to Switzerland, and at twenty-six published his celebrated "Institutes," which he dedicated to Francis I., hoping to convert him to the Protestant faith. After a short residence in Italy, at the court of the Duchess of Ferrara, he took up his abode at Geneva, and his great career began.

Geneva, a city of the Allobroges in the time of Cæsar, possessed at this time about twenty thousand inhabitants, and was a free state, having a constitution somewhat like that of Florence when it was under the control of Savonarola. It had rebelled against the Duke of Savoy, who seems to have been in the fifteenth century its patron ruler. The government of this little Savoyard state became substantially like that which existed among the Swiss cantons. The supreme power resided in the council of Two Hundred, which alone had the power to make or abolish laws. There was a lesser council of Sixty, for diplomatic objects only.

The first person who preached the reformed doctrines in Geneva was the missionary Farel, a French nobleman, spiritual, romantic, and zealous. He had great success, although he encountered much opposition and wrath. But the reformed doctrines were already established in Zurich, Berne, and Basle, chiefly through the preaching of Ulrich Zwingli, and Œcolampadius. The apostolic Farel welcomed with great cordiality the arrival of Calvin, then already known as an extraordinary man, though only twenty-eight years of age. He came to Geneva poor, and remained poor all his life. All his property at his death amounted to only two hundred dollars. As a minister in one of the churches, he soon began to exert a marvellous influence. He must have been eloquent, for he was received with enthusiasm. This was in 1536. But he soon met with obstacles. He was worried by the Anabaptists; and even his orthodoxy was impeached by one Coroli, who made much mischief, so that Calvin was obliged to publish his Genevan Catechism in Latin. He also offended many by his outspoken rebuke of sin, for he aimed at a complete reformation of morals, like Latimer in London and like Savonarola at Florence. He sought to reprove amusements which were demoralizing, or thought to be so in their influence. The passions of the people were excited, and the city was torn by parties; and such was the reluctance to submit to the discipline of the ministers that they refused to administer the sacraments. This created such a ferment that the syndics expelled Calvin and Farel from the city. They went at first to Berne, but the Bernese would not receive them. They then retired to Basle, wearied, wet, and hungry, and from Basle they went to Strasburg. It was in this city that Calvin dwelt three years, spending his time in lecturing on divinity, in making contributions to exegetical theology, in perfecting his "Institutes," forming a close alliance with Melancthon and other leading reformers. So pre-occupied was he with his labors as a commentator of the Scriptures, that he even contemplated withdrawing from the public service of religion.

Calvin was a scholar as well as theologian, and quiet labors in his library were probably more congenial to his tastes than active parochial duties. His highest life was amid his books, in serene repose and lofty contemplation. At this time he had an extensive correspondence, his advice being much sought for its wisdom and moderation. His judgment was almost unerring, since he was never led away by extravagances or enthusiasm: a cold, calm man even among his friends and admirers. He had no passions; he was all intellect. It would seem that in his exile he gave lectures on divinity, being invited by the Council of Strasburg; and also interested himself in reference to the Sacrament of the Lord's Supper, which he would withhold from the unworthy. He lived quietly in his retreat, and was much respected by the people of the city where he dwelt.

In 1539 a convention was held at Frankfort, at which Calvin was present as the envoy of the city of Strasburg. Here, for the first time, he met Melancthon; but there was no close intimacy between them until these two great men met in the following year at a Diet which was summoned at Worms by the Emperor Charles V., in order to produce concord between the Catholics and Protestants, and which was afterwards removed to Ratisbon. Melancthon represented one party, and Doctor Eck the other. Melancthon and Bucer were inclined to peace; and Cardinal Contarini freely offered his hand, agreeing with the reformers to adopt the idea of Justification as his starting point, allowing that it proceeds from faith, without any merit of our own; but, like Luther and Calvin, he opposed any attempt at union which might compromise the truth, and had no faith in the movement. Neither party, as it was to be expected, was satisfied. The main subject of the dispute was in reference to the Eucharist. Calvin denied the real presence of Christ in the Sacrament, regarding it as a symbol,— though one of special divine influence. But on this point the Catholics have ever been uncompromising from the times of

Berengar. Nor was Luther fully emancipated from the Catholic doctrine, modifying without essentially changing it. Calvin maintained that "This is my body" meant that it signified "my body." In regard to original sin and free-will, as represented by Augustine, there was no dispute; but much difficulty attended the interpretation of the doctrine of Justification. The greatest difficulty was in reference to the doctrine of Transubstantiation, which was rejected by the reformers because it had not the sanction of the Scriptures; and when it was found that this caused insuperable difficulties about the Lord's Supper, it was thought useless to proceed to other matters, like confession, masses for the dead, and the withholding the cup from the laity. There was not so great a difference between the Catholic and Protestant theologians concerning the main body of dogmatic divinity as is generally supposed. The fundamental questions pertaining to God, the Trinity, the mission and divinity of Christ, original sin, free-will, grace, predestination, had been formulated by Thomas Aquinas with as much severity as by Calvin. The great subjects at issue, in a strictly theological view, were Justification and the Eucharist. Respecting free-will and predestination, the Catholic theologians have never been agreed among themselves, — some siding with Augustine, like Aquinas, Bernard, and Anselm; and some with Pelagius, like Abélard and Lainez the Jesuit at the

Council of Trent (a council assembled by the Pope, with the concurrence of Charles V. of Germany and Francis I. of France), the decrees of which, against the authority of Augustine in this matter, seem to be now the established faith of the Roman Catholic Church.

After the Diet of Ratisbon, Calvin returned to Geneva, at the eager desire of the people. The great Council summoned him to return; every voice was raised for him. "Calvin, that learned and righteous man," they said, "it is he whom we would have as the minister of the Lord." Yet he did not willingly return; he preferred his quiet life at Strasburg, but obeyed the voice of conscience. On the 13th of September, 1541, he returned to his penitent congregation, and was received by the whole city with every demonstration of respect; and a cloth cloak was given him as a present, which he seemed to need.

The same year he was married to a widow, Idelette de Burie, who was a worthy, well-read, high-minded woman, with whom he lived happily for nine years, until her death. She was superior to Luther's wife, Catherine Bora, in culture and dignity, and was a helpmate who never opposed her husband in the slightest matter, always considering his interests. Esteem and friendship seem to have been the basis of this union, —not passionate love, which Calvin did not think much of. When his wife died it seems he mourned for her with decent grief, but did not seek a second marriage, perhaps because he was unable to support a wife on his small stipend as she would wish and expect. He rather courted poverty, and refused reasonable gratuities. His body was attenuated by fasting and study, like that of Saint Bernard. When he was completing his "Institutes," he passed days without eating and nights without sleeping. And as he practised poverty he had a right to inculcate it. He kept no servant, lived in a small tenement, and was always poorly clad. He derived no profit from any of his books, and the only present he ever consented to receive was a silver goblet from the Lord of Varennes. Luther's stipend was four hundred and fifty florins; and he too refused a yearly gift from the booksellers of four hundred dollars, not wishing to receive a gratuity for his writings. Calvin's salary was only fifty dollars a year, with a house, twelve measures of corn, and two pipes of wine; for tea and coffee were then unknown in Europe, and wine seems to have been the usual beverage, after water. He was pre-eminently a conscientious man, not allowing his feelings to sway his judgment. He was sedate and dignified and cheerful; though Bossuet accuses him of a surly disposition,— *un genre triste, un esprit chagrin.* Though formal and stern, women never shrank from familiar conversation with him on the subject of religion. Though intolerant of error, he cherished no personal animosities. Calvin was more refined than Luther, and never like him gave vent to coarse expressions. He had not Luther's physical strength, nor his versatility of genius; nor as a reformer was he so violent. " Luther aroused; Calvin tranquillized." The one stormed the great citadel of error, the other furnished the weapons for holding it after it was taken. The former was more popular; the latter appealed to a higher intelligence. The Saxon reformer was more eloquent; the Swiss reformer was more dialectical. The one advocated unity; the other theocracy. Luther was broader; Calvin engrafted on his reforms the Old Testament observances. The watchword of the one was Grace; that of the other was Predestination. Luther cut knots; Calvin made systems. Luther destroyed; Calvin legislated. His great principle of government was aristocratic. He wished to see both Church and State governed by a select few of able men. In all his writings we see no trace of popular sovereignty. He interested himself, like Savonarola, in political institutions, but would separate the functions of the magistracy from those of the clergy; and he clung to the notion of a theocratic government, like Jewish legislators and the popes themselves. The idea of a theocracy was the basis of Calvin's system of legislation, as it was that of Leo I. He desired that the temporal power should rule in the name of God, — should be the arm by which spiritual principles should be enforced. He did not object to the spiritual domination of the popes, so far as it was in accordance with the word of God. He wished to realize the grand idea which the Middle Ages sought for, but sought for in vain, — that the Church must always remain the mother of spiritual principles; but he objected to the exercise of temporal power by churchmen, as well as to the interference of the temporal power in matters purely spiritual, — virtually the doctrine of Anselm and Becket. But, unlike Becket, Calvin would not screen clergymen accused of crime from temporal tribunals; he rather sought the humiliation of the clergy in temporal matters. He also would destroy inequalities of rank, and do away with church dignitaries, like bishops and deans and archdeacons; and he instituted twice as many laymen as clergymen in ecclesiastical assemblies. But he gave to the clergy the exclusive right to excommunicate, and to regulate the administration of the sacraments. He was himself a high-churchman in his spirit, both in reference to the divine institution of the presbyterian form of government and the ascendancy of the Church as a great power in the world.

Calvin exercised a great influence on the civil polity of Geneva, although it was established before he came to the city. He undertook to frame for the State a code of morals. He limited the freedom of the citizens, and turned the old democratic constitution into an oligarchy. The general assembly, which met twice a year, nominated syndics, or judges; but nothing was proposed in the general assembly which had not previously been considered in the council of the Two Hundred; and nothing in the latter which had not been brought before the council of Sixty; nor even in this, which had not been approved by the lesser council. The four syndics, with their council of sixteen, had power of life and death, and the whole public business of the state was in their hands. The supreme legislation was in the council of Two Hundred; which was much influenced by ecclesiastics, or the consistory. If a man not forbidden to take the Sacrament neglected to receive it, he was condemned to banishment for a year. One was condemned to do public penance if he omitted a Sunday service. The military garrison was summoned to prayers twice a day. The judges punished severely all profanity, as blasphemy. A mason was put in prison three days for simply saying, when falling from a building, that it must be the work of the Devil. A young girl who insulted her mother was publicly punished and kept on bread-and-water; and a peasant-boy who called his mother a devil was publicly whipped. A child who struck his mother was beheaded; adultery was punished with death; a woman was publicly scourged because she sang common songs to a psalm-tune; and another because she dressed herself, in a frolic, in man's attire. Brides were not allowed to wear wreaths in their bonnets; gamblers were set in the pillory, and card-playing and nine-pins were denounced as gambling. Heresy was punished with death; and in sixty years one hundred and fifty people were burned to death, in Geneva, for witchcraft. Legislation extended to dress and private habits; many innocent amusements were altogether suppressed; also holidays and theatrical exhibitions. Excommunication was as much dreaded as in the Mediæval church.

In regard to the worship of God, Calvin was opposed to splendid churches, and to all ritualism. He retained psalm-singing, but abolished the organ; he removed the altar, the crucifix, and muniments from the churches, and closed them during the week-days, unless the minister was present. He despised what we call art, especially artistic music; nor did he have much respect for artificial sermons, or the art of speaking. He himself preached *ex tempore*, nor is there evidence that he ever wrote a sermon.

Respecting the Eucharist, Calvin took a middle course between Luther and Zwingli, — believing neither in the actual presence of Christ in the consecrated bread, nor regarding it as a mere symbol, but a means by which divine grace is imparted; a mirror in which we may contemplate Christ. Baptism he considered only as an indication of divine grace, and not essential to salvation; thereby differing from Luther and the Catholic church. Yet he was as strenuous in maintaining these sacraments as a Catholic priest, and made excommunication as fearful a weapon as it was in the Middle Ages. For admission to the Lord's Supper, and thus to the membership of the visible Church, it would seem that his requirements were not rigid, but rather very simple, like those of the primitive Christians, — namely, faith in God and faith in Christ, without any subtile and metaphysical creeds, such as one might expect from his inexorable theological deductions. But he would resort to excommunication as a discipline, as the only weapon which the Church could use to bind its members together, and which had been used from the beginning; yet he would temper severity with mildness and charity, since only God is able to judge the heart. And herein he departed from the customs of the Middle Ages, and did not regard the excommunicated as lost, but to be prayed for by the faithful. No one, he maintained, should be judged as deserving eternal death who was still in the hands of God. He made a broad distinction between excommunication and anathema; the latter, he maintained, should never, or very rarely, be pronounced, since it takes away the hope of forgiveness, and consigns one to the wrath of God and the power of Satan. He regarded the Sacrament of the Lord's Supper as a means to help manifold infirmities,—as a time of meditation for beholding Christ the crucified; as confirming reconciliation with God; as a visible sign of the body of Christ, recognizing his actual but spiritual presence. Luther recognized the bodily presence of Christ in the Eucharist, while he rejected transubstantiation and the idea of worshipping the consecrated wafer as the real God. This difference in the opinion of the reformers as to the Eucharist led to bitter quarrels and controversies, and divided the Protestants. Calvin pursued a middle and moderate course, and did much to harmonize the Protestant churches. He always sought peace and moderation; and his tranquillizing measures were not pleasant to the Catholics, who wished to see divisions among their enemies.

Calvin had a great dislike of ceremonies, festivals, holidays, and the like. For images he had an aversion amounting to horror. Christmas was the only festival he retained. He was even slanderously accused of wishing to abolish the Sabbath, the observance of which he inculcated with the strictness of the Puritans. He introduced congregational singing, but would not allow the ear or the eye to be distracted. The music was simple, dispensing with organs and instruments and all elaborate and artistic display. It is needless to say that this severe simplicity of worship has nearly passed away, but it cannot be doubted that the changes which the reformers made produced the deepest impression on the people in a fervent and religious age. The psalms and hymns of the reformers were composed in times of great religious excitement. Calvin was far behind Luther, who did not separate the art of music from religion; but Calvin made a divorce of art from public worship. Indeed, the Reformation was not favorable to art in any form except in sacred poetry; it declared those truths which save the soul, rather than sought those arts which adorn civilization. Hence its churches were barren of ornaments and symbols, and were cold and repulsive when the people were not excited by religious truths. Nor did they favor eloquence in the ordinary meaning of that word. Pulpit eloquence was simple, direct, and without rhetorical devices; seeking effect not in gestures and postures and modulated voice, but earnest appeals to the heart and conscience. The great Catholic preachers of the eighteenth century — like Bossuet and Bourdaloue and Massillon — surpassed the Protestants as rhetoricians.

The simplicity which marked the worship of God as established by Calvin was also a feature in his system of church government. He dispensed with bishops, archdeacons, deans, and the like. In his eyes every man who preached the word was a presbyter, or elder;

and every presbyter was a bishop. A deacon was an officer to take care of the poor, not to preach. And it was necessary that a minister should have a double call,— both an inward call and an outward one,— or an election by the people in union with the clergy. Paul and Barnabas set forth elders, but the people indicated their approval by lifting up their hands. In the Presbyterianism which Calvin instituted he maintained that the Church is represented by the laity as well as by the clergy. He therefore gave the right of excommunication to the congregation in conjunction with the clergy. In the Lutheran Church, as in the Catholic, the right of excommunication was vested in the clergy alone. But Calvin gave to the clergy alone the right to administer the sacraments; nor would he give to the Church any other power of punishment than exclusion from the Lord's Supper, and excommunication. His organization of the Church was aristocratic, placing the power in the hands of a few men of approved wisdom and piety. He had no sympathy with democracy, either civil or religious, and he formed a close union between Church and State,— giving to the council the right to choose elders and to confirm the election of ministers. As already stated, he did not attempt to shield the clergy from the civil tribunals. The consistory, which assembled once a week, was formed of elders and preachers, and a messenger of the civil court summoned before it the persons whose presence was required. No such power as this would be tolerated in these times. But the consistory could not itself inflict punishment; that was the province of the civil government. The elders and clergy inflicted no civil penalties, but simply determined what should be heard before the spiritual and what before the civil tribunal. A syndic presided in the spiritual assembly at first, but only as a church elder. The elders were chosen from the council, and the election was confirmed by the great council, the people, and preachers; so that the Church was really in the hands of the State, which appointed the clergy. It would thus seem that Church and State were very much mixed up together by Calvin, who legislated in view of the circumstances which surrounded him, and not for other times or nations. This subordination of the Church to the State, which was maintained by all the reformers, was established in opposition to the custom of the Catholic Church, which sought to make the State subservient to the Church. And the lay government of the Church, which entered into the system of Calvin, was owing to the fear that the clergy, when able to stand alone, might become proud and ambitious; a fear which was grounded on the whole history of the Church.

Although Calvin had an exalted idea of the spiritual dignity of the Church, he allowed a very dangerous interference of the State in ecclesiastical affairs, even while he would separate the functions of the clergy from those of the magistrates. He allowed the State to pronounce the final sentence on dogmatic questions, and hence the power of the synod failed in Geneva. Moreover, the payment of ministers by the State rather than by the people, as in this country, was against the old Jewish custom, which Calvin so often borrowed, — for the priests among the Jews were independent of the kings. But Calvin wished to destroy caste among the clergy, and consequently spiritual tyranny. In his legislation we see an intense hostility to the Roman Catholic Church,— one of the animating principles of the Reformers; and hence the Reformers, in their hostility to Rome, went from Sylla into Charybdis. Calvin, like all churchmen, exalted naturally the theocratic idea of the old Jewish and Mediæval Church, and yet practically put the Church into the hands of laymen. In one sense he was a spiritual dictator, and like Luther a sort of Protestant pope; and yet he built up a system which was fatal to spiritual power such as had existed among the Catholic priesthood. For their sacerdotal spiritual power he would substitute a moral power, the result of personal bearing and sanctity. It is amusing to hear some people speak of Calvin as a ghostly spiritual father; but no man ever fought sacerdotalism more earnestly than he. The logical sequence of his ecclesiastical reforms was not the aristocratic and Erastian Church of Scotland, but the Puritans in New England, who were Independents and not Presbyterians.

Yet there is an inconsistency even in Calvin's régime; for he had the zeal of the old Catholic Church in giving over to the civil power those he wished to punish, as in the case of Servetus. He even intruded into the circle of social life, and established a temporal rather than a spiritual theocracy; and while he overthrew the episcopal element, he made a distinction, not recognized in the primitive church, between clergy and laity. As for religious toleration, it did not exist in any country or in any church; there was no such thing as true evangelical freedom. All the Reformers attempted, as well as the Catholics, a compulsory unity of faith; and this is an impossibility. The Reformers adopted a catechism, or a theological system, which all communicants were required to learn and accept. This is substantially the acceptance of what the Church ordains. Creeds are perhaps a necessity in well-organized ecclesiastical bodies, and are not unreasonable; but it should not be forgotten that they are formulated doctrines made by men, on what is supposed to be the meaning of the Scriptures, and are not consistent with the right of private judgment when pushed out to its ultimate logical consequence. When we remember how few men are capable of interpreting Scripture for themselves, and how few are disposed to exercise this right, we can see why the formulated catechism proved useful in securing unity of belief; but when Protestant divines insisted on the acceptance of the articles of faith which they deduced from the Scriptures, they did not differ materially from the Catholic clergy in persisting on the acceptance of the authority of the Church as to matters of doctrine. Probably a church organization is impossible without a formulated creed. Such a creed has existed from the time of the Council of Nice, and is not likely ever to be abandoned by any Christian Church in any future age, although it may be modified and softened with the advance of knowledge. However, it is difficult to conceive of the unity of the Church as to faith, without a creed made obligatory on all the members of a communion to accept, and it always has been regarded as a useful and even necessary form of Christian instruction for the people. Calvin himself attached great importance to catechisms, and prepared one even for children.

He also put a great value on preaching, instead of the complicated and imposing ritual of the Catholic service; and in most Protestant churches from his day to ours preaching, or religious instruction, has occupied the most prominent part of the church service;

and it must be conceded that while the Catholic service has often degenerated into mere rites and ceremonies to aid a devotional spirit, so the Protestant service has often become cold and rationalistic,—and it is not easy to say which extreme is the worse.

Thus far we have viewed Calvin in the light of a reformer and legislator, but his influence as a theologian is more remarkable. It is for his theology that he stands out as a prominent figure in the history of the Church. As such he showed greater genius; as such he is the most eminent of all the reformers; as such he impressed his mind on the thinking of his own age and of succeeding ages,—an original and immortal man. His system of divinity embodied in his "Institutes" is remarkable for the radiation of the general doctrines of the Church around one central principle, which he defended with marvellous logical power. He was not a fencer like Abélard, displaying wonderful dexterity in the use of sophistries, overwhelming adversaries by wit and sarcasm; arrogant and self-sufficient, and destroying rather than building up. He did not deify the reason, like Erigina, nor throw himself on authority like Bernard. He was not comprehensive like Augustine, nor mystical like Bonaventura. He had the spiritual insight of Anselm, and the dialectical acumen of Thomas Aquinas; acknowledging no master but Christ, and implicitly receiving whatever the Scriptures declared. He takes his original position neither from natural reason nor from the authority of the church, but from the word of God; and from declarations of Scripture, as he interprets them, he draws sequences and conclusions with irresistible logic. In an important sense he is one-sided, since he does not take cognizance of other truths equally important. He is perfectly fearless in pushing out to its most logical consequences whatever truth he seizes upon; and hence he appears to many gifted and learned critics to draw conclusions from accepted premises which apparently conflict with consciousness or natural reason; and hence there has ever been repugnance to many of his doctrines, because it is impossible, it is said, to believe them.

In general, Calvin does not essentially differ from the received doctrines of the Church as defended by its greatest lights in all ages. His peculiarity is not in making a digest of divinity, — although he treated all the great subjects which have been discussed from Athanasius to Aquinas. His "Institutes" may well be called an exhaustive system of theology. There is no great doctrine which he has not presented with singular clearness and logical force. Yet it is not for a general system of divinity that he is famous, but for making prominent a certain class of subjects, among which he threw the whole force of his genius.

In fact all the great lights of the Church have been distinguished for the discussion of particular doctrines to meet the exigencies of their times. Thus Athanasius is identified with the Trinitarian controversy, although he was a minister of theological knowledge in general. Augustine directed his attention more particularly to the refutation of Pelagian heresies and human Depravity. Luther's great doctrine was Justification by Faith, although he took the same ground as Augustine. It was the logical result of the doctrines of Grace which he defended which led to the overthrow, in half of Europe, of that extensive system of penance and self-expiation which marked the Roman Catholic Church, and on which so many glaring abuses were based. As Athanasius rendered a great service to the Church by establishing the doctrine of the Trinity, and Augustine a still greater service by the overthrow of Pelagianism, so Luther undermined the papal pile of superstition by showing eloquently,—what indeed had been shown before,—the true ground of justification. When we speak of Calvin, the great subject of Predestination arises before our minds, although on this subject he made no pretention to originality. Nor did he differ materially from Augustine, or Gottschalk, or Thomas Aquinas before him, or Pascal and Edwards after him. But no man ever presented this complicated and mysterious subject so ably as he.

It is not for me to discuss this great topic. I simply wish to present the subject historically,— to give Calvin's own views, and the effect of his deductions on the theology of his age; and in giving Calvin's views I must shelter myself under the wings of his best biographer, Doctor Henry of Berlin, and quote the substance of his exposition of the peculiar doctrines of the Swiss, or rather French, theologian.

According to Henry, Calvin maintained that God, in his sovereign will and for his own glory, elected one part of the human race to everlasting life, and abandoned the other part to everlasting death; that man, by the original transgression, lost the power of free-will, except to do evil; that it is only by Divine Grace that freedom to do good is recovered; but that this grace is bestowed only on the elect, and elect not in consequence of the foreknowledge of God, but by his absolute decree before the world was made.

This is the substance of those peculiar doctrines which are called Calvinism, and by many regarded as fundamental principles of theology, to be received with the same unhesitating faith as the declarations of Scripture from which those doctrines are deduced. Augustine and Aquinas accepted substantially the same doctrines, but they were not made so prominent in their systems, nor were they so elaborately worked out.

The opponents of Calvin, including some of the brightest lights which have shone in the English church, — such men as Jeremy Taylor, Archbishop Whately, and Professor Mosley, — affirm that these doctrines are not only opposed to free-will, but represent God as arbitrarily dooming a large part of the human race to future and endless punishment, withholding from them his grace, by which alone they can turn from their sins, creating them only to destroy them: not as the potter moulds the clay for vessels of honor and dishonor, but moulding the clay in order to destroy the vessels he has made, whether good or bad; which doctrine they affirm conflicts with the views usually held out in the Scriptures of God as a God of love, and also conflicts with all natural justice, and is therefore one-sided and narrow.

The premises from which this doctrine is deduced are those Scripture texts which have the authority of the Apostle Paul, such as these: "According as he hath chosen us in him before the foundation of the world;" "For whom he did foreknow he also did predestinate;" "Jacob have I loved and Esau have I hated;" "He hath mercy on whom he will have mercy, and whom he will he hardeneth;" "Hath not the potter power over his clay?" No one denies that from these texts the Predestination of Calvin as well as Augustine — for they both had similar views — is

From a contemporaneous painting

JOHN CALVIN

logically drawn. It has been objected that both of these eminent theologians overlooked other truths which go in parallel lines, and which would modify the doctrine,—even as Scripture asserts in one place the great fact that the will is free, and in another place that the will is shackled. The Pelagian would push out the doctrine of free-will so as to ignore the necessity of grace; and the Augustinian would push out the doctrine of the servitude of the will into downright fatalism. But these great logicians apparently shrink from the conclusions to which their logic leads them. Both Augustine and Calvin protest against fatalism, and both assert that the will is so far free that the sinner acts without constraint; and consequently the blame of his sins rests upon himself, and not upon another. The doctrines of Calvin and Augustine logically pursued would lead to the damnation of infants; yet, as a matter of fact, neither maintained that to which their logic led. It is not in human nature to believe such a thing, even if it may be dogmatically asserted.

And then, in regard to sin: no one has ever disputed the fact that sin is rampant in this world, and is deserving of punishment. But theologians of the school of Augustine and Calvin, in view of the fact, have assumed the premise — which indeed cannot be disputed — that sin is against an infinite God. Hence, that sin against an infinite God is itself infinite; and hence that, as sin deserves punishment, an infinite sin deserves infinite punishment,—a conclusion from which consciousness recoils, and which is nowhere asserted in the Bible. It is a conclusion arrived at by metaphysical reasoning, which has very little to do with practical Christianity, and which, imposed as a dogma of belief, to be accepted like plain declarations of Scripture, is an insult to the human understanding. But this conclusion, involving the belief that inherited sin *is infinite*, and deserving of infinite punishment, appals the mind. For relief from this terrible logic, the theologian adduces the great fact that Christ made an atonement for sin,—another cardinal declaration of the Scripture,—and that believers in this atonement shall be saved. This Bible doctrine is exceedingly comforting, and accounts in a measure for the marvellous spread of Christianity. The wretched people of the old Roman world heard the glad tidings that Christ died for them, as an atonement for the sins of which they were conscious, and which had chained them to despair. But another class of theologians deduced from this premise, that, as Christ's death was an infinite atonement for the sins of the world, so all men, and consequently all sinners, would be saved. This was the ground of the original Universalists, deduced from the doctrines which Augustine and Calvin had formulated. But they overlooked the Scripture declaration which Calvin never lost sight of, that salvation was only for those who believed. Now inasmuch as a vast majority of the human race, including infants, have not believed, it becomes a logical conclusion that all who have not believed are lost. Logic and consciousness then come into collision, and there is no relief but in consigning these discrepancies to the realm of mystery.

I allude to these theological difficulties simply to show the tyranny to which the mind and soul are subjected whenever theological deductions are invested with the same authority as belongs to original declarations of Scripture; and which, so far from being systematized, do not even always apparently harmonize. Almost any system of belief can be logically deduced from Scripture texts. It should be the work of theologians to harmonize them and show their general spirit and meaning, rather than to draw conclusions from any particular class of subjects. Any system of deductions from texts of Scripture which are offset by texts of equal authority but apparently different meaning, is necessarily one-sided and imperfect, and therefore narrow. That is exactly the difficulty under which Calvin labored. He seems, to a large class of Christians of great ability and conscientiousness, to be narrow and one-sided, and is therefore no authority to them; not, be it understood, in reference to the great fundamental doctrines of Christianity, but in his views of Predestination and the subjects interlinked with it. And it was the great error of attaching so much importance to mere metaphysical divinity that led to such a revulsion from his peculiar system in after times. It was the great wisdom of the English reformers, like Cranmer, to leave all those metaphysical questions open, as matters of comparatively little consequence, and fall back on unquestioned doctrines of primitive faith, that have given so great vitality to the English Church, and made it so broad and catholic. The Puritans as a body, more intellectual than the mass of the Episcopalians, were led away by the imposing and entangling dialectics of the scholastic Calvin, and came unfortunately to attach as much importance to such subjects as free-will and predestination — questions most complicated — as they did to "the weightier matters of the law;" and when pushed by the logic of opponents to the *decretum horribile*," have been compelled to fall back on the Catholic doctrine of mysteries, as something which could never be explained or comprehended, but which it is a Christian duty to accept as a mystery. The Scriptures certainly speak of mysteries, like regeneration; but it is one thing to marvel how a man can be born again by the Spirit of God, — a fact we see every day, — and quite another thing to make a mystery to be accepted as a matter of faith of that which the Bible has nowhere distinctly affirmed, and which is against all ideas of natural justice, and arrived at by a subtle process of dialectical reasoning.

But it was natural for so great an intellectual giant as Calvin to make his startling deductions from the great truths he meditated upon with so much seriousness and earnestness. Only a very lofty nature would have revelled as he did, and as Augustine did before him and Pascal after him, in those great subjects which pertain to God and his dispensations. All his meditations and formulated doctrines radiate from the great and sublime idea of the majesty of God and the comparative insignificance of man. And here he was not so far apart from the great sages of antiquity, before salvation was revealed by Christ. "Canst thou by searching find out God?" "What is man that Thou art mindful of him?"

And here I would remark that theologians and philosophers have ever been divided into two great schools, — those who have had a tendency to exalt the dignity of man, and those who would absorb man in the greatness of the Deity. These two schools have advocated doctrines which, logically carried out to their ultimate sequences, would produce a Grecian humanitarianism on the one hand, and a sort of Bramanism on the other, — the one making man the arbiter of his own destiny, independently of divine agency, and the other making the Deity the only power of the universe. With one school, God as the only controlling agency is a fiction, and man himself is infinite in faculties; the other holds that God is everything and man is nothing. The distinction between these two schools, both of which have had great defenders, is fundamental, — such as that between Augustine and Pelagius, between Bernard and Abélard, and between Calvin and Lainez. Among those who have inclined to the doctrine of the majesty of God and the littleness of man were the primitive monks and the Indian theosophists, and the orthodox scholastics of the Middle Ages, — all of whom were comparatively indifferent to material pleasure and physical progress, and sought the salvation of the soul and the favor of God beyond all temporal blessings. Of the other class have been the Greek philosophers and the rationalizing schoolmen and the modern lights of science.

Now Calvin was imbued with the lofty spirit of the Fathers of the Church and the more religious and contemplative of the schoolmen and the saints of the Middle Ages, when he attached but little dignity to man unaided by divine grace, and was absorbed with the idea of the sovereignty of God, in whose hands man is like clay in the hands of the potter. This view of God pervaded the whole spirit of his theology, making it both lofty and yet one-sided. To him the chief end of man was to glorify God, not to develop his own intellectual faculties, and still less to seek the pleasures and excitements of the world. Man was a sinner before an infinite God, and he could rise above the polluting influence of sin only by the special favor of God and his divinely communicated grace. Man was so great a sinner that he deserved an eternal punishment, only to be rescued as a brand plucked from the fire, as one of the elect before the world was made. The vast majority of men were left to the uncovenanted mercies of Christ, — the redeemer, not of the race, but of those who believed.

To Calvin therefore, as to the Puritans, the belief in a personal God was everything; not a compulsory belief in the general existence of a deity who, united with Nature, reveals himself to our consciousness; not the God of the pantheist, visible in all the wonders of Nature; not the God of the rationalist, who retires from the universe which he has made, leaving it to the operation of certain unchanging and universal laws: but the God whom Abraham and Moses and the prophets saw and recognized, and who by his special providence rules the destinies of men. The most intellectual of the reformers abhorred the deification of the reason, and clung to that exalted supernaturalism which was the life and hope of blessed saints and martyrs in bygone ages, and which in "their contests with mail-clad infidelity was like the pebble which the shepherd of Israel hurled against the disdainful boaster who defied the power of Israel's God." And he was thus brought into close sympathy with the realism of the Fathers, who felt that all that is valuable in theology must radiate from the recognition of Almighty power in the renovation of society, and displayed, not acccording to our human notions of law and progress and free-will, but supernaturally and mysteriously, according to his sovereign will, which is above law, since God is the author of law. He simply erred in enforcing a certain class of truths which must follow from the majesty of the one great First Cause, lofty as these truths are, to the exclusion of another class of truths of great importance; which gives to his system incompleteness and one-sidedness. Thus he was led to undervalue the power of truth itself in its contest with error. He was led into a seeming recognition of two wills in God, — that which wills the salvation of all men, and that which wills the salvation of the elect alone. He is accused of a leaning to fatalism, which he heartily denied, but which seems to follow from his logical conclusions. He entered into an arena of metaphysical controversy which can never be settled. The doctrines of free-will and necessity can never be reconciled by mortal reason. Consciousness reveals the freedom of the will as well as the slavery to sin. Men are conscious of both; they waste their time in attempting to reconcile two apparently opposing facts,—like our pious fathers at their New England firesides, who were compelled to shelter themselves behind mystery.

The tendency of Calvin's system, it is maintained by many, is to ascribe to God attributes which according to natural justice would be injustice and cruelty, such as no father would exercise on his own children, however guilty. Even good men will not accept in their hearts doctrines which tend to make God less compassionate than man. There are not two kinds of justice. The intellect is appalled when it is affirmed that one man *justly* suffers the penalty of another man's sin,—although the world is full of instances of men suffering from the carelessness or wickedness of others, as in a wicked war or an unnecessary railway disaster. The Scripture law of retribution, as brought out in the Bible and sustained by consciousness, is the penalty a man pays for personal and voluntary transgression. Nor will consciousness accept the doctrine that the sin of a mortal—especially under strong temptation and with all the bias of a sinful nature—is infinite. Nothing which a created mortal can do is infinite; it is only finite: the infinite belongs to God alone. Hence an infinite penalty for a finite sin conflicts with consciousness and is nowhere asserted in the Bible, which is transcendently more merciful and comforting than many theological systems of belief, however powerfully sustained by dialectical reasoning and by the most excellent men. Human judgments or reasonings are fallible on moral questions which have two sides; and reasonings from texts which present different meanings when studied by the lights of learning and science are still more liable to be untrustworthy. It would seem to be the supremest necessity for theological schools to unravel the meaning of divine declarations, and present doctrines in their relation with apparently conflicting texts, rather than draw out a perfect and consistent system, philosophically considered, from any one class of texts. Of all things in this wicked and perplexing world the science of theology should be the most cheerful and inspiring, for it involves inquiries on the loftiest subjects which can interest a thoughtful mind.

But whatever defects the system of doctrines which Calvin elaborated with such transcendent ability may have, there is no question as to its vast influence on the thinking of the sixteenth and seventeenth centuries. The schools of France and Holland and Scotland and England and America were animated by his genius and authority. He was a burning and a shining light, if not for all ages, at least for the unsettled times in which he lived. No theologian ever had a greater posthumous power than he for nearly three hundred years, and he is still one of the great authorities of the church universal. John Knox sought his counsel and was influenced by his advice in the great reform he made in Scotland. In France the words Calvinist and Huguenot are synonymous. Cranmer, too, listened to his counsels, and had great respect for his learning and sanctity. Among the Puritans he has reigned like an oracle. Oliver Cromwell embraced his doctrines, as also did Sir Matthew Hale. Ridicule or abuse of Calvin is as absurd as the ridicule or abuse with which Protestants so long assailed Hildebrand or Innocent III. No one abuses Pascal or Augustine, and yet the theological views of all these are substantially the same.

In one respect I think that Calvin has received more credit than he deserves. Some have maintained that he was a sort of father of republicanism and democratic liberty. In truth he had no popular sympathies, and leaned towards an aristocracy which was little short of an oligarchy. He had no hand in establishing the political system of Geneva; it was established before he went there. He was not even one of those thinkers who sympathized with true liberty of conscience. He persecuted heretics like a mediæval Catholic divine. He would have burned a Galileo as he caused the death of Servetus, which need not have happened but for him. Calvin could have saved Servetus if he had pleased; but he complained of him to the magistrates, knowing that his condemnation and death would necessarily follow. He had neither the humanity of Luther nor the toleration of Saint Augustine. He was the impersonation of intellect, — like Newton, Leibnitz, Spinoza, and Kant, — which overbore the impulses of his heart. He had no passions except zeal for orthodoxy. So pre-eminently did intellect tower above the passions that he seemed to lack sympathy; and yet, such was his exalted character, he was capable of friendship. He was remarkable for every faculty of the mind except wit and imagination. His memory was almost incredible; he remembered everything he ever read or heard; he would, after long intervals, recognize persons whom he had never seen but once or twice. When employed in dictation, he would resume the thread of his discourse without being prompted, after the most vexatious interruptions. His judgment was as sound as his memory was retentive; it was almost infallible, — no one was ever known to have been misled by it. He had a remarkable analytical power, and also the power of generalization. He was a very learned man, and his Commentaries are among the most useful and valued of his writings, showing both learning and judgment; his exegetical works have scarcely been improved. He had no sceptical or rationalistic tendencies, and therefore his Commentaries may not be admired by men of "advanced thought," but his annotations will live when those of Ewald shall be forgotten; they still hold their place in the libraries of biblical critics. For his age he was a transcendent critic; his various writings fill five folio volumes. He was not so voluminous a writer as Thomas Aquinas, but less diffuse; his style is lucid, like that of Voltaire.

Considering the weakness of his body Calvin's labors were prodigious. There was never a more industrious man, finding time for everything, — for an amazing correspondence, for pastoral labors, for treatises and essays, for commentaries and official duties. No man ever accomplished more in the same space of time. He preached daily every alternate week; he attended meetings of the Consistory and of the Court of Morals; he interested himself in the great affairs of his age; he wrote letters to all parts of Christendom.

Reigning as a religious dictator, and with more influence than any man of his age, next to Luther, Calvin was content to remain poor, and was disdainful of money and all praises and rewards. This was not an affectation, not the desire to imitate the great saints of Christian antiquity to whom poverty was a cardinal virtue; but real indifference, looking upon money as *impedimenta*, as camp equipage is to successful generals. He was not conscious of being poor with his small salary of fifty dollars a year, feeling that he had inexhaustible riches within him; and hence he calmly and naturally took his seat among the great men of the world as their peer and equal, without envy of the accidents of fortune and birth. He was as indifferent to money and luxuries as Socrates when he walked barefooted among the Athenian aristocracy, or Basil when he retired to the wilderness; he rarely gave vent to extravagant grief or joy, seldom laughed, and cared little for hilarities; he knew no games or sports; he rarely played with children or gossiped with women; he loved without romance, and suffered bereavement without outward sorrow. He had no toleration for human infirmities, and was neither social nor genial; he sought a wife, not so much for communion of feeling as to ease him of his burdens, — not to share his confidence, but to take care of his house. Nor was he fond, like Luther, of music and poetry. He had no taste for the fine arts; he never had a poet or an artist for his friend or companion. He could not look out of his window without seeing the glaciers of the Alps, but seemed to be unmoved by their unspeakable grandeur; he did not revel in the glories of nature or art, but gave his mind to abstract ideas and stern practical duties. He was sparing of language, simple, direct, and precise, using neither sarcasm, nor ridicule, nor exaggeration. He was far from being eloquent according to popular notions of oratory, and despised the jingle of words and phrases and tricks of rhetoric; he appealed to reason rather than the passions, to the conscience rather than the imagination.

Though mild, Calvin was also intolerant. Castillo, once his friend, assailed his doctrine of Decrees, and was obliged to quit Geneva, and was so persecuted that he died of actual starvation; Perrin, captain-general of the republic, danced at a wedding, and was thrown into prison; Bolsec, an eminent physician, opposed the doctrine of Predestination, and was sentenced to perpetual imprisonment; Gruet spoke lightly of the ordinances of religion, and was beheaded; Servetus was a moral and learned and honest man, but could not escape the flames. Had he been willing to say, as the flames consumed his body, "Jesus, thou eternal Son of God, have mercy on me!" instead of, "Jesus, thou son of the eternal God!" he might have been spared. Calvin was as severe on those who refused to accept his logical deductions from acknowledged truths as he was on those who denied the fundamental truths themselves. But toleration was rare in his age, and he was not beyond it. He was not even beyond the ideas of the Middle Ages in some important points, such as those which pertained to divine justice,— the wrath rather than the love of God. He lived too near the Middle Ages to be emancipated from the ideas which enslaved such a man as Thomas Aquinas. He had very little patience with frivolous amusements or degrading pursuits. He attached great dignity to the ministerial office, and set a severe example of decorum and propriety in all his public ministrations. He was a type of the early evangelical divines, and was the father of the old Puritan strictness and narrowness and fidelity to trusts. His very faults grew out of virtues pushed to extremes. In our times such a man would not be selected as a travelling companion, or a man at whose house we would wish to keep the Christmas holidays. His unattractive austerity perhaps has been made too much of by his enemies, and grew out of his unimpulsive temperament, — call it cold if we must, — and also out of his stern theology, which marked the ascetics of the Middle Ages. Few would now approve of his severity of discipline any more than they would feel inclined to accept some of his theological deductions.

I question whether Calvin lived in the hearts of his countrymen, or they would have erected some monument to his memory. In our times a statue has been erected to Rousseau in Geneva; but Calvin was buried without ceremony and with exceeding simplicity. He was a warrior who cared nothing for glory or honor, absorbed in devotion to his Invisible King, not indifferent to the exercise of power, but only as he felt he was the delegated messenger of Divine Omnipotence scattering to the winds the dust of all mortal grandeur. With all his faults, which were on the surface, he was the accepted idol and oracle of a great party, and stamped his genius on his own and succeeding ages. Whatever the Presbyterians have done for civilization, he comes in for a share of the honor. Whatever foundations the Puritans laid for national greatness in this country, it must be confessed that they caught inspiration from his decrees. Such a great master of exegetical learning and theological inquiry and legislative wisdom will be forever held in reverence by lofty characters, although he may be no favorite with the mass of mankind. If many great men and good men have failed to comprehend either his character or his system, how can a pleasure-loving and material generation, seeking to combine the glories of this world with the promises of the next, see much in him to admire, except as a great intellectual dialectician and system-maker in an age with which it has no sympathy? How can it appreciate his deep spiritual life, his profound communion with God, his burning zeal for the defence of Christian doctrine, his sublime self-sacrifice, his holy resignation, his entire consecration to a great cause? Nobody can do justice to Calvin who does not know the history of his times, the circumstances which surrounded him, and the enemies he was required to fight. No one can comprehend his character or mission who does not feel it to be supremely necessary to have a definite, positive system of religious belief, based on the authority of the Scriptures as a divine inspiration, both as an anchor amid the storms and a star of promise and hope.

And, after all, what is the head and front of Calvin's offending? — that he was cold, unsocial, and ungenial in character; and that, as a theologian, he fearlessly and inexorably pushed out his deductions to their remotest logical sequences. But he was no more austere than Chrysostom, no more ascetic than Basil, not even sterner in character than Michael Angelo, or more unsocial than Pascal or Cromwell or William the Silent. We lose sight of his defects in the greatness of his services and the exalted dignity of his character. If he was severe to adversaries, he was kind to friends; and when his feeble body was worn out by his protracted labors, at the age of fifty-three, and he felt that the hand of death was upon him, he called together his friends and fellow-laborers in reform, — the magistrates and ministers of Geneva, — imparted his last lessons, and expressed his last wishes, with the placidity of a Christian sage. Amid tears and sobs and stifled groans he discoursed calmly on his approaching departure, gave his affectionate benedictions, and commended them and his cause to Christ; lingering longer than was expected, but dying in the highest triumphs of Christian faith, May 27, 1564, in the arms of his faithful and admiring Beza, as the rays of the setting-sun gilded with their glory his humble chamber of toil and spiritual exaltation.

No man who knows anything will ever sneer at Calvin. He is not to be measured by common standards. He was universally regarded as the greatest light of the theological world. When we remember his transcendent abilities, his matchless labors, his unrivalled influence, his unblemished morality, his lofty piety, and soaring soul, all flippant criticism is contemptible and mean. He ranks with immortal benefactors, and needs least of all any apologies for his defects. A man who stamped his opinions on his own age and succeeding ages can be regarded only as a very extraordinary genius. A frivolous and pleasure-seeking generation may not be attracted by such an impersonation of cold intellect, and may rear no costly monument to his memory; but his work remains as the leader of the loftiest class of Christian enthusiasts that the modern world has known, and the founder of a theological system which still numbers, in spite of all the changes of human thought, some of the greatest thinkers and ablest expounders of Christian doctrine in both Europe and America. To have been the spiritual father of the Puritans for three hundred years is itself a great evidence of moral and intellectual excellence, and will link his name with some of the greatest movements that have marked our modern civilization. From Plymouth Rock to the shores of the Pacific Ocean we still see the traces of his marvellous genius, and his still more wonderful influence on the minds of men and on the schools of Christian theology; so that he will ever be regarded as the great doctor of the Protestant Church.

AUTHORITIES.

Henry's Life of Calvin, translated by Stebbings; Dyer's Life of Calvin; Beza's Life of Calvin; Drelincourt's Defence of Calvin; Bayle; Maimbourg's Histoire du Calvinisme; Calvin's Works; Ruchat; D'Aubigné's History of the Reformation; Burnet's Reformation; Mosheim; Biographie Universelle, article on Servetus; Schlosser's Leben Bezas; McCrie's Life of Knox; Original Letters (Parker Society).

FRANCIS BACON.

A. D. 1561–1626.

THE NEW PHILOSOPHY.

FRANCIS BACON.

THE NEW PHILOSOPHY.

IT is not easy to present the life and labors of
"The wisest, brightest, meanest of mankind."
So Pope sums up the character of the great Lord Bacon, as he is generally but improperly called; and this verdict, in the main, has been confirmed by Lords Macaulay and Campbell, who seem to delight in keeping him in that niche of the temple of fame where the poet has placed him,—contemptible as a man, but venerable as the philosopher, radiant with all the wisdom of his age and of all preceding ages, the miner and sapper of ancient falsehoods, the pioneer of all true knowledge, the author of that inductive and experimental philosophy on which is based the glory of our age. Macaulay especially, in that long and brilliant article which appeared in the "Edinburgh Review" in 1837, has represented him as a remarkably worldly man, cold, calculating, selfish; a sycophant and a flat-

terer, bent on self-exaltation; greedy, careless, false; climbing to power by base subserviency; betraying friends and courting enemies; with no animosities he does not suppress from policy, and with no affections which he openly manifests when it does not suit his interests: so that we read with shame of his extraordinary shamelessness, from the time he first felt the cravings of a vulgar ambition to the consummation of a disgraceful crime; from the base desertion of his greatest benefactor to the public selling of justice as Lord High Chancellor of the realm; resorting to all the arts of a courtier to win the favor of his sovereign and of his minions and favorites; reckless as to honest debts; torturing on the rack an honest parson for a sermon he never preached; and, when obliged to confess his corruption, meanly supplicating mercy from the nation he had outraged, and favors from the monarch whose cause he had betrayed. The defects and delinquencies of this great man are bluntly and harshly put by Macaulay, without any attempt to soften or palliate them: as if he would consign his name and memory, not "to men's charitable speeches, to foreign nations, and to the next ages," but to an infamy as lasting and deep as that of Scroggs and of Jeffreys, or any of those hideous tyrants and monsters that disgraced the reigns of the Stuart kings.

And yet while the man is made to appear in such

hideous colors, his philosophy is exalted to the highest pinnacle of praise, as the greatest boon which any philosopher ever rendered to the world, and the chief cause of all subsequent progress in scientific discovery. And thus in brilliant rhetoric we have a painting of a man whose life was in striking contrast with his teachings, — a Judas Iscariot, uttering divine philosophy; a Seneca, accumulating millions as the tool of Nero; a fallen angel, pointing with rapture to the realms of eternal light. We have the most startling contradiction in all history, — glory in debasement, and debasement in glory; the most selfish and worldly man in England, the "meanest of mankind," conferring on the race one of the greatest blessings it ever received, — not accidentally, not in repentance and shame, but in exalted and persistent labors, amid public cares and physical infirmities, from youth to advanced old age; living in the highest regions of thought, studious and patient all his days, even when neglected and unrewarded for the transcendent services he rendered, not as a philosopher merely, but as a man of affairs and as a responsible officer of the Crown. Has there ever been, before or since, such an anomaly in human history, — so infamous in action, so glorious in thought; such a contradiction between life and teachings, — so that many are found to utter indignant protests against such a representation of humanity, justly feeling that such a portrait, however much it may be admired for its brilliant colors, and however difficult to be proved false, is nevertheless an insult to the human understanding? The heart of the world will not accept the strange and singular belief that so bad a man could confer so great a boon, especially when he seemed bent on bestowing it during his whole life, amid the most harassing duties. If it accepts the boon, it will strive to do justice to the benefactor, as he himself appealed to future ages; and if it cannot deny the charges which have been arrayed against him,—especially if it cannot exculpate him,—it will soar beyond technical proofs to take into consideration the circumstances of the times, the temptations of a corrupt age, and the splendid traits which can with equal authority be adduced to set off against the mistakes and faults which proceeded from inadvertence and weakness rather than a debased moral sense,—even as the defects and weaknesses of Cicero are lost sight of in the acknowledged virtues of his ordinary life, and the honest and noble services he rendered to his country and mankind.

Bacon was a favored man; he belonged to the upper ranks of society. His father, Sir Nicholas Bacon, was a great lawyer, and reached the highest dignities, being Lord Keeper of the Great Seal. His mother's sister was the wife of William Cecil, the great Lord Burleigh, the most able and influential of Queen Elizabeth's ministers. Francis Bacon was the youngest son of the Lord Keeper, and was born in London, Jan. 22, 1561. He had a sickly and feeble constitution, but intellectually was a youthful prodigy; and at nine years of age, by his gravity and knowledge, attracted the admiring attention of the Queen, who called him her young Lord Keeper. At the age of ten we find him stealing away from his companions to discover the cause of a singular echo in the brick conduit near his father's house in the Strand. At twelve he entered the University of Cambridge; at fifteen he quitted it, already disgusted with its pedantries and sophistries; at sixteen he rebelled against the authority of Aristotle, and took up his residence at Gray's Inn; the same year, 1576, he was sent to Paris in the suite of Sir Amias Paulet, ambassador to the court of France, and delighted the salons of the capital by his wit and profound inquiries; at nineteen he returned to England, having won golden opinions from the doctors of the French Sanhedrim, who saw in him a second Daniel; and in 1582 he was admitted as a barrister of Gray's Inn, and the following year composed an essay on the Instauration of Philosophy. Thus, at an age when young men now leave the university, he had attacked the existing systems of science and philosophy, proudly taking in all science and knowledge for his realm.

About this time his father died, without leaving him, a younger son, a competence. Nor would his great relatives give him an office or sinecure by which he might be supported while he sought truth, and he was forced to plod at the law, which he never liked, resisting the blandishments and follies by which he was surrounded; and at intervals, when other young men of his age and rank were seeking pleasure, he was studying Nature, science, history, philosophy, poetry, — everything, even the whole domain of truth, — and with such success that his varied attainments were rather a hindrance to an appreciation of his merits as a lawyer and his preferment in his profession.

In 1586 he entered parliament, sitting for Taunton, and also became a bencher at Gray's Inn; so that at twenty-six he was in full practice in the courts of Westminster, also a politician, speaking on almost every question of importance which agitated the House of Commons for twenty years, distinguished for eloquence as well as learning, and for a manly independence which did not entirely please the Queen, from whom all honors came.

In 1591, at the age of thirty-one, he formed the acquaintance of Essex, about his own age, who, as the favorite of the Queen, was regarded as the most influential man in the country. The acquaintance ripened into friendship; and to the solicitation of this powerful patron, who urged the Queen to give Bacon a high office, she is said to have replied: "He has indeed great wit and much learning, but in law, my lord, he is not deeply read,"—an opinion perhaps put into her head by his rival Coke, who did indeed know law but scarcely anything else, or by that class of old-fashioned functionaries who could not conceive how a man could master more than one thing. We should however remember that Bacon had not reached the age when great offices were usually conferred in the professions, and that his efforts to be made solicitor-general at the age of thirty-one, and even earlier, would now seem unreasonable and importunate, whatever might be his attainments. Disappointed in not receiving high office, he meditated a retreat to Cambridge; but his friend Essex gave him a villa in Twickenham, which he soon mortgaged, for he was in debt all his life, although in receipt of sums which would have supported him in comfort and dignity were it not for his habits of extravagance,—the greatest flaw in his character, and which was the indirect cause of his disgrace and fall. He was even arrested for debt when he enjoyed a lucrative practice at the courts. But nothing prevented him from pursuing his literary and scientific studies, amid great distractions,—for he was both a leader at the bar and a leader of the House of Commons; and if he did not receive the rewards to which he felt entitled, he was always consulted by Elizabeth in great legal difficulties.

It was not until the Queen died, and Bacon was forty-seven years old, that he became solicitor-general (1607), in the fourth year of the reign of James, one year after his marriage with Alice Barnham, an alderman's daughter, "a handsome maiden," and "to his liking." Besides this office, which brought him £1000 a year, he about this time had a windfall as clerk of the Star Chamber, which added £2000 to his income, at that time from all sources about £4500 a year,—a very large sum for those times, and making him really a rich man. Six years afterward he was made attorney-general, and in the year 1617 he was made Lord Keeper, and the following year he was raised to the highest position in the realm, next to that of Archbishop of Canterbury, as Lord Chancellor, at the age of fifty-seven, and soon after was created Lord Verulam. That is his title, but the world persists in calling him Lord Bacon. In 1620, two years after the execution of Sir Walter Raleigh, which Bacon advised, he was in the zenith of his fortunes and fame, having been lately created Viscount St. Albans, and having published the "Novum Organum," the first instalment of the "Instauratio Magna," at which he had been working the best part of his life,—some thirty years,—"A New Logic, to judge or invent by induction, and thereby to make philosophy and science both more true and more active."

Then began to gather the storms which were to wreck his fortunes. The nation now was clamorous for reform; and Coke, the enemy of Bacon, who was then the leader of the Reform party in the House of Commons, stimulated the movement. The House began its scrutiny with the administration of justice; and Bacon could not stand before it, for as the highest judge in England he was accused of taking bribes before rendering decisions, and of many cases of corruption so glaring that no defence was undertaken; and the House of Lords had no alternative but to sentence him to the Tower and fine him, to degrade him from his office, and banish him from the precincts of the court, — a fall so great, and the impression of it on the civilized world so tremendous, that the case of a judge accepting bribes has rarely since been known.

Bacon was imprisoned but a few days, his ruinous fine of £40,000 was remitted, and he was even soon after received at court; but he never again held office. He was hopelessly disgraced; he was a ruined man; and he bitterly felt the humiliation, and acknowledged the justice of his punishment. He had now no further object in life than to pursue his studies, and live comfortably in his retirement, and do what he could for future ages.

But before we consider his immortal legacy to the world, let us take one more view of the man, in order that we may do him justice, and remove some of the cruel charges against him as "the meanest of mankind."

It must be borne in mind that, from the beginning of his career until his fall, only four or five serious charges have been made against him, — that he was extravagant in his mode of life; that he was a sycophant and office-seeker; that he deserted his patron Essex; that he tortured Peacham, a Puritan clergyman, when tried for high-treason; that he himself was guilty of corruption as a judge.

In regard to the first charge, it is unfortunately too true; he lived beyond his means, and was in debt most of his life. This defect, as has been said, was the root of much evil; it destroyed his independence, detracted from the dignity of his character, created enemies, and led to a laxity of the moral sense which prepared the way for corruption, — thereby furnishing another illustration of that fatal weakness which degrades any man when he runs races with the rich, and indulges in a luxury and ostentation which he cannot afford. It was the curse of Cicero, of William Pitt, and of Daniel Webster. The first lesson which every public man should learn, especially if honored with important trusts, is to live within his income. However inconvenient and galling, a stringent economy is necessary. But this defect is a very common one, particularly when men are luxurious, or brought into intercourse with the rich, or inclined to be hospitable and generous, or have a great imagination and a sanguine temperament. So that those who are most liable to fall into this folly have many noble qualities to offset it, and it is not a stain which marks the "meanest of mankind." Who would call Webster the meanest of mankind because he had an absurd desire to live like an English country gentleman?

In regard to sycophancy, — a disgusting trait, I admit, — we should consider the age, when everybody cringed to sovereigns and their favorites. Bacon never made such an abject speech as Omer Talon, the greatest lawyer in France, did to Louis XIII., in the Parliament of Paris. Three hundred years ago everybody bowed down to exalted rank: witness the obsequious language which all authors addressed to patrons in the dedication of their books. How small the chance of any man rising in the world, who did not court favors from those who had favors to bestow! Is that the meanest or the most uncommon thing in this world? If so, how ignominious are all politicians who flatter the people and solicit their votes? Is it not natural to be obsequious to those who have offices to bestow? This trait is not commendable, but is it the meanest thing we see?

In regard to Essex, nobody can approve of the ingratitude which Bacon showed to his noble patron. But, on the other hand, remember the good advice which Bacon ever gave him, and his constant efforts to keep him out of scrapes. How often did he excuse him to his royal mistress, at the risk of incurring her displeasure? And when Essex was guilty of a thousand times worse crime than ever Bacon committed,—even high-treason, in a time of tumult and insurrection,— and it became Bacon's task as prosecuting officer of the Crown to bring this great culprit to justice, was he required by a former friendship to sacrifice his duty and his allegiance to his sovereign, to screen a man who had perverted the affection of the noblest woman who ever wore a crown, and came near involving his country in a civil war? Grant that Essex had bestowed favors, and was an accomplished and interesting man,—was Bacon to ignore his official duties? He may have been too harsh in his procedure; but in that age all criminal proceedings were harsh and inexorable,—there was but little mercy shown to culprits, especially to traitors. If Elizabeth could bring herself, out of respect to her wounded honor and slighted kindness and the dignity of the realm and the majesty of the law, to surrender into the hands of justice one whom she so tenderly loved and magnificently rewarded, even when the sacrifice cost her both peace and life, snapped the last cord which bound her to this world, — may we not forgive Bacon for the part he played? Does this fidelity to an official and professional duty, even if he were harsh, make him "the meanest of mankind"?

In regard to Peacham, it is true he was tortured, according to the practice of that cruel age; but Bacon had no hand in the issuing of the warrant against him for high-treason, although in accordance with custom he, as prosecuting officer of the Crown, examined Peacham under torture before his trial. The parson was convicted; but the sentence of death was not executed upon him, and he died in jail.

And in regard to corruption, — the sin which cast Bacon from his high estate, though fortunately he did not fall like Lucifer, never to rise again, — may not the verdict of the poet and the historian be rather exaggerated? Nobody has ever attempted to acquit Bacon for taking bribes. Nobody has ever excused him. He did commit a crime; but in palliation it might be said that he never decided against justice, and that it was customary for great public functionaries to accept presents. Had he taken them after he had rendered judgment instead of before, he might have been acquitted; for out of the seven thousand cases which he decided as Lord-Chancellor, not one of them has been reversed: so that he said of himself, "I was the justest judge that England has had for fifty years; and I suffered the justest sentence that had been inflicted for two hundred years." He did not excuse himself. His ingenuousness of confession astonished everybody, and moved the hearts of his judges. It was his misfortune to be in debt; he had pressing creditors; and in two cases he accepted presents before the decision was made, but was brave enough to decide against those who bribed him, — *hinc illæ lacrymæ.* A modern corrupt official generally covers his tracks; and many a modern judge has been bribed to decide against justice, and has escaped ignominy, even in a country which claims the greatest purity and the loftiest moral standard. We admit that Bacon was a sinner; but was he a sinner above all others who cast stones at Jerusalem?

In reference to these admitted defects and crimes, I only wish to show that even these do not make him "the meanest of mankind." What crimes have sullied many of those benefactors whom all ages will admire and honor, and whom, in spite of their defects, we call good men, — not bad men to be forgiven for their services, but excellent and righteous on the whole! See Abraham telling lies to the King of Egypt; and Jacob robbing his brother of his birthright; and David murdering his bravest soldier to screen himself from adultery; and Solomon selling himself to false idols to please the wicked women who ensnared him; and Peter denying his Master; and Marcus Aurelius persecuting the Christians; and Constantine putting to death his own son; and Theodosius slaughtering the citizens of Thessalonica; and Isabella establishing the Inquisition; and Sir Mathew Hale burning witches; and Cromwell stealing a sceptre; and Calvin murdering Servetus; and Queen Elizabeth lying and cheating and swearing in the midst of her patriotic labors for her country and civilization. Even the sun passes through eclipses. Have the spots upon the career of Bacon hidden the brightness of his general beneficence? Is he the meanest of men because he had great faults? When we speak of mean men, it is those whose general character is contemptible.

Now, see Bacon pursuing his honorable career amid rebuffs and enmities and jealousies, toiling in Herculean tasks without complaint, and waiting his time; always accessible, affable, gentle, with no vulgar pride, if he aped vulgar ostentation; calm, beneficent, studious, without envy or bitterness; interesting in his home, courted as a friend, admired as a philosopher, generous to the poor, kind to the servants who cheated him, with an unsubdued love of Nature as well as of books; not negligent of religious duties, a believer in God and immortality; and though broken in spirit, like a bruised reed, yet soaring beyond all his misfortunes to study the highest problems, and bequeathing his knowledge for the benefit of future ages! Can such a man be stigmatized as "the meanest of mankind"? Is it candid and just for a great historian to indorse such a verdict, to gloss over Bacon's virtues, and make like an advocate at the bar, or an ancient sophist, a special plea to magnify his defects, and stain his noble name with an infamy as deep as would be inflicted upon an enemy of the human race? And all for what?—just to make a rhetorical point, and show the writer's brilliancy and genius in making a telling contrast between the man and the philosopher. A man who habitually dwelt in the highest regions of thought during his whole life, absorbed in lofty contemplations, all from love of truth itself and to benefit the world, could not have had a mean or sordid soul. "As a man thinketh, so is he." We admit that he was a man of the world, politic, self-seeking, extravagant, careless about his debts and how he raised money to pay them; but we deny that he was a bad judge on the whole, or was unpatriotic, or immoral in his private life, or mean in his ordinary dealings, or more cruel and harsh in his judicial transactions than most of the public functionaries of his rough and venal age. We admit it is difficult to controvert the charges which Macaulay arrays against him, for so accurate and painstaking an historian is not likely to be wrong in his facts; but we believe that they are uncandidly stated, and so ingeniously and sophistically put as to give on the whole a wrong impression of the man, — making him out worse than he was, considering his age and circumstances. Bacon's character, like that of most great men, has two sides; and while we are compelled painfully to admit that he had many faults, we shrink from classing him among bad men, as is implied in Pope's characterization of him as "the meanest of mankind."

We now take leave of the man, to consider his legacy to the world. And here again we are compelled to take issue with Macaulay, not in regard to the great fact that Bacon's inquiries tended to a new revelation of Nature, and by means of the method called *induction,* by which he sought to establish fixed principles of science that could not be controverted, but in reference to the *ends* for which he labored. "The aim of Bacon," says Macaulay, "was utility, — fruit; the multiplication of human enjoyments, . . . the mitigation of human sufferings, . . . the prolongation of life by new inventions," —*dotare vitam humanum novis inventis et copiis;* "the conquest of Nature," — dominion over the beasts of the field and the fowls of the air; the application of science to the subjection of the outward world; progress in useful arts, — in those arts which enable us to become strong, comfortable, and rich in houses, shops, fabrics, tools, merchandise, new vegetables, fruits, and animals: in short, a philosophy which will "not raise us above vulgar wants, but will supply those wants." "And as an acre in Middlesex is worth more than a principality in Utopia, so the smallest practical good is better than any magnificent effort to realize an impossibility;" and "hence the first shoemaker has rendered more substantial service to mankind than all the sages of Greece. All they could do was to fill the world with long beards and long words; whereas Bacon's philosophy has lengthened life, mitigated pain, extinguished disease, built bridges, guided the thunderbolts, lightened the night with the splendor of the day, accelerated motion, annihilated distance, facilitated intercourse; enabled men to descend to the depths of the earth, to traverse the land in cars which whirl without horses, and the ocean in ships which sail against the wind." In other words, it was his aim to stimulate mankind, not to seek unattainable truth, but useful truth; that is, the science which produces railroads, canals, cultivated farms, ships, rich returns for labor, silver and gold from the mines,—all that purchase the joys of material life and fit us for dominion over the world in which we live. Hence anything which will curtail our sufferings and add to our pleasures or our powers, should be sought as the highest good. Geometry is desirable, not as a noble intellectual exercise, but as a handmaid to natural philosophy. Astronomy

After the painting by P. Van Somer

LORD FRANCIS BACON

is not to assist the mind to lofty contemplation, but to enable mariners to verify degrees of latitude and regulate clocks. A college is not designed to train and discipline the mind, but to utilize science, and become a school of technology. Greek and Latin exercises are comparatively worthless, and even mathematics, unless they can be converted into practical use. Philosophy, as ordinarily understood, — that is, metaphysics, — is most idle of all, since it does not pertain to mundane wants. Hence the old Grecian philosopher labored in vain; and still more profitless were the disquisitions of the scholastics of the Middle Ages, since they were chiefly used to prop up unintelligible creeds. Theology is not of much account, since it pertains to mysteries we cannot solve. It is not with heaven or hell, or abstract inquiries, or divine certitudes, that we have to do, but the things of earth, — things that advance our material and outward condition. To be rich and comfortable is the end of life, — not meditations on abstract and eternal truth, such as elevate the soul or prepare it for a future and endless life. The certitudes of faith, of love, of friendship, are of small value when compared with the blessings of outward prosperity. Utilitarianism is the true philosophy, for this confines us to the world where we are born to labor, and enables us to make acquisitions which promote our comfort and ease. The chemist and the manufacturer are our greatest benefactors, for they make for us oils and gases and paints, — things we must have. The philosophy of Bacon is an immense improvement on all previous systems, since it heralds the jubilee of trades, the millennium of merchants, the schools of thrift, the apostles of physical progress, the pioneers of enterprise, — the Franklins and Stephensons and Tyndalls and Morses of our glorious era. Its watchword is progress. All hail, then, to the electric telegraph and telephones and Thames tunnels and Crystal Palaces and Niagara bridges and railways over the Rocky Mountains! The day of our deliverance is come; the nations are saved; the Brunels and the Fieldses are our victors and leaders! Crown them with Olympic leaves, as the heroes of our great games of life. And thou, O England! exalted art thou among the nations, — not for thy Oxfords and Westminsters; not for thy divines and saints and martyrs and poets; not for thy Hookers and Leightons and Cranmers and Miltons and Burkes and Lockes; not for thy Reformation; not for thy struggles for liberty, — but for thy Manchesters and Birminghams, thy Portsmouth shipyards, thy London docks, thy Liverpool warehouses, thy mines of coal and iron, thy countless mechanisms by which thou bringest the wealth of nations into thy banks, and art enabled to buy the toil of foreigners and to raise thy standards on the farthest battlements of

India and China. These conquests and acquisitions are real, are practical; machinery over life, the triumph of physical forces, dominion over waves and winds, — these are the great victories which consummate the happiness of man; and these are they which flow from the philosophy which Bacon taught.

Now Macaulay does not directly say all these things, but these are the spirit and gist of the interpretation which he puts upon Bacon's writings. The philosophy of Bacon leads directly to these blessings; and these constitute its great peculiarity. And it cannot be denied that the new era which Bacon heralded was fruitful in these very things, — that his philosophy encouraged this new development of material forces; but it may be questioned whether he had not something else in view than mere utility and physical progress, and whether his method could not equally be applied to metaphysical subjects; whether it did not pertain to the whole domain of truth, and take in the whole realm of human inquiry. I believe that Bacon was interested, not merely in the world of matter, but in the world of mind; that he sought to establish principles from which sound deductions might be made, as well as to establish reliable inductions. Lord Campbell thinks that a perfect system of ethics could be made out of his writings, and that his method is equally well adapted to examine and classify the phenomena of the mind. He separated the legitimate paths of human inquiry, giving his attention to poetry and politics and metaphysics, as well as to physics. Bacon does not sneer as Macaulay does at the ancient philosophers; he bears testimony to their genius and their unrivalled dialectical powers, even if he regards their speculations as frequently barren. He does not flippantly ridicule the *homoousian* and the *homoiousian* as mere words, but the expression and exponent of profound theological distinctions, as every theologian knows them to be. He does not throw dirt on metaphysical science if properly directed, still less on noble inquiries after God and the mysteries of life. He is subjective as well as objective. He treats of philosophy in its broadest meaning, as it takes in the province of the understanding, the memory, and the will, as well as of man in society. He speaks of the principles of government and of the fountains of law; of universal justice, of eternal spiritual truth. So that Playfair judiciously observes (and he was a scientist) "that it was not by sagacious anticipations of science, afterwards to be made in physics, that his writings have had so powerful an influence, as in his knowledge of the limits and resources of the human understanding. It would be difficult to find another writer, prior to Locke, whose works are enriched with so many just observations on mere intellectual phenomena. What he says of the laws of memory, of imagination, has never been surpassed in subtlety. No man ever more carefully studied the operation of his own mind and the intellectual character of others." Nor did Bacon despise metaphysical science, only the frivolous questions that the old scholastics associated with it, and the general barrenness of their speculations. He surely would not have disdained the subsequent inquiries of Locke, or Berkeley, or Leibnitz, or Kant. True, he sought definite knowledge,— something firm to stand upon, and which could not be controverted. No philosophy can be sound when the principle from which deductions are made is not itself certain or very highly probable, or when this principle, pushed to its utmost logical sequence, would lead to absurdity, or even to a conflict with human consciousness. To Bacon the old methods were wrong, and it was his primal aim to reform the scientific methods in order to arrive at truth; not truth for utilitarian ends chiefly, but truth for its own sake. He loved truth as Palestrina loved music, or Raphael loved painting, or Socrates loved virtue.

Now the method which was almost exclusively employed until Bacon's time is commonly called the *deductive* method; that is, some principle or premise was assumed to be true, and reasoning was made from this assumption. No especial fault was found with the reasoning of the great masters of logic like Aristotle and

Thomas Aquinas, for it never has been surpassed in acuteness and severity. If their premises were admitted, their conclusions would follow as a certainty. What was wanted was to establish the truth of premises, or general propositions. This Bacon affirmed could be arrived at only by *induction;* that is, the ascending from ascertained individual facts to general principles, by extending what is true of particulars to the whole class in which they belong. Bacon has been called the father of inductive science, since he would employ the inductive method. Yet he is not truly the father of induction, since it is as old as the beginnings of science. Hippocrates, when he ridiculed the quacks of his day, and collected the facts and phenomena of disease, and inferred from them the proper treatment of it, was as much the father of induction as Bacon himself. The error the ancients made was in not collecting a sufficient number of facts to warrant a sound induction. And the ancients looked out for facts to support some preconceived theory, from which they reasoned syllogistically. The theory could not be substantiated by any syllogistic reasonings, since conclusions could never go beyond assumptions; if the assumptions were wrong, no ingenious or elaborate reasoning would avail anything towards the discovery of truth, but could only uphold what was assumed. This applied to theology as well as to science. In the Dark Ages it was well for the teachers of mankind to uphold the dogmas of the Church, which they did with masterly dialectical skill. Those were ages of Faith, and not of Inquiry. It was all-important to ground believers in a firm faith of the dogmas which were deemed necessary to support the Church and the cause of religion. They were regarded as absolute certainties. There was no dispute about the premises of the scholastic's arguments; and hence his dialectics strengthened the mind by the exercise of logical sports, and at the same time confirmed the faith.

The world never saw a more complete system of dogmatic theology than that elaborated by Thomas Aquinas. When the knowledge of the Greek and Hebrew was rare and imperfect, and it was impossible to throw light by means of learning and science on the texts of Scripture, it was well to follow the interpretation of such a great light as Augustine, and assume his dogmas as certainties, since they could not then be controverted; and thus from them construct a system of belief which would confirm the faith. But Aquinas, with his Aristotelian method of syllogism and definitions, could not go beyond Augustine. Augustine was the fountain, and the water that flowed from it in ten thousand channels could not rise above the spring; and as everybody appealed to and believed in Saint Augustine, it was well to construct a system from him to confute the heretical, and which the heretical would respect. The scholastic philosophy which some ridicule, in spite of its puerilities and sophistries and syllogisms, preserved the theology of the Middle Ages, perhaps of the Fathers. It was a mighty bulwark of the faith which was then accepted. No honors could be conferred on its great architects that were deemed extravagant. The Pope and the clergy saw in Thomas Aquinas the great defender of the Church, — not of its abuses, but of its doctrines. And if no new light can be shed on the Scripture text from which assumptions were made; if these assumptions cannot be assailed, if they are certitudes, — then we can scarcely have better text-books than those furnished to the theologians of the Middle Ages, for no modern dialetician can excel them in severity of logic. The great object of modern theologians should be to establish the authenticity and meaning of the Scripture texts on which their assumptions rest; and this can be done only by the method which Bacon laid down, which is virtually a collation and collection of facts,— that is, divine declarations. Establish the meaning of these without question, and we have *principia* from which we may deduce creeds and systems, the usefulness of which cannot be exaggerated, especially in an age of agnosticism. Having fundamental principles which cannot be gainsaid, we may philosophically draw deductions. Bacon did not make war on deduction, when its fundamental truths are established. Deduction is as much a necessary part of philosophy as induction: it is the peculiarity of the Scotch metaphysicians, who have ever deduced truths from those previously established. Deduction even enters into modern science as well as induction. When Cuvier deduced from a bone the form and habits of the mastodon; when Kepler deduced his great laws, all from the primary thought that there must be some numerical or geographical relation between the times, distances, and velocities of the revolving bodies of the solar system; when Newton deduced, as is said, the principle of gravitation from the fall of an apple; when Leverrier sought for a new planet from the perturbations of the heavenly bodies in their orbits,—we feel that deduction is as much a legitimate process as induction itself.

But deductive logic is the creation of Aristotle; and it was the authority of Aristotle that Bacon sought to subvert. The inductive process is also old, of which Bacon is called the father. How are these things to be reconciled and explained? Wherein and how did Bacon adapt his method to the discovery of truth, which was his principal aim, — that method which is the great cause of modern progress in science, the way to it being indicated by him pre-eminently?

The whole thing consists in this, that Bacon pointed

out the right road to truth, — as a board where two roads meet or diverge indicates the one which is to be followed. He did not make a system, like Descartes or Spinoza or Newton: he showed the way to make it on sound principles. "He laid down a systematic analysis and arrangement of inductive evidence." The syllogism, the great instrument used by Aristotle and the Schoolmen, "is, from its very nature, incompetent to prove the ultimate premises from which it proceeds; and when the truth of these remains doubtful, we can place no confidence in the conclusions drawn from them." Hence, the first step in the reform of science is to review its ultimate principles; and the first condition of a scientific method is that it shall be competent to conduct such an inquiry; and this method is applicable, not to physical science merely, but to the whole realm of knowledge. This, of course, includes poetry, art, intellectual philosophy, and theology, as well as geology and chemistry.

And it is this breadth of inquiry — directed to subjective as well as objective knowledge — which made Bacon so great a benefactor. The defect in Macaulay's criticism is that he makes Bacon interested in mere outward phenomena, or matters of practical utility, — a worldly utilitarian of whom Epicureans may be proud. In reality he soared to the realm of Plato as well as of Aristotle. Take, for instance, his *Idola*

Mentis Humanæ, or "Phantoms of the Human Mind," which compose the best-known part of the "Novum Organum." "The Idols of the Tribe" would show the folly of attempting to penetrate further than the limits of the human faculties permit, as also "the liability of the intellect to be warped by the will and affections, and the like." The "Idols of the Den" have reference to "the tendency to notice differences rather than resemblances, or resemblances rather than differences, in the attachment to antiquity or novelty, in the partiality to minute or comprehensive investigations." "The Idols of the Market-Place" have reference to the tendency to confound words with things, which has ever marked controversialists in their learned disputations. In what he here says about the necessity for accurate definitions, he reminds us of Socrates rather than a modern scientist; this necessity for accuracy applies to metaphysics as much as it does to physics. "The Idols of the Theatre" have reference to perverse laws of demonstration which are the strongholds of error. This school deals in speculations and experiments confined to a narrow compass, like those of the alchemists, — too imperfect to elicit the light which should guide.

Bacon having completed his discussion of the *Idola*, then proceeds to point out the weakness of the old philosophies, which produced leaves rather than fruit, and were stationary in their character. Here he would seem to lean towards utilitarianism, were it not that he is as severe on men of experiment as on men of dogma. "The men of experiment are," says he, "like ants,— they only collect and use; the reasoners resemble spiders, who make cobwebs out of their own substance. But the bee takes a middle course; it gathers the material from the flowers, but digests it by a power of its own. . . . So true philosophy neither chiefly relies on the powers of the mind, nor takes the matter which it gathers and lays it up in the memory, whole as it finds it, but lays it up in the understanding, to be transformed and digested." Here he simply points out the laws by which true knowledge is to be attained. He does not extol physical science alone, though doubtless he had a preference for it over metaphysical inquiries. He was an Englishman, and the English mind is objective rather than subjective, and is prone to over-value the outward and the seen, above the inward and unseen; and perhaps for the same reason that the Old Testament seems to make prosperity the greatest blessing, while adversity seems to be the blessing of the New Testament.

One of Bacon's longest works is the "Silva Sylvarum," — a sort of natural history, in which he treats of the various forces and productions of Nature, — the air, the sea, the winds, the clouds, plants and animals, fire and water, sounds and discords, colors and smells, heat and cold, disease and health; but which varied subjects he presents to communicate knowledge, with no especial utilitarian end.

"The Advancement of Learning" is one of Bacon's most famous productions, but I fail to see in it an objective purpose to enable men to become powerful or rich or comfortable; it is rather an abstract treatise, as dry to most people as legal disquisitions, and with no more reference to rising in the world than "Blackstone's Commentaries" or "Coke upon Littleton." It is a profound dissertation on the excellence of learning; its great divisions treating of history, poetry, and philosophy, — of metaphysical as well as physical philosophy; of the province of understanding, the memory, the will, the reason, and the imagination; and of man in society, — of government, of universal justice, of the fountains of law, of revealed religion.

And if we turn from the new method by which he would advance all knowledge, and on which his fame as a philosopher chiefly rests, — that method which has led to discoveries that even Bacon never dreamed of, not thinking of the fruit he was to bestow, but only the way to secure it, — even as a great inventor thinks more of his invention than of the money he himself may reap from it, as a work of creation to benefit the world rather than his own family, and in the work of which his mind revels in a sort of intoxicated delight, like a true poet when he constructs his lines, or a great artist when he paints his picture, — a pure subjective joy, not an anticipated gain; — if we turn from this "method" to most of his other writings, what do we find? Simply the lucubrations of a man of letters, the moral wisdom of the moralist, the historian, the biographer, the essayist. In these writings we discover no more worldliness than in Macaulay when he wrote his "Milton," or Carlyle when he penned his "Burns," — even less, for Bacon did not write to gain a living, but to please himself and give vent to his burning thoughts. In these he had no worldly aim to reach, except perhaps an imperishable fame. He wrote as Michael Angelo sculptured his Moses; and he wrote not merely amid the cares and duties of a great public office, with other labors which might be called Herculean, but even amid the pains of disease and the infirmities of age, — when rest, to most people, is the greatest boon and solace of their lives.

Take his Essays, — these are among his best-known works, — so brilliant and forcible, suggestive and rich, that even Archbishop Whately's commentaries upon them are scarcely an addition. Surely these are not on material subjects, and indicate anything but a worldly or sordid nature. In these famous Essays, so luminous with the gems of genius, we read not such worldly-wise exhortations as Lord Chesterfield impressed upon his son, not the gossiping frivolities of Horace Walpole, not the cynical wit of Montaigne, but those great certitudes which console in affliction, which kindle hope, which inspire lofty resolutions,—anchors of the soul, pillars of faith, sources of immeasurable joy, the glorious ideals of true objects of desire, the eternal unities of truth and love and beauty; all of which reveal the varied experiences of life and the riches of deeply-pondered meditation on God and Christianity, as well as knowledge of the world and the desirableness of its valued gifts. How beautiful are his thoughts on death, on adversity, on glory, on anger, on friendship, on fame, on ambition, on envy, on riches, on youth and old age, and divers other subjects of moral import, which show the elevation of his soul, and the subjective as well as the objective turn of his mind; not dwelling on what he should eat and what he should drink and wherewithal he should be clothed, but on the truths which appeal to our higher nature, and which raise the thoughts of men from earth to heaven, or at least to the realms of intellectual life and joy.

And then, it is necessary that we should take in view other labors which dignified Bacon's retirement, as well as those which marked his more active career as a lawyer and statesman,—his histories and biographies, as well as learned treatises to improve the laws of England; his political discourses, his judicial charges, his theological tracts, his speeches and letters and prayers;

all of which had relation to benefit others rather than himself. Who has ever done more to instruct the world, — to enable men to rise not in fortune merely, but in virtue and patriotism, in those things which are of themselves the only reward? We should consider these labors, as well as the new method he taught to arrive at knowledge, in our estimate of the sage as well as of the man. He was a moral philosopher, like Socrates. He even soared into the realm of supposititious truth, like Plato. He observed Nature, like Aristotle. He took away the syllogism from Thomas Aquinas, — not to throw contempt on metaphysical inquiry or dialectical reasoning, but to arrive by a better method at the knowledge of first principles; which once established, he allowed deductions to be drawn from them, leading to other truths as certainly as induction itself. Yea, he was also a Moses on the mount of Pisgah, from which with prophetic eye he could survey the promised land of indefinite wealth and boundless material prosperity, which he was not permitted to enter, but which he had bequeathed to civilization. This may have been his greatest gift in the view of scientific men, — this inductive process of reasoning, by which great discoveries have been made after he was dead. But this was not his only legacy, for other things which he taught were as valuable, not merely in his sight, but to the eye of enlightened reason. There are other truths besides those of physical science; there is greatness in deduction as well as in induction. Geometry — whose successive and progressive revelations are so inspiring, and which have come down to us from a remote antiquity, which are even now taught in our modern schools as Euclid demonstrated them, since they cannot be improved — is a purely deductive science. The scholastic philosophy, even if it was barren and unfruitful in leading to new truths, yet confirmed what was valuable in the old systems, and by the severity of its logic and its dialectical subtleties trained the European mind for the reception of the message of Luther and Bacon; and this was based on deductions, never wrong unless the premises are unsound. Theology is deductive reasoning from truths assumed to be fundamental, and is inductive only so far as it collates Scripture declarations, and interprets their meaning by the aid which learning brings. Is not this science worthy of some regard? Will it not live when all the speculations of evolutionists are forgotten, and occupy the thoughts of the greatest and profoundest minds so long as anything shall be studied, so long as the Bible shall be the guide of life? Is it not by deduction that we ascend from Nature herself to the God of Nature? What is more certain than deduction when the principles from which it reasons are indisputably established?

Is induction, great as it is, especially in the explorations of Nature and science, always certain? Are not most of the sciences which are based upon it progressive? Have we yet learned the ultimate principles of political economy, or of geology, or of government, or even of art? The theory of induction, though supposed by Dr. Whewell to lead to certain results, is regarded by Professor Jevons as leading to results only "almost certain." "All inductive inference is merely probable," says the present professor of logic, Thomas Fowler, in the University of Oxford.

And although it is supposed that the inductive method of Bacon has led to the noblest discoveries of modern times, is this strictly true? Galileo made his discoveries in the heavens before Bacon died. Physical improvements must need follow such inventions as gunpowder and the mariners' compass, and printing and the pictures of Italy, and the discovery of mines and the revived arts of the Romans and Greeks, and the glorious emancipation which the Reformation produced. Why should not the modern races follow in the track of Carthage and Alexandria and Rome, with the progress of wealth, and carry out inventions as those cities did, and all other civilized peoples since Babel towered above the plains of Babylon? Physical developments arise from the developments of man, whatever method may be recommended by philosophers. What philosophical teachings led to the machinery of the mines of California, or to that of the mills of Lowell? Some think that our modern improvements would have come whether Bacon had lived or not. But I would not disparage the labors of Bacon in pointing out the method which leads to scientific discoveries. Granting that he sought merely utility, an improvement in the outward condition of society, which is the view that Macaulay takes, I would not underrate his legacy. And even supposing that the blessings of material life—"the acre of Middlesex"—are as much to be desired as Macaulay, with the complacency of an eminently practical and prosperous man, seems to argue, I would not sneer at them. Who does not value them? Who will not value them so long as our mortal bodies are to be cared for? It is a pleasant thing to ride in "cars without horses," to feel in winter the genial warmth of grates and furnaces, to receive messages from distant friends in a moment of time, to cross the ocean without discomfort, with the "almost certainty" of safety, and save our wives and daughters from the ancient drudgeries of the loom and the knitting-needle. Who ever tires in gazing at a locomotive as it whirls along with the power of destiny? Who is not astonished at the triumphs of the engineer, the wonders of an ocean-steamer, the marvellous tunnels under lofty mountains? We feel that Titans have been sent to ease us of our burdens.

But great and beneficent as are these blessings, they are not the only certitudes, nor are they the greatest. An outward life of ease and comfort is not the chief end of man. The interests of the soul are more important than any comforts of the body. The higher life is only reached by lofty contemplation on the true, the beautiful, and the good. Subjective wisdom is worth more than objective knowledge. What are the great realities, — machinery, new breeds of horses, carpets, diamonds, mirrors, gas? or are they affections, friendships, generous impulses, inspiring thoughts? Look to Socrates: what raised that barefooted, ugly-looking, impecunious, persecuted, cross-questioning, self-constituted teacher, without pay, to the loftiest pedestal of Athenian fame? What was the spirit of the truths *he* taught? Was it objective or subjective truth; the way to become rich and comfortable, or the search for the indefinite, the infinite, the eternal, — Utopia, not Middlesex, — that which fed the wants of the immaterial soul, and enabled it to rise above temptation and vulgar rewards? What raised Plato to the highest pinnacle of intellectual life? Was it definite and practical knowledge of outward phenomena; or was it "a longing after love, in the contemplation of which the mortal soul sustains itself, and becomes participant in the glories of immortality"? What were realities to Anselm, Bernard, and Bonaventura? What gave beauty and placidity to Descartes and Leibnitz and Kant? It may be very dignified for a modern savant to sit serenely on his tower of observation, indifferent to all the lofty speculations of the great men of bygone ages; yet those profound questions pertaining to the λογος and the τα οντα, which had such attractions for Augustine and Pascal and Calvin, did have as real bearing on human life and on what is best worth knowing, as the scales of a leuciscus cephalus or the limbs of a magnified animalculus, or any of the facts of which physical science can boast. The wonders of science are great, but so also are the secrets of the soul, the mysteries of the spiritual life, the truths which come from divine revelation. Whatever most dignifies humanity, and makes our labors sweet, and causes us to forget our pains, and kindles us to lofty contemplations, and prompts us to heroic sacrifice, is the most real and the most useful. Even the leaves of a barren and neglected philosophy may be in some important respects of more value than all the boasted fruit of utilitarian science. Is that which is most useful always the most valuable,—that, I mean, which gives the highest pleasure? Do we not plant our grounds with the acacia, the oak, the cedar, the elm, as well as with the apple, the pear, and the cherry? Are not flowers and shrubs which beautify the lawn as desirable as beans and turnips and cabbages? Is not the rose or tulip as great an addition to even a poor man's cottage as his bed of onions or patch of potatoes? What is the scale to measure even mortal happiness? What is the marketable value of friendship or of love? What makes the dinner of herbs sometimes more refreshing than the stalled ox? What is the material profit of a first love? What is the value in tangible dollars and cents of a beautiful landscape, or a speaking picture, or a marble statue, or a living book, or the voice of eloquence, or the charm of earliest bird, or the smile of a friend, or the promise of immortality? In what consisted the real glory of the country we are never weary of quoting, — the land of Phidias and Pericles and Demosthenes? Was it not in immaterial ideas, in patriotism, in heroism, in conceptions of ideal beauty, in speculations on the infinite and unattainable, in the songs which still inspire the minds of youth, in the expression which made marble live, in those conceptions of beauty and harmony which still give shape to the temples of Christendom? Was Rome more glorious with her fine roads and tables of thuja-root, and Falernian wines, and oysters from the Lucrine Lake, and chariots of silver, and robes of purple and rings of gold, — these useful blessings which are the pride of an Epicurean civilization? And who gave the last support, who raised the last barrier, against that inundation of destructive pleasures in which some see the most valued fruits of human invention, but which proved a canker that prepared the way to ruin? It was that pious Emperor who learned his wisdom from a slave, and who set a haughty defiance to all the grandeur and all the comforts of the highest position which earth could give, and spent his leisure hours in the quiet study of those truths which elevate the soul,— truths not taught by science or nature, but by communication with invisible powers.

Ah, what indeed is reality; what is the higher good; what is that which perishes never; what is that which assimilates man to Deity? Is it houses, is it lands, is it gold and silver, is it luxurious couches, is it the practical utilitarian comforts that pamper this mortal body in its brief existence? or is it women's loves and patriots' struggles, and sages' pious thoughts, affections, noble aspirations, Bethanies, the serenities of virtuous old age, the harmonies of unpolluted homes, the existence of art, of truth, of love; the hopes which last when sun and stars decay? Tell us, ye women, what are realities to you, — your carpets, your plate, your jewels, your luxurious banquets; or your husbands' love, your friends' esteem, your children's reverence? And ye, toiling men of business, what is really your highest joy,— your piles of gold, your marble palaces; or the pleasures of your homes, the approbation of your consciences, your hopes of future bliss? Yes, you are dreamers, like poets and philosophers, when you call yourselves pack-horses. Even you are only sustained in labor by intangible rewards that you can neither see nor feel. The most practical of men and women can really only live in those ideas which are deemed indefinite and unreal. For what do the busiest of you run away from money-making, and ride in cold or heat, in dreariness or discomfort, — dinners, or greetings of love and sympathy? On what are such festivals as Christmas and Thanksgiving Day based? — on consecrated sentiments that have more force than any material gains or ends. These, after all, are realities to you as much as ideas were to Plato, or music to Beethoven, or patriotism to Washington. Deny these as the higher certitudes, and you rob the soul of its dignity, and life of its consolations.

AUTHORITIES.

Bacon's Works, edited by Basil Montagu; Bacon's Life, by Basil Montagu; Bacon's Life, by James Spedding; Bacon's Life, by Thomas Fowler; Dr. Abbott's Introduction to Bacon's Essays, in Contemporary Review, 1876; Macaulay's famous essay in Edinburgh Review, 1839; Archbishop Whately's annotations of the Essays of Bacon; the general Histories of England.

GALILEO.

A. D. 1564–1642.

ASTRONOMICAL DISCOVERIES.

GALILEO.

ASTRONOMICAL DISCOVERIES.

AMONG the wonders of the sixteenth century was the appearance of a new star in the northern horizon, which, shining at first with a feeble light, gradually surpassed the brightness of the planet Jupiter; and then changing its color from white to yellow and from yellow to red, after seventeen months, faded away from the sight, and has not since appeared. This celebrated star, first seen by Tycho Brahe in the constellation Cassiopeia, never changed its position, or presented the slightest perceptible parallax. It could not therefore have been a meteor, nor a planet regularly revolving round the sun, nor a comet blazing with fiery nebulous light, nor a satellite of one of the planets, but a fixed star, far beyond our solar system. Such a phenomenon created an immense sensation, and has never since been satisfactorily explained by philosophers. In the infancy of astronomical science it was regarded by astrologers as a sign to portend the birth of an extraordinary individual.

Though the birth of some great political character was supposed to be heralded by this mysterious star, its prophetic meaning might with more propriety apply to the extraordinary man who astonished his contemporaries by discoveries in the heavens, and who forms the subject of this lecture; or it poetically might apply to the brilliancy of the century itself in which it appeared. The sixteenth century cannot be compared with the nineteenth century in the variety and scope of scientific discoveries; but, compared with the ages which had preceded it, it was a memorable epoch, marked by the simultaneous breaking up of the darkness of mediæval Europe, and the bursting forth of new energies in all departments of human thought and action. In that century arose great artists, poets, philosophers, theologians, reformers, navigators, jurists, statesmen, whose genius has scarcely since been surpassed. In Italy it was marked by the triumphs of scholars and artists; in Germany and France, by reformers and warriors; in England, by that splendid constellation that shed glory on the reign of Elizabeth. Close upon the artists who followed Da Vinci, to Salvator Rosa, were those scholars of whom Emanuel Chrysoloras, Erasmus, and Scaliger were the representatives, — going back to the classic fountains of Greece and Rome, reviving a study for antiquity, breathing a new spirit into universities, enriching vernacular tongues, collecting and collating manuscripts, translating the Scriptures, and stimulating the learned to emancipate themselves from the trammels of the scholastic philosophers.

Then rose up the reformers, headed by Luther, consigning to destruction the emblems and ceremonies of mediæval superstition, defying popes, burning bulls, ridiculing monks, exposing frauds, unravelling sophistries, attacking vices and traditions with the new arms of reason, and asserting before councils and dignitaries the right of private judgment and the supreme authority of the Bible in all matters of religious faith.

And then appeared the defenders of their cause, by force of arms maintaining the great rights of religious liberty in France, Germany, Switzerland, Holland, and England, until Protestantism was established in half of the countries that had for more than a thousand years servilely bowed down to the authority of the popes. Genius stimulates and enterprise multiplies all the energies and aims of emancipated millions. Before the close of the sixteenth century new continents are colonized, new modes of warfare are introduced, manuscripts are changed into printed books, the comforts of life are increased, governments are more firmly established, and learned men are enriched and honored. Feudalism has succumbed to central power, and barons revolve around their sovereign at court rather than compose an independent authority. Before that century had been numbered with the ages past, the Portuguese had sailed to the East Indies, Sir Francis Drake had circumnavigated the globe, Pizarro had conquered Peru, Sir Walter Raleigh had colonized Virginia, Ricci had penetrated to China, Lescot had planned the palace of the Louvre, Raphael had painted the Transfiguration, Michael Angelo had raised the dome of St. Peter's, Giacomo della Porta had ornamented the Vatican with mosaics, Copernicus had taught the true centre of planetary motion, Dumoulin had introduced into French jurisprudence the principles of the Justinian code, Ariosto had published the "Orlando Furioso," Cervantes had written "Don Quixote," Spenser had dedicated his "Fairy Queen," Shakspeare had composed his immortal dramas, Hooker had devised his "Ecclesiastical Polity," Cranmer had published his Forty-two Articles, John Calvin had dedicated to Francis I. his celebrated "Institutes," Luther had translated the Bible, Bacon had begun the "Instauration of Philosophy," Bellarmine had systematized the Roman Catholic theology, Henry IV. had signed the Edict of Nantes, Queen Elizabeth had defeated the Invincible Armada, and William the Silent had achieved the independence of Holland.

Such were some of the lights and some of the enterprises of that great age, when the profoundest questions pertaining to philosophy, religion, law, and government were discussed with the enthusiasm and fresh-

After the painting by J. Sustermans, Uffizi, Florence
GALILEO GALILEI

ness of a revolutionary age; when men felt the inspiration of a new life, and looked back on the Middle Ages with disgust and hatred, as a period which enslaved the human soul. But what peculiarly marked that period was the commencement of those marvellous discoveries in science which have enriched our times and added to the material blessings of the new civilization. Tycho Brahe, Copernicus, Galileo, Kepler, and Bacon inaugurated the era which led to progressive improvements in the physical condition of society, and to those scientific marvels which have followed in such quick succession and produced such astonishing changes that we are fain to boast that we have entered upon the most fortunate and triumphant epoch in our world's history.

Many men might be taken as the representatives of this new era of science and material inventions, but I select Galileo Galilei as one of the most interesting in his life, opinions, and conflicts.

Galileo was born at Pisa, in the year 1564, the year that Calvin and Michael Angelo died, four years after the birth of Bacon, in the sixth year of the reign of Elizabeth, and the fourth of Charles IX., about the time when the Huguenot persecution was at its height, and the Spanish monarchy was in its most prosperous state, under Philip II. His parents were of a noble but impoverished Florentine family; and his father, who was a man of some learning, — a writer on the science of music, — gave him the best education he could afford. Like so many of the most illustrious men, he early gave promise of rare abilities. It was while he was a student in the university of his native city that his attention was arrested by the vibrations of a lamp suspended from the ceiling of the cathedral; and before he had quitted the church, while the choir was chanting mediæval anthems, he had compared those vibrations with his own pulse, which after repeated experiments, ended in the construction of the first pendulum, — applied not as it was by Huygens to the measurement of time, but to medical science, to enable physicians to ascertain the rate of the pulse. But the pendulum was soon brought into the service of the clockmakers, and ultimately to the determination of the form of the earth, by its minute irregularities in diverse latitudes, and finally to the measurement of differences of longitude by its connection with electricity and the recording of astronomical observations. Thus it was that the swinging of a cathedral lamp, before the eye of a man of genius, has done nearly as much as the telescope itself to advance science, to say nothing of its practical uses in common life.

Galileo had been destined by his father to the profession of medicine, and was ignorant of mathematics. He amused his leisure hours with painting and music, and in order to study the principles of drawing he found it necessary to acquire some knowledge of geometry, much to the annoyance of his father, who did not like to see his mind diverted from the prescriptions of Hippocrates and Galen. The certain truths of geometry burst upon him like a revelation, and after mastering Euclid he turned to Archimedes with equal enthusiasm. Mathematics now absorbed his mind, and the father was obliged to yield to the bent of his genius, which seemed to disdain the regular professions by which social position was most surely effected. He wrote about this time an essay on the Hydrostatic Balance, which introduced him to Guido Ubaldo, a famous mathematician, who induced him to investigate the subject of the centre of gravity in solid bodies. His treatise on this subject secured an introduction to the Grand Duke of Tuscany, who perceived his merits, and by whom he was appointed a lecturer on mathematics at Pisa, but on the small salary of sixty crowns a year.

This was in 1589, when he was twenty-five, an enthusiastic young man, full of hope and animal spirits, the charm of every circle for his intelligence, vivacity, and wit; but bold and sarcastic, contemptuous of ancient dogmas, defiant of authority, and therefore no favorite with Jesuit priests and Dominican professors. It is said that he was a handsome man, with bright golden locks, such as painters in that age loved to perpetuate upon the canvas; hilarious and cheerful, fond of good cheer, yet a close student, obnoxious only to learned dunces and narrow pedants and treadmill professors and bigoted priests, — all of whom sought to molest him, yet to whom he was either indifferent or sarcastic, holding them and their formulas up to ridicule. He now directed his inquiries to the mechanical doctrines of Aristotle, to whose authority the schools had long bowed down, and whom he too regarded as one of the great intellectual giants of the world, yet not to be credited without sufficient reasons. Before the "Novum Organum" was written, he sought, as Bacon himself pointed out, the way to arrive at truth, — a foundation to stand upon, a principle tested by experience, which, when established by experiment, would serve for sure deductions.

Now one of the principles assumed by Aristotle, and which had never been disputed, was, that if different weights of the same material were let fall from the same height, the heavier would reach the ground sooner than the lighter, and in proportion to the difference of weight. This assumption Galileo denied, and asserted that, with the exception of a small difference owing to the resistance of the air, both would fall to the ground in the same space of time. To prove his position by actual experiment, he repaired to the leaning tower of Pisa, and demonstrated that he was right and Aristotle was wrong. The Aristotelians would not believe the evidence of their own senses, and ascribed the effect to some unknown cause. To such a degree were men enslaved by authority. This provoked Galileo, and led him to attack authority with still greater vehemence, adding mockery to sarcasm; which again exasperated his opponents, and doubtless laid the foundation of that personal hostility which afterwards pursued him to the prison of the Inquisition. This blended arrogance and asperity in a young man was offensive to the whole university, yet natural to one who had overturned one of the favorite axioms of the greatest master of thought the world had seen for nearly two thousand years; and the scorn and opposition with which his discovery was received increased his rancor, so that he, in his turn, did not render justice to the learned men arrayed against him, who were not necessarily dull or obstinate because they would not at once give up the opinions in which they were educated, and which the learned world still accepted. Nor did they oppose and hate him for his new opinions, so much as from dislike of his personal arrogance and bitter sarcasms.

At last his enemies made it too hot for him at Pisa. He resigned his chair (1591), but only to accept a higher position at Padua, on a salary of one hundred and eighty florins, — not, however, adequate to his support, so that he was obliged to take pupils in mathematics. To show the comparative estimate of that age of science, the fact may be mentioned that the professor of scholastic philosophy in the same university was paid fourteen hundred florins. This was in 1592; and the next year Galileo invented the thermometer, still an imperfect instrument, since air was not perfectly excluded. At this period his reputation seems to have been established as a brilliant lecturer rather than as a great discoverer, or even as a great mathematician; for he was immeasurably behind Kepler, his contemporary, in the power of making abstruse calculations and numerical combinations. In this respect Kepler was inferior only to Copernicus, Newton, and Laplace in our times, or Hipparchus and Ptolemy among the ancients; and it is to him that we owe the discovery of those great laws of planetary motion from which there is no appeal, and which have never been rivalled in importance except those made by Newton himself, — laws which connect the mean distance of the planets from the sun with the times of their revolutions; laws which show that the orbits of planets are elliptical, not circular; and that the areas described by lines drawn from the moving planet to the sun are proportionable to the times employed in the motion. What an infinity of calculation, in the infancy of science, — before the invention of logarithms, — was necessary to arrive at these truths! What fertility of invention was displayed in all his hypotheses; what patience in working them out; what magnanimity in discarding those which were not true! What power of guessing, even to hit upon theories which could be established by elaborate calculations, — all from the primary thought, the grand axiom, which Kepler was the first to propose, that there must be some numerical or geometrical relations among the times, distances, and velocities of the revolving bodies of the solar system! It would seem that although his science was deductive, he invoked the aid of induction also : a great original genius, yet modest like Newton; a man who avoided hostilities, yet given to the most boundless enthusiasm on the subjects to which he devoted his life. How intense his raptures! "Nothing holds me," he writes, on discovering his great laws; "I will indulge in my sacred fury. I will boast of the golden vessels I have stolen from the Egyptians. If you forgive me, I rejoice. If you are angry, it is all the same to me. The die is cast; the book is written, — to be read either now, or by posterity, I care not which. It may well wait a century for a reader, as God has waited six thousand years for an observer."

We do not see this sublime repose in the attitude of Galileo, — this falling back on his own conscious greatness, willing to let things take their natural course; but rather, on the other hand, an impatience under contradiction, a vehement scorn of adversaries, and an intellectual arrogance that gave offence, and impeded his career, and injured his fame. No matter how great a man may be, his intellectual pride is always offensive; and when united with sarcasm and mockery it will make bitter enemies, who will pull him down.

Galileo, on his transfer to Padua, began to teach the doctrines of Copernicus, — a much greater genius than he, and yet one who provoked no enmities, although he made the greatest revolution in astronomical knowledge that any man ever made, since he was in no haste to reveal his discoveries, and stated them in a calm and inoffensive way. I doubt if new discoverers in science meet with serious opposition when men themselves are not attacked, and they are made to appeal to calm intelligence, and war is not made on those Scripture texts which seem to controvert them. Even theologians receive science when science is not made to undermine theological declarations, and when the divorce of science from revelation, reason from faith, as two distinct realms, is vigorously insisted upon. Pascal incurred no hostilities for his scientific investigations, nor Newton, nor Laplace. It is only when scientific men sneer at the Bible because its declarations cannot always be harmonized with science, that the hostilities of theologians are provoked. And it is only when theologians deny scientific discoveries that seem to conflict with texts of Scripture, that opposition arises among scientific men. It would seem that the doctrines of Copernicus were offensive to churchmen on this narrow ground. It was hard to believe that the earth revolved around the sun, when the opinions of the learned for two thousand years were unanimous that the sun revolved around the earth. Had both theologian and scientist let the Bible alone, there would not have been a bitter war between them. But scientists were accused by theologians of undermining the Bible; and the theologians were accused of stupid obstinacy, and were mercilessly exposed to ridicule.

That was the great error of Galileo. He made fun and sport of the theologians, as Samson did of the Philistines; and the Philistines of Galileo's day cut off his locks and put out his eyes when the Pope put him into their power,— those Dominican inquisitors who made a crusade against human thought. If Galileo had shown more tact and less arrogance, possibly those Dominican doctors might have joined the chorus of universal praise; for they were learned men, although devoted to a bad system, and incapable of seeing truth when their old authorities were ridiculed and set at nought. Galileo did not deny the Scriptures, but his spirit was mocking; and he seemed to prejudiced people to undermine the truths which were felt to be vital for the preservation of faith in the world. And as some scientific truths seemed to be adverse to Scripture declarations, the transition was easy to a denial of the inspiration which was claimed by nearly all Christian sects, both Catholic and Protestant.

The intolerance of the Church in every age has driven many scientists into infidelity; for it cannot be doubted that the tendency of scientific investigation has been to make scientific men incredulous of divine inspiration, and hence to undermine their faith in dogmas which good men have ever received, and which are supported by evidence that is not merely probable but almost certain. And all now that seems wanting to harmonize science with revelation is, on the one hand, the re-examination of the Scripture texts on which are based the principia from which deductions are made, and which we call theology; and, on the other hand, the rejection of indefensible statements which are at war with both science and consciousness, except in those matters which claim special supernatural agency, which we can neither prove nor disprove by reason; for supernaturalism claims to transcend the realm of reason altogether in what relates to the government of God,— ways that no searching will ever enable us to find out with our limited faculties and obscured understanding. When the two realms of reason and faith are kept distinct, and neither encroaches on the other, then the discoveries and claims of science will meet with but little opposition from theologians, and they will be left to be sifted by men who alone are capable of the task.

Thus far science, outside of pure mathematics, is made up of theories which are greatly modified by advancing knowledge, so that they cannot claim in all respects to be eternally established, like the laws of Kepler and the discoveries of Copernicus, — the latter of which were only true in the main fact that the earth revolves around the sun. But even he retained epicycles and excentrics, and could not explain the unequal orbits of planetary motion. In fact he retained many of the errors of Hipparchus and Ptolemy. Much, too, as we are inclined to ridicule the astronomy of the ancients because they made the earth the centre, we should remember that they also resolved the orbits of the heavenly bodies into circular motions, discovered the precession of the equinoxes, and knew also the apparent motions of the planets and their periods. They could predict eclipses of the sun and moon, and knew that the orbit of the sun and planets was through a belt in the heavens, of a few degrees in width, which they called the Zodiac. They did not know, indeed, the difference between real and apparent motion, nor the distance of the sun and stars, nor their relative size and weight, nor the laws of motion, nor the principles of gravitation, nor the nature of the Milky Way, nor the existence of nebulæ, nor any of the wonders which the telescope reveals; but in the severity of their mathematical calculations they were quite equal to modern astronomers.

If Copernicus revolutionized astronomy by proving the sun to be the centre of motion to our planetary system, Galileo gave it an immense impulse by his discoveries with the telescope. These did not require such marvellous mathematical powers as made Kepler and Newton immortal, — the equals of Ptolemy and Hipparchus in mathematical demonstration, — but only accuracy and perseverance in observations. Doubtless he was a great mathematician, but his fame rests on his observations and the deductions he made from them. These were more easily comprehended, and had an objective value which made him popular: and for these discoveries he was indebted in a great measure to the labors of others, — it was mechanical invention applied to the advancement of science. The utilization of science was reserved to our times; and it is this utilization which makes science such a handmaid to the enrichment of its votaries, and holds it up to worship in our laboratories and schools of technology and mines, — not merely for itself, but also for the substantial fruit it yields.

It was when Galileo was writing treatises on the

Structure of the Universe, on Local Motion, on Sound, on Continuous Quantity, on Light, on Colors, on the Tides, on Dialing, — subjects that also interested Lord Bacon at the same period, — and when he was giving lectures on these subjects with immense *éclat*, frequently to one thousand persons (scarcely less than what Abélard enjoyed when he made fun of the more conservative schoolmen with whom he was brought in contact), that he heard, while on a visit to Venice, that a Dutch spectacle-maker had invented an instrument which was said to represent distant objects nearer than they usually appeared. This was in 1609, when he, at the age of fifty-five, was the idol of scientific men, and was in the enjoyment of an ample revenue, giving only sixty half-hours in the year to lectures, and allowed time to prosecute his studies in that "sweet solitariness" which all true scholars prize, and without which few great attainments are made. The rumor of the invention excited in his mind the intensest interest. He sought for the explanation of the fact in the doctrine of refraction. He meditated day and night. At last he himself constructed an instrument, — a leaden organ pipe with two spectacle glasses, both plain on one side, while one of them had its opposite side convex, and the other its second side concave.

This crude little instrument, which magnified but three times, he carries in triumph back to Venice. It is regarded as a scientific toy, yet everybody wishes to see an instrument by which the human eye indefinitely multiplies its power. The Doge is delighted, and the Senate is anxious to secure so great a curiosity. He makes a present of it to the Senate, after he has spent a month in showing it round to the principal people of that wealthy city; and he is rewarded for his ingenuity with an increase of his salary, at Padua, to one thousand florins, and is made professor for life.

He now only thinks of making discoveries in the heavens; but his instrument is too small. He makes another and larger telescope, which magnifies eight times, and then another which magnifies thirty times; and points it to the moon. And how indescribable his satisfaction, for he sees what no mortal had ever before seen, — ranges of mountains, deep hollows, and various inequalities! These discoveries, it would seem, are not favorably received by the Aristotelians; however, he continues his labors, and points his telescope to the planets and fixed stars, — but the magnitude of the latter remain the same, while the planets appear with disks like the moon. Then he directs his observations to the Pleiades, and counts forty stars in the cluster, when only six were visible to the naked eye; in the Milky Way he descries crowds of minute stars.

Having now reached the limit of discovery with his present instrument, he makes another of still greater power, and points it to the planet Jupiter. On the 7th of January, 1610, he observes three little stars near the body of the planet, all in a straight line and parallel to the ecliptic, two on the east and one on the west of Jupiter. On the next observation he finds that they have changed places, and are all on the west of Jupiter; and the next time he observes them they have changed again. He also discovers that there are four of these little stars revolving round the planet. What is the explanation of this singular phenomenon? They cannot be fixed stars, or planets; they must then be moons. Jupiter is attended with satellites like the earth, but has four instead of one! The importance of this last discovery was of supreme value, for it confirmed the heliocentric theory. Old Kepler is filled with agitations of joy; all the friends of Galileo extol his genius; his fame spreads far and near; he is regarded as the ablest scientific man in Europe.

His enemies are now dismayed and perplexed. The principal professor of philosophy at Padua would not even look through the wonderful instrument. Sissi of Florence ridicules the discovery. "As," said he, "there are only seven apertures of the head,—two eyes, two ears, two nostrils, and one mouth,—and as there are only seven days in the week and seven metals, how can there be seven planets?"

But science, discarded by the schools, fortunately

finds a refuge among princes. Cosimo de' Medici prefers the testimony of his senses to the voice of authority. He observes the new satellites with Galileo at Pisa, makes him a present of one thousand florins, and gives him a mere nominal office, — that of lecturing occasionally to princes, on a salary of one thousand florins for life. He is now the chosen companion of the great, and the admiration of Italy. He has rendered an immense service to astronomy. "His discovery of the satellites of Jupiter," says Herschel, "gave the holding turn to the opinion of mankind respecting the Copernican system, and pointed out a connection between speculative astronomy and practical utility."

But this did not complete the catalogue of his discoveries. In 1610 he perceived that Saturn appeared to be triple, and excited the curiosity of astronomers by the publication of his first "Enigma," — *Altissimam planetam tergeminam observavi.* He could not then perceive the rings; the planet seemed through his telescope to have the form of three concentric O's. Soon after, in examining Venus, he saw her in the form of a crescent: *Cynthiæ figuras æmulatur mater amorum,* — "Venus rivals the phases of the moon."

At last he discovers the spots upon the sun's disk, and that they all revolve with the sun, and therefore that the sun has a revolution in about twenty-eight days, and may be moving on in a larger circle, with all its attendant planets, around some distant centre.

Galileo has now attained the highest object of his ambition. He is at the head, confessedly, of all the scientific men of Europe. He has an ample revenue; he is independent, and has perfect leisure. Even the Pope is gracious to him when he makes a visit to Rome; while cardinals, princes, and ambassadors rival one another in bestowing upon him attention and honors.

But there is no height of fortune from which a man may not fall; and it is usually the proud, the ostentatious, and the contemptuous who do fall, since they create envy, and are apt to make social mistakes. Galileo continued to exasperate his enemies by his arrogance and sarcasms. "They refused to be dragged at his chariot-wheels." "The Aristotelian professors," says Brewster, "the temporizing Jesuits, the political churchmen, and that timid but respectable body who at all times dread innovation, whether it be in legislation or science, entered into an alliance against the philosophical tyrant who threatened them with the penalties of knowledge." The church dignitaries were especially hostile, since they thought the tendency of Galileo's investigations was to undermine the Bible. Flanked by the logic of the schools and the popular interpretation of Scripture, and backed by the civil power, they were eager for war. Galileo wrote a letter to his friend the Abbé Castelli, the object of which was "to prove that the Scriptures were not intended to teach science and philosophy," but to point out the way of salvation. He was indiscreet enough to write a longer letter of seventy pages, quoting the Fathers in support of his views, and attempting to show that Nature and Scripture could not speak a different language. It was this reasoning which irritated the dignitaries of the Church more than his discoveries, since it is plain that the literal language of Scripture upholds the doctrine that the sun revolves around the earth. He was wrong or foolish in trying to harmonize revelation and science. He should have advanced his truths of science and left them to take care of themselves. He should not have meddled with the dogmas of his enemies: not that he was wrong in doing so, but it was not politic or wise; and he was not called upon to harmonize Scripture with science.

So his enemies busily employed themselves in collecting evidence against him. They laid their complaints before the Inquisition of Rome, and on the occasion of paying a visit to that city, he was summoned before that tribunal which has been the shame and the reproach of the Catholic Church. It was a tribunal utterly incompetent to sit upon his case, since it was ignorant of science. In 1615 it was decreed that Galileo should renounce his obnoxious doctrines, and pledge himself neither to defend nor publish them in future. And Galileo accordingly, in dread of prison, appeared before Cardinal Bellarmine and declared that he would renounce the doctrines he had defended. This cardinal was not an ignorant man. He was the greatest theologian of the Catholic Church; but his bitterness and rancor in reference to the new doctrines were as marked as his scholastic learning. The Pope, supposing that Galileo would adhere to his promise, was gracious and kind.

But the philosopher could not resist the temptation of ridiculing the advocates of the old system. He called them "paper philosophers." In private he made a mockery of his persecutors. One Saisi undertook to prove from Suidas that the Babylonians used to cook eggs by whirling them swiftly on a sling; to which he replied: "If Saisi insists on the authority of Suidas, that the Babylonians cooked eggs by whirling them on a sling, I will believe it. But I must add that we have eggs and slings, and strong men to whirl them, yet they will not become cooked; nay, if they were hot at first, they more quickly became cool; and as there is nothing wanting to us but to be Babylonians, it follows that being Babylonians is the true cause why the eggs became hard." Such was his prevailing mockery and ridicule. "Your Eminence," writes one of his friends to the Cardinal D'Este, "would be delighted if you could hear him hold forth in the midst of fifteen or twenty, all violently attacking him, sometimes in one house, and sometimes in another; but he is armed after such a fashion that he laughs them all to scorn."

Galileo, after his admonition from the Inquisition, and his promise to hold his tongue, did keep comparatively quiet for a while, amusing himself with mechanics, and striving to find out a new way of discovering longitude at sea. But the want of better telescopes baffled his efforts; and even to-day it is said "that no telescope has yet been made which is capable of observing at sea the eclipses of Jupiter's satellites, by which on shore this method of finding longitude has many advantages."

On the accession of a new Pope (1623), Urban VIII., who had been his friend as Cardinal Barberini, Galileo, after eight years of silence, thought that he might now venture to publish his great work on the Ptolemaic and Copernican systems, especially as the papal censor also had been his friend. But the publication of the book was delayed nearly two years, so great were the obstacles to be surmounted, and so prejudiced and hostile was the Church to the new views. At last it appeared in Florence in 1632, with a dedication to the Grand Duke,—not the Cosimo who had rewarded him, but his son Ferdinand, who was a mere youth. It was an unfortunate thing for Galileo to do. He had pledged his word not to advocate the Copernican theory, which was already sufficiently established in the opinions of philosophers. The form of the book was even offensive, in the shape of dialogues, where some of the chief speakers were his enemies. One of them he ridiculed under the name of Simplicio. This was supposed to mean the Pope himself, — so they made the Pope believe, and he was furious. Old Cardinal Bellarmine roared like a lion. The whole Church, as represented by its dignitaries, seemed to be against him. The Pope seized the old weapons of the Clements and the Gregories to hurl upon the daring innovator; but delayed to hurl them, since he dealt with a giant, covered not only by the shield of the Medici, but that of Minerva. So he convened a congregation of cardinals, and submitted to them the examination of the detested book. The author was summoned to Rome to appear before the Inquisition, and answer at its judgment-seat the charges against him as a heretic. The Tuscan ambassador expostulated with his Holiness against such a cruel thing, considering Galileo's age, infirmities, and fame, — all to no avail. He was obliged to obey the summons. At the age of seventy this venerated philosopher, infirm, in precarious health, appeared before the Inquisition of cardinals, not one of whom had any familiarity with abstruse speculations, or even with mathematics.

Whether out of regard to his age and infirmities, or to his great fame and illustrious position as the greatest philosopher of his day, the cardinals treat Galileo with unusual indulgence. Though a prisoner of the Inquisition, and completely in its hands, with power of life and death, it would seem that he is allowed every personal comfort. His table is provided by the Tuscan ambassador; a servant obeys his slightest nod; he sleeps in the luxurious apartment of the fiscal of that dreaded body; he is even liberated on the responsibility of a cardinal; he is permitted to lodge in the palace of the ambassador; he is allowed time to make his defence: those holy Inquisitors would not unnecessarily harm a hair of his head. Nor was it probably their object to inflict bodily torments: these would call out sympathy and degrade the tribunal. It was enough to threaten these torments, to which they did not wish to resort except in case of necessity. There is no evidence that Galileo was personally tortured. He was indeed a martyr, but not a sufferer except in humiliated pride. Probably the object of his enemies was to silence him, to degrade him, to expose his name to infamy, to arrest the spread of his doctrines, to bow his old head in shame, to murder his soul, to make him stab himself, and be his own executioner, by an act which all posterity should regard as unworthy of his name and cause.

After a fitting time has elapsed, — four months of dignified session, — the mind of the Holy Tribunal is made up. Its judgment is ready. On the 22d of June, 1633, the prisoner appears in penitential dress at the convent of Minerva, and the presiding cardinal, in his scarlet robes, delivers the sentence of the Court, — that Galileo, as a warning to others, and by way of salutary penance, be condemned to the formal prison of the Holy Office, and be ordered to recite once a week the seven Penitential Psalms for the benefit of his soul, — apparently a light sentence, only to be nominally imprisoned a few days, and to repeat those Psalms which were the life of blessed saints in mediæval times. But this was nothing. He was required to recant, to abjure the doctrines he had taught; not in private, but publicly before the world. Will he recant? Will he subscribe himself an imposter? Will he abjure the doctrines on which his fame rests? Oh, tell it not in Gath! The timid, infirm, life-loving old patriarch of science falls. He is not great enough for martyrdom. He chooses shame. In an evil hour this venerable sage falls down upon his knees before the assembled cardinals, and reads aloud this recantation: "I, Galileo Galilei, aged seventy, on my knees before you most reverend lords, and having my eye on the Holy Gospel, which I do touch with my lips, thus publish and declare, that I believe, and always have believed, and always will believe every article which the Holy Catholic Roman Church holds and teaches. And as I have written a book in which I have maintained that the sun is the centre, which doctrine is repugnant to the Holy Scriptures, I, with sincere heart and unfeigned faith, do abjure and detest, and curse the said error and heresy, and all other errors contrary to said Holy Church, whose penance I solemnly swear to observe faithfully, and all other penances which have been or shall be laid upon me."

It would appear from this confession that he did not declare his doctrines false, only that they were in opposition to the Scriptures; and it is also said that as he arose from his knees he whispered to a friend, "It does move, nevertheless." As some excuse for him, he acted with the certainty that he would be tortured if he did not recant; and at the worst he had only affirmed that his scientific theory was in opposition to the Scriptures. He had not denied his master, like Peter; he had not recanted the faith like Cranmer; he had simply yielded for fear of bodily torments, and therefore was not sincere in the abjuration which he made to save his life. Nevertheless, his recantation was a fall, and in the eyes of the scientific world perhaps greater than that of Bacon. Galileo was false to philosophy and himself. Why did he suffer himself to be conquered by priests he despised? Why did so bold and witty and proud a man betray his cause? Why did he not accept the penalty of intellectual freedom, and die, if die he must? What was life to him, diseased, infirm, and old? What had he more to gain? Was it not a good time to die and consummate his protests? Only one hundred and fifty years before, one of his countrymen had accepted torture and death rather than recant his religious opinions. Why could not Galileo have been as great in martyrdom as Savonarola? He was a renowned philosopher and brilliant as a man of genius, — but he was a man of the world; he loved ease and length of days. He could ridicule and deride opponents, — he could not suffer pain. He had a great intellect, but not a great soul. There were flaws in his morality; he was anything but a saint or hero. He was great in mind, and yet he was far from being great in character. We pity him, while we exalt him. Nor is the world harsh to him; it forgives him for his services. The worst that can be said, is that he was not willing to suffer and die for his opinions: and how many philosophers are there who are willing to be martyrs?

Nevertheless, in the eyes of philosophers he has disgraced himself. Let him then return to Florence, to his own Arceti. He is a silenced man. But he is silenced, not because he believed with Copernicus, but because he ridiculed his enemies and confronted the Church, and in the eyes of blinded partisans had attacked divine authority. Why did Copernicus escape persecution? The Church must have known that there was something in his discoveries, and in those of Galileo, worthy of attention. About this time Pascal wrote: "It is vain that you have procured the condemnation of Galileo. That will never prove the earth to be at rest. If unerring observation proves that it turns round, not all mankind together can keep it from turning, or themselves from turning with it."

But let that persecution pass. It is no worse than other persecutions, either in Catholic or Protestant ranks. It was no worse than burning witches. Not only is intolerance in human nature, but there is a repugnance among the learned to receive new opinions when these interfere with their ascendency. The opposition to Galileo's discoveries was no greater than that of the Protestant Church, half a century ago, to some of the inductions of geology. How bitter the hatred, even in our times, to such men as Huxley and Darwin! True, they have not proved their theories as Galileo did; but they gave as great a shock as he to the minds of theologians. All science is progressive, yet there are thousands who oppose its progress. And if learning and science should establish a different meaning to certain texts from which theological deductions are drawn, and these premises be undermined, there would be the same bitterness among the defenders of the present system of dogmatic theology. Yet theology will live, and never lose its dignity and importance; only, some of its present assumptions may be discarded. God will never be dethroned from the world he governs; but some of his ways may appear to be different from what was once supposed. And all science is not only progressive, but it appears to be bold and scornful and proud, — at least, its advocates are and ever have been contemptuous of all other departments of knowledge but its own. So narrow and limited is the human mind in the midst of its triumphs. So full of prejudices are even the learned and the great.

Let us turn then to give another glance at the fallen philosopher in his final retreat at Arceti. He lives under restrictions. But they allow him leisure and choice wines, of which he is fond, and gardens and friends; and many come to do him reverence. He amuses his old age with the studies of his youth and manhood, and writes dialogues on Motion, and even discovers the phenomena of the moon's libration; and by means of the pendulum he gives additional importance to astronomical science. But he is not allowed to leave his retirement, not even to visit his friends in Florence. The wrath of the Inquisition still pursues him, even in his villa at Arceti in the suburbs of Florence. Then renewed afflictions come. He loses his daughter, who was devoted to him; and her death nearly plunges him into despair. The bulwarks of his heart break down; a flood of grief overwhelms his stricken soul. His appetite leaves him; his health forsakes him; his infirmities increase upon him. His right eye loses its power, — that eye that had seen more of the heavens than the eyes of all who had gone before him. He becomes blind and deaf, and cannot sleep, afflicted with rheumatic pains and maladies forlorn. No more for him is rest, or peace, or bliss; still less the glories of his brighter days, — the sight of glittering fields, the gems of heaven, without which

> " Neither breath of Morn, when she ascends
> With charm of earliest birds, nor rising sun
> On this delightful land, nor herb, fruit, flower
> Glistering with dew, nor fragrance after showers,
> Nor grateful evening mild, . . . is sweet."

No more shall he gaze on features that he loves, or stars, or trees, or hills. No more to him

> " Returns
> Day, or the sweet approach of even or morn,
> Or sight of vernal bloom, or summer's rose,
> Or flocks, or herds, or human face divine;
> But clouds, instead, and ever-during dark
> Surround " [him].

It was in those dreary desolate days at Arceti,

> " Unseen
> In manly beauty Milton stood before him,
> Gazing in reverent awe, — Milton, his guest,

Just then come forth, all life and enterprise;
While he in his old age, . . .
   . . . exploring with his staff,
His eyes upturned as to the golden sun,
His eyeballs idly rolling."

This may have been the punishment of his recantation, — not Inquisitorial torture, but the consciousness that he had lost his honor. Poor Galileo! thine illustrious visitor, when *his* affliction came, could cast his sightless eyeballs inward, and see and tell "things unattempted yet in prose or rhyme," — not

" Rocks, caves, lakes, bogs, fens, and shades of death,
. . . .
Where all life dies, death lives, and Nature breeds
. . . .
Gorgons, and Hydras, and Chimeras dire,"

but of "eternal Providence," and "Eden with surpassing glory crowned," and "our first parents," and of "salvation," "goodness infinite," of "wisdom," which when known we need no higher though all the stars we know by name, —

" All secrets of the deep, all Nature's works,
Or works of God in heaven, or air, or sea."

And yet, thou stricken observer of the heavenly bodies! hadst thou but known what marvels would be revealed by the power of thy wondrous instrument after thou should'st be laid lifeless and cold beneath the marble floor of Sante Croce, at the age of seventy-eight, without a monument, without even the right of burial in consecrated ground, having died a prisoner of the Inquisition, yet not without having rendered to astronomical science services of utmost value,—even thou might have died rejoicing, as one of the great benefactors of the world. And thy discoveries shall be forever held in gratitude; they shall herald others of even greater importance. Newton shall prove that the different planets are attracted to the sun in the inverse ratio of the squares of their distances; that the earth has a force on the moon identical with the force of gravity, and that all celestial bodies, to the utmost boundaries of space, mutually attract each other; that all particles of matter are governed by the same law,—the great law of gravitation, by which "astronomy," in the language of Whewell, "passed from boyhood to manhood, and by which law the great discoverer added more to the realm of science than any man before or since his day." And after Newton shall pass away, honored and lamented, and be buried with almost royal pomp in the vaults of Westminster, Halley and other mathematicians shall construct lunar tables, by which longitude shall be accurately measured on the pathless ocean. Lagrange and Laplace shall apply the Newtonian theory to determine the secular inequalities of celestial motion;

they shall weigh absolutely the amount of matter in the planets; they shall show how far their orbits deviate from circles; and they shall enumerate the cycles of changes detected in the circuit of the moon. Clairaut shall remove the perplexity occasioned by the seeming discrepancy between the observed and computed motions of the moon's perigee. Halley shall demonstrate the importance of observations of the transit of Venus as the only certain way of obtaining the sun's parallax, and hence the distance of the sun from the earth; he shall predict the return of that mysterious body which we call a comet. Herschel shall construct a telescope which magnifies two thousand times, and add another planet to our system beyond the mighty orb of Saturn. Römer shall estimate the velocity of light from the eclipses of Jupiter's satellites. Bessell shall pass the impassable gulf of space and measure the distance of some of the fixed stars, although such is the immeasurable space between the earth and those distant suns that the parallax of only about thirty has yet been discovered with our finest instruments, — so boundless is the material universe, so vast are the distances, that light, travelling one hundred and sixty thousand miles with every pulsation of the blood, will not reach us from some of those remote worlds in one hundred thousand years. So marvellous shall be the victories of science, that the perturbations of the planets in their courses shall reveal the existence of a new one more distant than Uranus, and Leverrier shall tell at what part of the heavens that star shall first be seen.

So far as we have discovered, the universe which we have observed with telescopic instruments has no limits that mortals can define, and in comparison with its magnitude our earth is less than a grain of sand, and is so old that no genius can calculate and no imagination can conceive when it had a beginning. All that we know is, that suns exist at distances we cannot define. But around what centre do they revolve? Of what are they composed? Are they inhabited by intelligent and immortal beings? Do we know that they are not eternal, except from the divine declaration that there *was* a time when the Almighty fiat went forth for this grand creation? Creation involves a creator; and can the order and harmony seen in Nature's laws exist without Supreme intelligence and power? Who, then, and what, is God? "Canst thou by searching find out Him? Knowest thou the ordinances of Heaven? Canst thou bind the sweet influences of the Pleiades, or loose the bands of Orion?" What an atom is this world in the light of science! Yet what dignity has man by the light of revelation! What majesty and power and glory has God! What goodness, benevolence, and love, that even a sparrow cannot fall to the ground without

His notice, — that we are the special objects of His providence and care! Is there an imagination so lofty that will not be oppressed with the discoveries that even the telescope has made?

Ah, to what exalted heights reason may soar when allied with faith! How truly it should elevate us above the evils of this brief and busy existence to the conditions of that other life, —

> "When the soul,
> Advancing ever to the Source of light
> And all perfection, lives, adores, and reigns
> In cloudless knowledge, purity, and bliss!"

AUTHORITIES.

Delambre, Histoire de l'Astronomie; Arago, Histoire de l'Astronomie; Life of Galileo, in Cabinet Library; Life of Galileo, by Brewster; Lives of Galileo, by Italian and Spanish Literary Men; Whewell's History of Inductive Sciences; Plurality of Worlds; Humboldt's Cosmos; Nichols' Architecture of the Heavens; Chalmers' Astronomical Discourses; Life of Kepler, Library of Useful Knowledge; Brewster's Life of Tycho Brahe, of Kepler, and of Sir Isaac Newton; Mitchell's Stellar and Planetary Worlds; Bradley's Correspondence; Airy's Reports; Voiron's History of Astronomy; Philosophical Transactions; Everett's Oration on Galileo; Life of Copernicus; Bayly's Astronomy; Encyclopædia Britannica, Art. *Astronomy*; Proctor's Lectures.